1966

EROS AND PSYCHE

PHOENIX

SUPPLEMENTARY VOLUMES

EROS AND PSYCHE

STUDIES IN
PLATO, PLOTINUS,
AND ORIGEN

JOHN M. RIST

PHOENIX

JOURNAL OF THE CLASSICAL
ASSOCIATION OF CANADA
SUPPLEMENTARY VOLUME VI

UNIVERSITY OF TORONTO PRESS

EDITORIAL COMMITTEE

© UNIVERSITY OF TORONTO PRESS 1964
Printed in Canada

TO ANNA

PREFACE

THIS book clearly could never have existed without the unending inspiration of the Greek philosophers, especially of Plato and Plotinus. After them, I owe an unrepayable debt to my former teacher Mr. F. H. Sandbach, of Trinity College, Cambridge, on whose immense knowledge of antiquity I have often called, and whose high ideals of scholarship have often been a challenge. Professor A. H. Armstrong has offered a number of valuable and detailed suggestions, and has drawn my attention to passages in the *Enneads* which I would otherwise have overlooked. My thanks go to him and also to Miss A. N. M. Rich and others who have read the manuscript. Last but not least, my wife, to whom this book is dedicated, has been a source of help both literary and practical at all stages of its composition.

The manuscript was prepared for publication by Dr. R. M. Schoeffel of the University of Toronto Press. He has lavished much care on it, and it owes many improvements to him. It has been published with the help of a grant from the Humanities Research Council of Canada using funds provided by the Canada Council.

J.M.R.

University College, University of Toronto

CONTENTS

cause and "Father"; quasi-lifelike terms applied to it,
69–73. Metaphors of emanation, 74. Difficulties in motive
for the One and the Demiourgos, 75–76. The One described in voluntarist terms; the view of Trouillard;
the One as Ἔρως, 76–79. Nygren on Ἔρως and Ἀγάπη,
79–80. The transcendence, immanence, and Ἔρως of
the One, 80–84. Plato and Plotinus on Ἔρως, 84–85.
Plotinus excludes doctrines of salvation, 85. The One
"supra-personal" rather than impersonal, 86–87.
    II. The mystical union as a clue to the understanding
of the One; two ways of approach; deification, 87–89.
Preliminary studies, including mathematics out of
deference to Plato, 89–91. The *via negativa* is platonic,
91–92. Plotinus' attitude to mystic union and δαίμονες,
92–94. Dialectic, 94. Ὁμοίωσις θεῷ, 94. Ecstasy described; Ἔρως as the link between the two approaches
to the One, 95–97. Higher replaces lower in union, 97–99.
No Christian influence, 99. The sublimations of heterosexual and homosexual love, 100–102. The Good and the
Beautiful, 103. Tactual imagery in the description of
ecstasy, 103. The transcendence of self and Plato's views
on immortality, 104–109. Forms of individuals and the
transcendence of self, 109–110. Ὁμοίωσις and Ἔρως in
Plato and Plotinus, 110–111. Plotinus, his contemporaries, and personal religion, 111–112.

PART TWO

I   Knowing How and Knowing That   115

The theory of Gould, 115–117. "Knowing how" in Plato,
117. Τέχνη and ἐπιστήμη, 118–120. Definitions of
σωφροσύνη, 120–121. Has the Platonic Socrates a theory
of the object?, 121–128. The *Memorabilia* on "knowing
how" and "knowing that," 128–130. The priority of
"knowing that," 130–137. Knowing oneself, 137. Gould's
distinction anachronistic, 138. Learning to "know how,"
139–141. Virtue as knowledge of the Good, 142.

II Virtue in the Middle and Late Dialogues   143

True opinion, virtue, and φρόνησις, 143–144. The kinds
of virtue, 144–148. Virtue as health or harmony, 148–150.
Ἐπιστήμη, φρόνησις, and ἀρετή, 150–155. Ὁμοίωσις
θεῷ and virtue, 155–156.

III The Disintegration of the Platonic Doctrine of
     Virtue and Knowledge   157

    1. Aristotle on the "theoretical" and practical life; mo-
tives for moral behaviour, 157–160.

CONTENTS   xi

EROS AND PSYCHE

LIST OF ABBREVIATIONS

AJP *American Journal of Philology*

CP *Classical Philology*

CQ *Classical Quarterly*

DK Diels-Kranz, *Fragmente der Vorsokratiker*

DTC *Dictionnaire de théologie catholique*

GCS *Die Griechischen Christlichen Schriftsteller der Ersten Drei Jahrhunderte.*

HTR *Harvard Theological Review*

JHI *Journal of the History of Ideas*

JHS *Journal of Hellenic Studies*

JRS *Journal of Roman Studies*

LSJ Liddell-Scott-Jones, *A Greek-English Lexicon*, 9th ed.

Mus. Helv. *Museum Helveticum*

PG *Patrologia Graeca*, ed. J. P. Migne

PR *Philosophical Review*

Rh. Mus. *Rheinisches Museum für Philologie*

RE *Paulys Real-Encyclopädie der classischen Altertumswissenschaft*

SVF *Stoicorum Veterum Fragmenta*, ed. von Arnim

TAPA *Transactions and Proceedings of the American Philological Association*

INTRODUCTION

O F all the philosophies of antiquity, Platonism had by far the most fluctuations. After Aristotle and Theophrastus, the Peripatetics concentrated almost exclusively on commentaries on their master and on the building up of various fields of specialized knowledge; the later Epicureans hardly added a word to the Founder's teaching, which they professed in the form of a creed; the Stoics only developed their doctrines when the criticisms of rivals, especially the Sceptics of the New Academy, made it essential for them to do so. The theories of the Platonists, however, varied radically. Speusippus, for example, the successor of Plato himself as head of the Academy, dispensed with the Theory of Forms. The next head, Xenocrates, revived it—only to amalgamate it with Plato's theory of the objects of mathematics.

Among the reasons for this unusual variety of doctrines even within the Old Academy is the fact that Plato's thought could not easily be reduced to a system or taught systematically. It contained within itself unresolved, but—as it is the purpose of this study to demonstrate— philosophically fruitful divergences of opinion on the highest topics: the Good, the nature of love, the aim of the life of virtue. Plato himself, by writing in dialogue form, gives an indication that he thought of his writings largely as compositions *ad hominem*. What is written here is intended to suggest that the unity of his thought consists only in certain general beliefs, such as that there are supra-sensible realities and that some aspect of the human soul is immortal. It protests, in passing, against those who look on Plato as the author of a series of tracts: one on the Theory of Forms, one on Aesthetics, another on Statesmanship, and so on.

The Theory of Forms is a faith: a faith expressed in general terms and not explained in detail. Plato himself, at sundry times in his life, suggested ways of understanding its relevance, but he probably did not regard even his final opinions as conclusive. Many of his successors, however, including Plotinus and Origen, assumed that they could "explain" or "correct" his "system" as though it were a compact and unified whole. Accordingly, they took parts of that supposed system out of context and welded them into their own theories. In doing so, by the very production of a system that was seldom self-contradictory and indistinct in detail, they were unplatonic even when expounding parts of the Platonic corpus. To extend the meaning of "unplatonic" in this direction is somewhat unusual, but none the less meaningful. To understand in particular instances the way Plotinus and Origen handled the Platonic originals and developed Platonic themes is a major object of this book.

PART ONE

PART ONE

Chapter One

PLATO AND NEOPLATONISM

WHEN considering the origin of Neoplatonism, interpreters have frequently tended to one of two extreme views. Some, well aware that Platonism and Neoplatonism are not the same thing, have been led to discover the "origins" of the theories of Plotinus among the motley of Oriental beliefs which were scattered throughout the Roman Empire in his day, or to over-emphasize the Stoic or Aristotelian elements in his system. Others have suggested that all, or almost all, the distinctive features of Neoplatonism are already to be found in Plato himself or in his immediate successors at the Academy, and that Plato clearly intended his works to be interpreted in a "Neoplatonic" sense.

The view to be proposed here is perhaps nearer to the latter, but is far from going the whole way with those who believe in a Neoplatonic Plato. It assumes that Plato influenced his successors in the following important ways: first, certain of his views were repeated and interpreted as he himself had intended; secondly, many others were repeated, but logical conclusions which Plato had not always made clear were brought out; furthermore it can then be shown that the developed form of these doctrines reveals certain inconsistencies in the Platonic originals. In these cases, by emphasizing the alternative that their Master had perhaps adumbrated but not followed up, the Neoplatonists were, in fact, formulating views which we may call "unplatonic," in the sense that they diverge from what is normally regarded as the Master's *conscious, positive* teaching. In the course of our enquiry into the development and history of certain of these "enlarged" notions, we shall also be able to see where Plato himself appeared to suggest too lofty a view, and where his successors, in enlarging upon certain aspects of his thought, rendered Platonism less abstract and thus more to the taste of the majority of men.

Before examining a number of Platonic themes, however, we must clarify our position on certain general issues of interpretation, and in particular on the treatment of those sections of Plato's works which are generally regarded as myths, for one of the greatest obstacles to an

enquiry into Neoplatonism is the commonly held view that the
Neoplatonists, both Christian and pagan, were unjustified in interpreting Platonic "myths" as though they contained dialectical explanations of Plato's views. The Neoplatonists, say their critics, made
the error of treating all Plato's writings as a sacred text which could
be expounded as exact philosophy whether their subject-matter was
in a "mythical" or a dialectical form.

Here arises the question of the distinction between myth and
allegory. It is commonly held that Plato used the former regularly and
despised the latter, whereas the Neoplatonists were prepared to use
both indiscriminately. To prove that Plato despised allegorical interpretations, scholars often quote a well-known passage from the
Phaedrus,[1] which, however, is irrelevant. Socrates does not say that he
disbelieves the rationalizing statements made by the expounders of
traditional mythology; rather he insists that he himself has no time to
spend on such things since his work in life is to follow the advice of the
Delphic God and learn to know himself. His dismissal of the rationalizing of mythology in favour of the study of his own soul is similar to
his rejection of the theories of the natural philosophers in the *Phaedo*.
We are not to assume that Socrates disbelieved such theories and rejected all possibility of their value; the truth is rather that he thought
that these theories were the product of irrelevant or unimportant enquiries which would divert the mind from the supreme study of
teleology.

In the *Cratylus*,[2] Plato condemns allegories that are based on a
study of etymology, and thus far he would have condemned the
Neoplatonists, but when it comes to the allegorizing of mythology, his
views are more restrained. In the *Republic*[3] he rejects certain tales on
moral grounds and will not accept a defence of them as allegories. His
objection, however, is not to the allegories themselves, for he never
denies that the myths *may* have an "undersense" (ὑπόνοια), but is
based on the fact that young people cannot distinguish what is allegory and what is not, and are thus liable to be corrupted.

As Tate[4] says: "Plato does not allegorize ancient myths and fables,"
but "he does not hesitate to make use of them in stating his own
philosophic views." Tate is right to suggest that those few poets
admitted to the Ideal State may make use of ὑπόνοιαι, for Socrates
himself frequently invites us to look into the inner meaning of the
words of the poets.[5] Thus, in general, to hold that Plato makes use of

---

[1] *Phaedrus* 229C ff.   [2] *Crat.* 407A.   [3] *Rep.* 2, 378D.
[4] Tate, "Plato," 142.   [5] *Apol.* 22BC; *Ion* 533D–534E; *Prot.* 342A–347A.

myth and condemns allegory is an over-simplification. His hesitations about allegorizing are caused not by a feeling that the procedure is nonsensical, but by an unwillingness to prefer it to more important studies and a fear of its failure to consider the moral welfare of the undiscriminating young. We can imagine circumstances where neither of these objections would apply; indeed Socrates' treatment of the passage of Simonides in the *Protagoras* comes near to being such an instance.

This is not to defend as correct—that is to say, in accordance with the Platonic spirit—all those Neoplatonic interpretations of Plato which assume him to be using allegory. Nevertheless a considerable degree of caution should be employed in condemning the Neoplatonists; each case should be judged on its merits, and with respect to the doctrine it teaches rather than to its conformity to an attitude supposed to have been Plato's.

Furthermore, during the course of this essay I have on occasions treated Plato's "mythical" and "dialectical" passages on the same footing, just as the Neoplatonists did, who, I maintain, should not be condemned as unplatonic for following this procedure. In order to defend my view, however, I must look briefly at the rôle Plato himself assigns to his myths and also say at once that in general terms I follow the views of P. Frutiger, as expressed in his book *Les Mythes de Platon*.

J. A. Stewart, in his book *The Myths of Plato*, writes as follows:[6] "The Neoplatonists did not understand the difference between myth and allegory. Allegory is dogma in picture-writing, but myth is not dogma and does not convey dogma. Dogma is gained and maintained by dialectic." This view, it is evident, seeks to maintain a sharp distinction between μῦθοι and λόγοι. Λόγοι are supposed to teach dogma, that is, the truth according to Plato; so far all is plain. But what are we to learn from the μῦθοι? It is obvious that if this sort of antithesis is to be maintained, they must tell us something which is, at best, less than the truth, and certain critics have gone so far as to insist that the value of the myths for an understanding of Platonism is quite small.

Such procedure has rightly been censured by Frutiger,[7] who tells us that the word "Μῦθος est employé sans aucune idée accessoire de fiction ou de légende" in a large number of Greek authors, both philosophers and non-philosophers, and that it is perfectly reasonable to believe Plato capable of the same usage. This should be a starting-point for a defence of the Neoplatonic method which attempts a semi-scholastic treatment of dialectic and "myth" alike.

[6]Stewart, *Myths* 242.　　　　　　　　[7]Frutiger, *Mythes* 16, n. 1.

My own view is that "myths" are a kind of δεύτερος πλοῦς. When Socrates uses this expression in the *Phaedo*, it is to describe his method of question and answer in contrast with the method of the φυσικοί. Ideally, we must suppose, he would have preferred the straightforward authoritative discourse, such as the physical philosophers were accustomed to give. But only if this discourse (λόγος), could bring out the truth. Socrates in the *Phaedo* chooses the δεύτερος πλοῦς of the dialectical method in preference to that of exposition, because although a true exposition is the best possible means to the philosopher's goal of truth, a false one is clearly the very worst. *Corruptio optimi pessima.* Dialectic, Socrates believes, though not as quick and efficient as a good exposition, has the great advantage of truthfulness and completeness over such inadequate "systems" as that of Anaxagoras.

In his commentary on the *Phaedo* (p. 137), Hackforth suggests that in the *Timaeus* Plato takes up the method of the πρῶτος πλοῦς and by its aid gives us "a discovery of the detailed operations of Mind throughout the universe." This opinion, though correct in its recognition of what a πρῶτος πλοῦς should do, is inaccurate in suggesting that this is what we have in the *Timaeus*. For Timaeus insists that his audience must be satisfied with a μῦθος.[8]

This μῦθος ought not to be regarded as the πρῶτος πλοῦς, although some of it deals with a subject-matter highly suited to that method. A πρῶτος πλοῦς, however, would be an exact account of facts and deductions as real and self-evident to Plato as the existence of Forms. This is not what we have in the *Timaeus*, which is still a μῦθος and thus only a different variety of δεύτερος πλοῦς. The δεύτερος πλοῦς of dialectic, as Socrates describes it in the *Phaedo*, does not attempt to deal with the truth about the universe as a whole in one broad sweep; it deals with points one at a time. The δεύτερος πλοῦς of the *Timaeus* myth does attempt the broad sweep, but lacks the element of certainty, passing as it does beyond the sphere where man's mind can find adequate proof. Both methods, then, are imperfect; both present the truth as nearly as Plato can expound it. It is therefore absurd to condemn the

[8] *Tim.* 29D. In *The Theory of Motion in Plato's Later Dialogues*, Professor Skemp, following and refining Frutiger, distinguishes (p. xv) two kinds of μῦθοι in the *Timaeus*. "The physics of the *Timaeus* is μῦθος and can never be λόγος: it must aspire to be εἰκὼς μῦθος. But in the creation story and the account of the activities of the Demiurge and the lesser souls we have μῦθος striving to become λόγος-μῦθος, indeed, which is potentially λόγος because it concerns ὄντως ὄντα (cf. 67, 110)." This distinction is of help towards an understanding of the rôle of the Demiourgos, and is in no way contrary to our more general remarks which follow.

Neoplatonists too readily because their interpretations of Plato are
often concerned with the μῦθος of the *Timaeus*.

The view that the myth of the *Timaeus* and the accounts of the
after-life in the *Gorgias*, *Phaedo*, and *Republic*, as well as that of the
soul in the *Phaedrus*, are meant to be taken seriously and believed as
the most likely hypothesis, is supported by Plato's words in *Phaedo*
114D: "Now to affirm confidently that these things are as I have told
them would not befit a man of good sense; yet seeing that the soul is
found to be immortal, I think it is befitting to affirm that this or something like it is the truth about our souls and their habitations. I think
too that we should do well in venturing—and a glorious venture it is—
to believe it to be so. And we should treat such tales as spells to pro-
nounce over ourselves, as in fact has been my own purpose all this
while in telling my long story." (Trans. Hackforth.)

Nothing could be more explicit than this passage. Admittedly, says
Socrates, many details may not be accurate, but the general outline
is most certainly near to reality, so near, in fact, that we should put
implicit faith in it—feed our minds upon it—as being the nearest
possible apprehension of the truth. Nothing could be clearer than that
Plato treats these myths in something like the way in which we regard
a scientific theory. Our experiments have shown, we say, that the
theory is so likely to be true that we ought to put our faith in it unless
and until it can be demonstrated to be incorrect. The onus of proof is
upon the opponent of the accepted theory.

Again, in the *Gorgias*[9], we read as follows: "Listen then, as they say,
to a very fine account (λόγου) which you, I suppose, will think of as a
story (μῦθος) but which I treat as an actual account (λόγον). For what I
am about to tell you I offer to you as the truth." Then follows the
eschatological myth, some details of which the *Phaedo* encourages us
to treat as inexact (for example, the identity of the judges, Minos and
Rhadamanthys) but which in its broad outline is a λόγος in the form
of a myth, and not a myth in the sense of a fiction or a vague tale
about what is only δοξαστόν. For the existence of our souls and their
fate is not δοξαστόν but a part of reality, and the souls of Minos,
Rhadamanthys and the other gods or θεῖοι ἄνθρωποι are akin to the
Forms and therefore real.

Plato's belief in the likelihood of the myth in the *Gorgias* is repeated
in 527A. "Possibly," he writes, "you regard this as an old wife's tale
and despise it, and there would be no wonder in our despising it if
with all our searching we could find somewhere anything better and

[9]*Gorgias* 523A.

truer than this. But as it is, you observe that you three, who are the wisest of the Greeks in our day—you and Polus and Gorgias—are unable to prove that we ought to live any other life than this, which is evidently advantageous also in the other world." (Trans. Lamb.)

From the above passages and arguments, therefore, it can be seen that the distinction between μῦθος and λόγος is not as easy to determine as Platonic scholars sometimes suppose, and that it is unjustifiable to assume that every time we find Plotinus, for example, citing and using "mythical" passages he is bound to be going beyond the Platonic view. This essay, therefore, will not attempt to establish in each specific case of Plotinus' quoting a Platonic "myth" whether he is justified in doing so or not. However, such cases only will be referred to as seem to be interpretations of the Platonic text which have some definite relation to Plato's own thoughts; in other words we shall look to the doctrine which Plotinus produces, and see whether, or rather in what sense, that is Platonic, rather than examine how he extracts his interpretations from particular Platonic texts.

The last observation to be made here on the subject of the "myths" is that scholars have too often not learned, from the difficulty of assigning passages to the one group or the other, to avoid drawing hard and fast lines between μῦθοι and λόγοι. In fact, since Plato's own day, disputes have raged as to which passages are "mythical" and which are not; for example, as to the ontological status of the Demiourgos in the *Timaeus*. Many of these questions are very little nearer being solved now than they were in 300 B.C. and it is not likely that they will become clearer in the next two thousand years than they have in the last, for they are unreal questions and have no definite answer. They are unreal because the λόγος–μῦθος distinction in Plato is unreal if these terms are supposed to refer respectively to the spheres of Truth and Opinion (or something inferior to Truth). Who would be justified in insisting that the proof of a scientific theory when written out was a λόγος but that the application of it was a μῦθος, if μῦθος is to have a pejorative sense? Yet this is exactly what the critics of Plato's myths have done when they have complained that the Neoplatonists have treated them as factual.

In recent times, very many aspects of Plato's thought have been described as "mythical" in a sense more pejorative even than that used in antiquity, and the difficulty of finding a truly Platonic explanation of Plato becomes greater as his teaching is more and more dissolved into "untrustworthy" myths. Here is J. A. Stewart again (p. 344): "I venture to think that the doctrine of ἀνάμνησις, in itself,

and in its setting, is not intended by Plato to be taken literally—that
it is not Dogma but Myth. This view, for which I may appeal to the
authority of Leibniz and Coleridge, seems to me to be borne out by the
passage in the *Meno* (81) dealing with ἀνάμνησις; ἀνάμνησις is presented
there, in accordance with Orphic belief, as becoming clearer and
clearer at each incarnation, till the soul at last attains to the blessed
life of a δαίμων. Can it be maintained that Plato is in earnest with all
the Orphic beliefs of this passage? And if not with all, with any?"

Apart from the use of the equivocal word "Orphic" in this passage,
it contains an example of just the sort of reasoning that we have found
Plato warning us against in the *Phaedo*.[10] There he admitted that certain parts of his account might not be entirely correct, but he insisted
that we should take notice of the main tenor of his suggestions, whereas here we find Stewart writing "And if not with all, with any?" The
contrast is striking. Stewart goes on to say: "To put the matter
briefly: I regard the whole doctrine of ἀνάμνησις and of ἰδέαι *qua* involved in that doctrine, as an Aetiological Myth—plausible, com-
forting and encouraging—to explain the fact that Man finds himself
in a World in which he can get on." From this it is but a short step to
Couturat's[11] suggestion that the whole doctrine of Ideas is "mythical."
Once we have taken that step we are obliged to assume, if we accept
the μῦθος–λόγος dichotomy, that of all his theories Plato himself felt
certain only of various logical demonstrations, such as those in the
Sophist. Yet it is inconceivable that he would have troubled to proceed
to logical investigations if he had not felt certain of the Ideas.

Such then is the position into which the λόγος–μῦθος dichotomy and
the attempts to classify all Plato's work under one of these two heads
can lead. It is surely time either to abandon the dichotomy or to give
up the study of Plato, for that is what a view such as that of Couturat
implies.

If we choose the former alternative, we are in no position to censure
the Neoplatonists for having done likewise. Indeed, their attitude may
be a confirmation of our own, for we have found that when required to
account for the dichotomy, we can see no Platonic justification for it.
Thus is cleared away an important obstacle to a proper investigation
of the relationship between Plato and Plotinus. Another and more
serious objection, slightly related to the one just discussed, and perhaps in the remote past an ancestor of it, remains and must be considered before any more positive views can be expressed.

[10]*Phaedo* 114D.
[11]Couturat, *De Plat. Mythis* 81.

This objection is simply the belief that modern scholarship is able to demonstrate exactly Plato's views on every philosophic topic, and hence to show that in very many cases these views were misconstrued by the Neoplatonists. Such arguments are often expressed in grandiose language and adopt a patronizing tone towards the supposedly misguided Neoplatonists. An example which displays these qualities and this mode of criticism is the following passage from Shorey[12] which deserves to be quoted at length:

The Neoplatonic mind combines with its dialectical impulse certain needs and aptitudes vaguely designated by such words as scholasticism, mysticism, enthusiasm, asceticism, pantheism, symbolism and the imaginative personification of abstractions. The dialectic yields pleasure from the mere exercise of ingenuity in the process, and from the cumulative intensity of the emotion of conviction which this semblance of reasoning generates. This subjective feeling is so strong that it requires little confirmation from without. Hence the imperturbable self-assurance of the Neoplatonic state of mind—the almost comic innocent serenity with which these "babe-like Jupiters", in Emerson's phrase, Plotinus, Proclus, Olympiodorus, Synesius and the rest, sit on their clouds and from age to age prattle to each other and to no contemporary . . . . Plato, as if in divinatory anticipation of the Neoplatonists and the Hegelians, calls the pseudo-dialectics of the One and the Many an eternal disease of language in the human mind.

Generally speaking, scholars pretend to ignore contributions to a topic couched in this kind of emotive language, believing themselves to be raised by their critical acumen high enough to be able to separate facts from partisan interpretation of facts; but in the case of the relation between Plato and the Neoplatonists, their usual judgment seems not uncommonly to go astray, and such untested generalities as those here suggested by Shorey have often been allowed to pass almost unchallenged.

Shorey, for example, is suggesting that "scholasticism, mysticism, enthusiasm, pantheism," and the rest are in some way Neoplatonic aberrations of which Plato was innocent. This is plainly incorrect. The laws of Athens are "imaginatively personified" in the *Crito*, symbolism is involved in the illustration of the Good by comparison with the Sun in the *Republic*, asceticism is continually in the background of the *Phaedo*, enthusiasm and mysticism abound in the *Phaedrus* and *Symposium*, while scholasticism might well be suspected in the second half of the *Parmenides*. As for pantheism, it is true that it cannot be found in Plato; neither can it in Plotinus.

Again, as this passage shows, the Neoplatonists have suffered because of certain superficial resemblances between the system of

[12]Shorey, *Platonism* 40.

Plotinus and that of Hegel, and the opponents of the latter, who hope perhaps to invoke the authority of Plato against him, find themselves compelled to detach Plato from all Neoplatonic associations.

Furthermore, such phrases as "the imaginative personification of abstractions" suggest that a serious philosopher such as Plotinus is being too easily confused with a writer of romance like Apuleius, who had a certain penchant for the exotic, including Platonism, but whose tastes ranged far beyond mere philosophy. Such confusion arises from the vague and perhaps misleading expressions "Platonism" and "Neoplatonism," since these terms tend to imply that all "Platonists" or "Neoplatonists" should be lumped together, distinctions in specific theories being disregarded. That every philosopher should be considered on his merits is generally admitted, but those who accept this in theory still avail themselves in practice of the cover afforded by such blanket terms as "Middle-" or "Neo-Platonist."

Finally, if the suggestion that the Neoplatonists "prattle to each other from age to age and to no contemporary" be taken at all seriously, it must be remembered that similar criticism could very easily be levelled at Plato himself, and perhaps at all great philosophers. Some leading contemporaries of Plato in the Academy, such as Speusippus and Eudoxus, did not accept the Master's system; yet Shorey would not, I think, suggest that this inability to convince them brings Plato any nearer to being a "babe-like Jupiter."

THE GOOD, THE FORMS, AND
EROS IN PLATO

I

IT is a commonplace to point out that the Homeric gods are anthropomorphic. Even in the sixth century this was clear to Xenophanes of Elea. We know that he maintained[1] that if cows and lions had gods and could describe them, their descriptions, physical and moral, would be in terms of cows and lions, with only the added attribute of immortality. The word ἀθάνατος would denote this distinguishing feature.

When the Greeks became self-conscious about their divinities, it was plain that such "overgrown humans" would prove unsatisfying. The curious thing is that to philosophers such as Plato the chief objection to the Olympians was not that they were men writ large, but that they were only "ordinary" men writ large; that is, that they were not divine exponents of Platonism. As Werner Jaeger has pointed out, this authoritarian assumption passed from Plato to Aristotle, whose "Unmoved Mover" he[2] describes as "truly a professor's god." If Xenophanes had lived in the post-Aristotelian era, he would have been perfectly justified in making the same criticism of the Aristotelian as he did of the Olympian God. Νόησις νοήσεως νόησις is plainly a translation into heaven of the ideal Aristotle would have liked to see, or maybe even to become, here on earth. Despite all objections, anthropomorphism had in a sense survived the attacks of the philosophers. What the latter had done, however, was to make the gods moral.[3]

Plato was a violent critic of the Olympians. If there were to be gods, they must, he decreed, be admirable. And he not only believed that gods existed, but desired, at least in his old age, to make his own belief into a law of the state, to be disobeyed at great peril. This extreme respect, however, does not mean that Plato had a grand vision of the distant majesty of the Deity which he felt it his duty to protect from the attacks of mortals. On the contrary, his respect for God goes

[1]Xenophanes fr. 15, *ap.* Clement *Strom.* 5.109.3.
[2]Jaeger, *Aristotle.* Cf. Arist. *Met.* Λ. 1071B2–1075A10.
[3]*Rep.* 2, and elsewhere.

hand in hand with a sense of the kinship of men and gods, with a belief that men too can raise themselves to the level of divinity, or rather can "know themselves" to be in a sense already divine. Plato's theology is not so much anthropomorphic as his notion of mankind is theomorphic. His gods are men as they can be and ought to be.

What is the remedy for the world's ills? is the question that Plato asks in the *Theaetetus*.[4] It is to try to escape from this world to that of the gods as soon as we can. In order to escape, we must become like gods as far as we may, that is, we must become just, holy, and wise. Now if men and gods were totally different orders of creature, such a course would be impossible. Plato would call it ὅμοιον εὐχαῖς. With the best will in the world, a garden slug cannot become a butterfly, whereas a caterpillar can and does become a butterfly simply because it has the potential of butterflyhood! In the same way men, according to Plato, have the potentiality of divinity. Perhaps the clearest statement of man's innate kinship with God occurs in the *Timaeus*.[5] Here we read that we must suppose that God has given each of us our own δαίμων. This δαίμων is none other than the most lordly part of our soul, that rational element which is situated in the head and which has the power of raising us, if only we give it the scope it demands, from earth to heaven. In words reminiscent of the *Theaetetus*, we are invited to think thoughts which are immortal and divine (ἀθάνατα καὶ θεῖα) and thus lay hold of our share of immortality (μετασχεῖν ἀθανασίας) to the utmost of our capacities.[6]

But Plato is a man of restraint, and though far from advocating a belief in the old maxim θνητὸς ὤν, θνητὰ φρόνει, he does not entirely confound human nature with divine. In the passages quoted above, we notice that he adds the words κατὰ τὸ δυνατόν in the *Theaetetus* and καθ' ὅσον ἐνδέχεται in the *Timaeus*. Similarly, in the *Republic*[7] there is the statement that the real philosopher who lives with what is divine and orderly will himself gain these admirable qualities so far as man can do so. In all these passages, Plato seems to be aware of the difficulties and dangers to man inherent in the notion of self-deification.[8] In the

---

[4]*Theaet.* 176AB. Cf. *Rep.* 10.613B.

[5]*Tim.* 90A ff.

[6]For the notion of ὁμοίωσις θεῷ, see also *Laws* 4. 716B.

[7]*Rep.* 6. 500C. θείῳ δὴ καὶ κοσμίῳ ὅ γε φιλόσοφος ὁμιλῶν κόσμιός τε καὶ θεῖος εἰς τὸ δυνατὸν ἀνθρώπῳ γίγνεται.

[8]In *Soph.* 216C, Plato distinguishes between θεῖος ἀνήρ and θεός. The philosopher is a θεῖος ἀνήρ. This implies that he is a δαίμων—not a god, since he is still living out an earthly existence, but more than man because his "daemonic" element (νοῦς) has attained complete possession of his soul. Cf. Mugnier, *Le sens du mot* Θεῖος 68 and Van Camp–Canart, *Le sens du mot* Θεῖος 195–196.

myth of the *Phaedrus*, however, a more lofty claim appears, though not in a direct form. There we find that the philosopher alone has wings,[9] since he is able to commune with those very things that make God divine. The implication is that it is the ability to understand and see the Forms in the ὑπερουράνιος τόπος that constitutes divinity, and that if man can gain this vision he too will be a god. It is true that here we find the phrase κατὰ δύναμιν, but the implication of this is not the same as κατὰ τὸ δυνατόν or καθ' ὅσον ἐνδέχεται. In the *Phaedrus*, the implication is that, so far as we can *remember* the Forms, we can be gods; elsewhere the emphasis is that we can only be godlike as far as our human nature permits. As we shall see, the *Phaedrus* teaches that a will to Goodness can make anyone in some sense a god.

Perhaps it may still be objected that there is no difference of meaning between the two phrases κατὰ δύναμιν and κατὰ τὸ δυνατόν. A consideration of the abilities of the Guardians in the *Republic* may show that there is, for it is evident that, in their case, the faculty of ἀνάμνησις reaches its consummation and that they gain the vision of the Forms and even of the Form of the Good. These Guardians must, then, if we follow the teaching of the *Phaedrus*, be no different in essentials from the Gods, for they are in full communion with what gives the Gods themselves their divinity. If human nature (ἀνθρωπίνη φύσις) made it impossible to reach this divine state, but compelled us to approximate to it (κατὰ τὸ δυνατόν), then there could never be such a person as a Platonic Guardian. If, however, as in the *Phaedrus*, our grasp of the Forms depends on the better or worse cultivation of memory and the faculty of recollection, then a few men, at least, have the power of becoming gods. The Guardians are such men, and it is probably with this in mind that Plato decrees that a Guardian at his death shall be honoured as a δαίμων, if Delphi approves, or at the least as fortunate and godlike (εὐδαίμων τε καὶ θεῖος).[10] Delphi, we must suppose, is able to tell whether a Guardian is a "true" philosopher and therefore a δαίμων, or whether he is not quite worthy of that degree of respect.

When the best of the Guardians have died, we must suppose that they return to the train of Zeus, where they were before being involved with earthly bodies. The Guardians are by nature φιλόσοφοι καὶ ἡγεμονικοί[11] and such pre-eminent souls are, as the *Phaedrus* tells us, devotees of the great leader[12] and supremely wise divinity. In this passage, Plato

---

[9] *Phaedrus* 249C.   [10] *Rep.* 7. 540C.   [11] *Phaedrus* 252E.

[12] In *Phaedrus* 246E, Zeus is described as the μέγας ἡγεμών. Hackforth, *Plato's Phaedrus* 99 n.3, reminds us that Μῆτις is the first wife of Zeus in Hesiod, *Theog.* 886.

speaks also of the "followers" of other Gods: of Hera, Ares, and Apollo.[13] That such persons are inferior to the "followers" of Zeus is certain. They are not philosophers, perhaps they are deficient intellectually, but they have practised ὁμοίωσις θεῷ as far as their inferior potentialities allow, and Plato seems, in the *Phaedrus* at least, not to exclude them from blessedness. Just as, in the *Symposium*, he certainly has some sympathy for the ἐρασταί of Phaedrus, so, as Hackforth reminds us, he feels admiration for such pairs of warrior-lovers as appear regularly in Spartan history and composed the famous Theban "Sacred Band."[14] Just as, in the *Republic*, the best of the Guardians are the followers of Zeus, so the others, and perhaps the ἐπίκουροι, may be the followers of Ares or of Hera. Even the artisans in the Ideal Republic are possibly the followers of some lesser divinity. So much, we may assume, can their will to Goodness achieve for them.

There is no megalomania in Plato. His Guardian is not a Superman who can recklessly set the laws at nought; and this alone is surprising when we compare him with some of his spurious modern descendants. Indeed it may seem strange that the Guardian's actions are in any way restricted, since he is a kind of god, and we may wonder what saved Plato from a closer resemblance to other delusions of grandeur. The answer is simple. It is that even gods are not the supreme elements of Being; that highest honour is reserved for the Forms. (We have seen already that it is only the ability to know the Forms that gives the Gods their divinity.) This belief that non-mental and non-personal entities are the ultimate Goods is what distinguishes Plato from most other philosophers and, which is important to our present investigation, from most of his leading disciples. Few of the later Platonists were able to maintain their Master's faith in such static abstracted ultimate principles. Even the One of Plotinus is, as we shall see, in some ways nearer to the everyday world. We shall be returning to this question many times during our study; let us content ourselves at the moment with saying that this is the feature which chiefly distinguishes the philosophy of Plato from the systems of the Neoplatonists.

If, according to Plato, we all have divinity within our grasp, why is the number of true philosophers so small? The answer is that, although τὸ λογιστικόν in our soul is indeed a δαίμων, it is usually quite powerless in the face of other more earthly elements and thus gains no opportunity to live the life it needs and to bring us to that blessedness for which we crave. This, however, is inadequate, for there is no doubt

[13]Ares in *Phaedrus* 252C, Hera and Apollo in 253D.
[14]Hackforth, *Plato's Phaedrus* 101.

that, with every possible advantage of enthusiasm and good instruction, most men could not complete many of the more elementary
stages in their desired advance to divinity. In other words, most men
are not intelligent enough to satisfy the exacting claims of Platonic
godhead. We can only say that Plato seems to have neglected this
point, and pass on.

For those few who are candidates for the honoured rôle of philosopher
and god, Plato is able to prescribe the exact syllabus, which is wholly
designed to purify the soul. It is most appropriate that the clearest
account of the purificatory importance of "Platonic studies" should
be in the *Phaedo*, for in that dialogue Socrates' views on the immortality of the soul are pitted against those of two Pythagoreans,
Simmias and Cebes, members of a school to which purification is of
supreme importance and from which some at least of Plato's own
opinions on the subject are undoubtedly derived. We read here that
any so-called virtue that is separate from wisdom is valueless, and
that in fact truth, moderation, justice, courage, and wisdom are a
kind of purification.[15] Without this purification we are uninitiated and
unsanctified (ἀμύητος καὶ ἀτέλεστος) and when we pass on to the other
world we shall be wallowing in the mire (ἐν βορβόρῳ). There is an echo
of this also in the *Republic*[16] where we are told that dialectic, which is
the coping-stone of wisdom, is able to draw the soul up to perfection
from that βόρβορος βαρβαρικός where it must dwell until it can be purified by study.

Moderation, justice, and courage can proceed from one of two things,
according to Plato: they can be the result of the true opinion (ἀληθὴς
δόξα) of a disciplined mind, or they can be the clearly visualized
Ideals of the Man of Wisdom. To the end of his life, Plato appears to
have maintained the Socratic position that Virtue is Knowledge; but
he made this advance on his Master's teaching, that he claimed to
know *what kind* of knowledge is required. This knowledge, he thought,
must be knowledge of the Forms; let a man once possess that and he
will at once establish his "civic" virtues of moderation, justice, and
courage on a permanent and stable base. Hence the detailed exposition
in the *Republic* of how those who have, as it were, already passed the
tests set by "civic virtue" grounded on "true opinion," may pass on
to those final purificatory studies which will make their master divine
(θεῖος).

We have already spoken of the Greek tendency towards anthropomorphism, from which even Aristotle, with his "professor's God," was

[15]*Phaedo* 69C.   [16]*Rep.* 7. 533D.

not free. Plato, too, tended to deduce the activities of his Gods from the activities of himself and his friends. His own primary interest in the field of study was in mathematics, and, remembering that he forbade those ignorant of geometry to enter the Academy, we find him seeing in mathematics the divine temper and therefore a *sine qua non* for the philosopher. This mathematical tendency, so deplored by Aristotle,[17] led Plato to make a mathematical "Form," that of the One, the equivalent of the Form of the Good, and to insist that the Gods are the most perfect exponents of this particular branch of knowledge. Leaving the question of the validity of this kind of egotism aside, we may turn to enquire in more detail what these mathematical studies involve.

The preliminary subjects are to be arithmetic, geometry plain and solid, plus astronomy and harmony regarded as branches of pure mathematics. These are the prerequisites for the dialectician and cannot be passed over. Without them, the *Republic* tells us, dialectic is valueless, if not meaningless.[18] What little dialectical method can be picked up without them can only be used as eristic. Furthermore, Plato never came to believe that this valuation of mathematics was unjustifiably high. If anything, a remark in the *Laws*[19] puts an even higher premium on it. No one, says Plato, can hope to become godlike (θεῖος) without a knowledge of arithmetic. Finally, we should consider the extraordinary remark of Socrates to Callicles in the *Gorgias*:[20] "Wise men say that heaven and earth, and gods and men, are held together by communion and friendship, by orderliness and moderation and by justice . . . . But you, I think, despite your cleverness, pay no attention to these things and have not noticed how powerful geometrical equality is among men and gods. You think you ought to practise self-seeking because you neglect the science of geometry." Such faith in the power of mathematics to put Callicles back on the straight and narrow path reveals how much importance Plato attached to the science as a means to man's spiritual advance.

In all justice, however, it should be remembered that Plato has another strong reason for selecting these particular studies apart from his predilection for them. He explains in the seventh book of the *Republic* that all branches of learning are of two kinds. Either the initial act of sense-perception is sufficient in itself for knowledge, or else it

---

[17]Arist. *Met.* A. 992B. Ἀλλὰ γέγονε τὰ μαθήματα τοῖς νῦν ἡ φιλοσοφία.

[18]*Rep.* 7. 533A8. δαίμονες (like νοῦς) come from God θείᾳ μοίρᾳ. Cf. ἔρως in *Phaedrus* 265B.

[19]*Laws* 7. 818C.   [20]*Gorgias* 507E–508A.

requires to be completed by analytical or comprehensive thought if it is
to attain to any degree of clarity. Plato is not interested, for example,
in counting the apples in a box and finding that there are one or two or
three. He is particularly interested in the nature of the unit, for he
sees that the same thing presents the appearance of one thing and of a
plurality of things at the same moment,[21] and in such notions as "big"
and "small" and "double." Study of these things, he believes, gives
the would-be philosopher a "synoptic"[22] view more developed than
that of the ordinary man, without which dialectic is impossible.

That such mathematical studies have a further value, and that they
appeal to the δαίμων within us, becomes clear from the *Timaeus*. There
we learn of the kinship between the divine element in our souls and the
Soul of the World. Both contain harmonies and revolutions, but those
in our souls are distorted at birth. If, then, we can study the harmonies and revolutions of the Universe, we shall be both feeding the
divine part in us and at the same time straightening out those distor-
tions that are inherent in our humanity. When we are thus in accord
with the Universe, we have reached the highest goal of life.[23]

Mathematical studies, however, will tell us little about the Forms
themselves, which as "lovers of wisdom" we are to make our ultimate
objective. All they can do is prepare our minds and dispositions for the
reception of that science which will allow us to share in the causes of
the divinity of the Gods. This mighty science is, of course, dialectic.
We are not concerned here with the precise meaning of Plato's
description of the working of this science in the *Republic* and elsewhere.[24] What we are concerned with is the results which he claims for
it, and which make it the coping-stone of all studies. Plato tells us that
there is no other method of investigation which both tries to grasp
the real nature of each individual Form and is unsatisfied with accepting unexamined axioms such as satisfy the geometers. Dialectic is able
to form a conception of the greatest of all the objects of study, which
is the Form of the Good, and by its light to understand the whole of
the rest of the real world without any aid from studies outside that
world. If it could not do this, Plato insists, it would be valueless. He
asserts[25] that the thinker whose dialectic fails to reach the Form of the

---

[21]*Rep.* 7. 525A.
[22]*Rep.* 7. 537C7. ὁ μὲν γὰρ συνοπτικὸς διαλεκτικός, ὁ δὲ μὴ οὔ.
[23]For this whole passage, see *Tim.* 90D.
[24]For this subject, see especially Robinson, *Plato's Earlier Dialectic*, which contains
a summary of the existing views.
[25]*Rep.* 7. 534C.

Good is not a philosopher at all, but a mere lover of "opinion," and
that he is, as it were, sleeping his life away in a pursuit which will
fail to give him any useful standard of values.

We see, then, that we have become perfect dialecticians; we are as
the Gods. At this point we may pause and wonder what our feelings
towards those Gods are while we are still striving towards their blessed
life. Are we to love them as perfect practitioners of Goodness? Apparently not, for as Professor Dodds[26] has pointed out, the notion of love
directed towards God is absent from the earliest Greek writers. The
word φιλόθεος is unknown in literature before Aristotle and is of rare
occurrence even there. Indeed, the Greeks appear not to have loved
their native Gods, at least as individuals. The *Magna Moralia*[27] tells
us that it would be absurd for a man to claim that he felt love for
Zeus, and Aristotle[28] insists that φιλία between man and God is impossible because of their difference in status. In at least one passage of
Plato we seem to be justified in believing that we have little cause to
love the Gods. After all, they are only doing what we are trying to do.
They are not to be our objects of devotion. That honour is to be reserved for the Forms. The Good is not good because the Gods love it;
rather the Gods love the Good because it is good. Such is the general
conclusion we can draw from the discussions of "the Holy" (τὸ ὅσιον) in
the *Euthyphro*.[29]

We are not then to love the Gods, but Wisdom and the Forms; and
this, as Plato must have been well aware, is a paradoxical notion. For
to most men love is a very personal emotion. Is it possible to experience love for realities which are in a sense abstractions? The
history of Platonism in the Ancient World shows, as we shall see, that
this kind of love was too rarefied to last. Plato was demanding an
emotional response beyond the range of most of even the greatest of
his admirers, and with this tacit condemnation many modern scholars
and critics would agree. Let us, for example, cite the words of Professor
Grube, who writes:

In another way too, Plato's conception of philosophic love is difficult for us to accept.
As we follow the philosopher on his upward journey, we feel that something has gone
wrong, that passionate oratory has somehow left love behind; that in the contempla-

---

[26]Dodds, *The Greeks* 35.
[27]*M.M.* 1208B 30. ἄτοπον γὰρ ἂν εἴη εἴ τις φαίη φιλεῖν τὸν Δία. The feeling of
the Athenians for their goddess was probably more national pride than love; it was
felt for Athena as representative of Athens, rather than for her own sake.
[28]Arist. *E.N.* 1159A 5ff.
[29]*Euthyphro* 10Aff.

tion of supreme beauty the philosopher may indeed find a sublime satisfaction, but we would hardly call this the satisfaction of love, which must surely be limited to relations between individuals. If we look closer we shall find that the point when we should part company with Plato is where Diotima reaches the beauty of "laws and institutions." Love, we feel, must have and retain some sort of physical basis and Plato has here . . . been carried away on the tide of his own magnificent metaphors.[30]

If this indictment is true, as I shall suggest is implied by the direction in which Platonism turned in the hands of Plotinus and Origen, it is a serious flaw in the Platonic system. What we should first consider is how far Plato himself was aware of the unusual and perhaps impossible direction of his thoughts and what steps he suggested, if any, to remedy it. Since this question will be bound up with our previous remarks on the purificatory studies—for plainly love is the only motive possible for a man to undertake such an arduous and demanding course and complete it successfully—we shall require a fairly detailed examination of the two dialogues in which Plato treats most fully of the subject of love, namely the *Symposium* and the *Phaedrus*.

Despite the fact that Plato was, by ancient standards, a voluminous author, he followed his master Socrates' belief in the superiority of the spoken to the written word, of oral instruction to the reading of books. In the *Phaedrus*,[31] he goes so far as to insist that the only benefit one can derive from the written word is that it is an aid to memory. Real philosophy can only be learned by personal instruction, as is made clear in the *Seventh Letter*,[32] where we learn that Plato has never written anything of the highest aspects of his philosophy. He says: "There is no treatise of mine on these subjects nor will I ever write one." Indeed they are not even describable in concrete terms, being above and beyond mere words. Plato did, however, lecture on these highest subjects (τὸ μέγιστον μάθημα), for we know from Simplicius that Aristotle and Speusippus, among others, published their notes upon them. His aim doubtless was to lead his pupils to gain from his discourses that communion with the subject which could arise from long application and which alone led to an intuitive grasp of the Forms.

If the study of books is valueless for the philosopher and personal instruction vital, some kind of pupil-master relationship is necessary. Plato believed that this relationship could be a sublimated form of love. He wanted to start from this love of individuals and transmute personal attraction into first a common love of learning, and then perhaps into a love of the Eternal Verities themselves without reference

[30]Grube, *Plato's Thought* 114.
[31]*Phaedrus* 275C.
[32]*Ep.* 7. 341C.

to the companion of one's studies, the love of former days. The last stage is a little doubtful even to Plato, who appears to waver on the issue of whether the original personal and in some degree physical elements can be *completely* discarded, as we shall see.

But first we must define our terms. What, we should ask, does Plato mean by "love"? The answer Plato gives in the *Symposium*[33] is at first as surprising to us as it was to the assembled company in the house of Agathon. In general, non-philosophical terms, we are accustomed to think of love as a Good-in-itself. This is part of our heritage from Christianity, and as I will later suggest, from Neoplatonism too. It is not, however, the view of Socrates, who, in the *Symposium*, pays much more attention to the *odi et amo* view of Catullus, to the feelings of bitter-sweetness that love can bring, to the notion that love is not a good because it is, in essence, unfulfilled.[34] Accordingly, when he hears it extravagantly praised by Agathon he claims to be amazed and hurriedly denies any knowledge of love-matters at all. This is, of course, his accustomed irony, and his friends recognize it as such. He pretends to have been guilty of the "foolish" notion that when eulogizing a particular person or thing it is necessary to adhere closely to the truth. Finally he owns that he is willing to speak after all, provided he be allowed to ask Agathon a few questions before he starts.

The next passage is of the utmost importance, for Socrates makes Agathon admit that if love were good and beautiful, as he has claimed it is, it would have no desire for union or possession of what is good and beautiful outside itself. He then hastily adds that it is not, of course, bad and ugly either, and thus must be an intermediate state. There follows his account of how he learned this truth from Diotima, the priestess of Mantinea, who was once his instructress on the subject of the true nature of love. Diotima insisted that love cannot even be a God, as most men seem to believe, since it is impossible that Gods should be deficient in Goodness and Beauty. He must therefore be something between a mortal and an immortal. He is a great spirit (δαίμων μέγας), a member of that class of semi-divine beings which includes the human soul, or at least the rational part of it. In the words of L. Robin, "La nature synthétique de l'Amour fait de lui un intermédiaire entre les qualités opposées que cette nature a pour fonction d'unir.[35]

Diotima continues her description of the nature of Love with an

---

[33]*Symp.* 201A–204D.
[34]For Ἔρως as a "lack," see also *Lysis* 217.
[35]Robin, *La Théorie platonicienne de l'Amour* 129

account of his birth. That his father was Poros or "Resource" and his mother Penia or "Poverty" is in itself a sufficient proof of his own nature. He unites in his own being the qualities of both his parents. He is, as Plato says, "always poor and far from being tender and beautiful. On the contrary he is hard and parched, shoeless and homeless. He always sleeps on the gound with no bedding, resting on doorsteps or beneath the stars on the open road." Such are the characteristics he derives from his mother. From his father, on the other hand, he inherits his bravery, impetuosity, and desire for wisdom.

Such is love. A doubtful divinity (δαίμων), we may think, and Socrates is perhaps to be pardoned for asking what use he is to mankind. Diotima, however, is able to explain that he alone can supply the motive by which we may reach out towards the Good and the Beautiful, that we may attain them and thus reach the happiness and blessedness of the Gods. When we reach that degree of perfection, we shall not love the Forms; we shall possess them. No God, says Plato, is a philosopher. He does not "love" Wisdom; he already possesses it and has thus lost all sense of desire—Ἔρως.[36]

This violent sense of need is what Plato primarily means by love, and to the casual reader his analysis of the nature of Ἔρως gives little trace of any non-appetitive ideal. However, when we come to consider the actions of the Gods and of those perfect mortals who have been able to follow the path of Ἔρως to its end, we find a considerably less egoistic, and, as the future was to show, more fruitful notion, that of Creation as a result of "Love perfected."[37] We shall be returning to this point again in our examination of Plato, and when we turn to the Neoplatonists we shall speak of Creation in more detail, but for the time being let us simply remember the possible dichotomy of Plato's thought on the nature of love, and the suggestion that, while he normally regards it as an appetitive emotion, there are traces of a less egoistic outlook.

With this general view in mind, let us turn to the "lover's progress" as Diotima describes it. First of all, he must love the ephemeral beauty of a particular person in this world. No one is able to avoid this preliminary stage, which Plato would like, we may suspect, to be able to suppress, but is too realistic to do so. From the individual beauty, our potential philosopher may come to realize that such passing beauty is

[36]*Symp.* 203E. θεῶν οὐδεὶς φιλοσοφεῖ οὐδ' ἐπιθυμεῖ σοφὸς γενέσθαι· Ἔστι γάρ.

[37]For a detailed examination of this view, see pp. 26–34 and compare Markus, "The Dialectic of Eros," 219–230.

more permanently grasped if it be recognized as quite widely distributed. So he becomes a lover of beautiful bodies in general. Next, he must make a great stride forward and come to set a higher value on the soul than on the body. This is in itself a considerable advance, and is probably to be equated with what Pausanias has earlier suggested as the highest point that love can attain, but for Plato it is still only a beginning, for from there we must proceed, he says, to contemplate Beauty, first as it appears in laws and observances (νόμοις καὶ ἐπιτηδεύμασιν), then in the branches of knowledge—by which he presumably means the studies undertaken by the Guardians in the *Republic* and the future philosophers in the Academy—and finally in Beauty itself. This is the goal that can be attained by those who love in the right way.[38] The philosopher has attained to the blessedness of the Gods through the mediation of love; he is now able to share with them the contemplation of the Eternal Forms.

It has often been claimed that the emphasis placed in the *Symposium* on the power of emotion is a counterblast to the simple body-soul dualism[39] and associated intellectualism of the *Phaedo*. We know how in that dialogue Socrates is made to declare that the purpose of philosophy is to provide a practice for death.[40] To accomplish this "practice" and to achieve any clear and true knowledge, we must, he insists, be rid of the body and see by the soul alone.[41] But even in this extreme dualist passage, the phrase "lovers of Wisdom" (ἐρασταὶ φρονήσεως) occurs and brings out what is at the back of Plato's mind in the *Symposium*. He is still as certainly opposed to the tyranny of the body as he is in the *Phaedo*, but he has grasped more firmly the notion that if the Soul can, as it were, win the support of love, which has previously been tied to the things of the "body," the "partisans of the Soul," that is the philosophers, will the more readily subdue bodily desires. Soul is willing to accept a purified notion of love; indeed she is shown to need such a powerful motive-force as the only means of attaining her ends. She is only willing to accept it, however, on her own terms, and these terms are that the physical bases shall gradually →

[38]*Symp.* 211B. διὰ τὸ ὀρθῶς παιδεραστεῖν.

[39]For the question whether this dualism was superseded by the theory of the tripartite soul, see, for example, Hackforth's translation of the *Phaedo* (Cambridge 1955) 49. Passages such as *Rep.* 10.611C and *Tim.* 43BC may show that Plato regarded the lower two sections of the soul as ultimately akin to the body, and that thus the dualism was maintained. Compare below, pp. 105–109.

[40]*Phaedo* 64A.

[41]*Phaedo* 66D. εἰ μέλλομέν ποτε καθαρῶς τι ἔσεσθαι, ἀπαλλακτέον αὐτοῦ καὶ αὐτῇ τῇ ψυχῇ θεατέον αὐτὰ τὰ πράγματα.

be eliminated. The perfect philosopher appears to outgrow Ἔρως even
in that "right form" which was the ladder which sustained his ascent.
If the Gods do not "love Wisdom, since they are already wise" it is
plain that they love nothing else. They "have" or "possess" their
wisdom; they do not "love" it. There seems to be an inadequacy in
Plato's appetitive theory.

Furthermore, if for the Gods, and therefore presumably for the perfect philosophers, the "physical basis" and the "love itself" are bypassed, we may wonder why such beings still trouble about the Realities at all. We shall suggest later that this lack of motive at the highest
level is one reason why Origen and other later Platonists reintroduced
the physical basis of Ἔρως in the form of the doctrine that the Soul is
the Bride of Christ.

Reverting to the *Symposium*, however, we find that Plato, at least,
is convinced that purified philosophic love is possible and that his
master Socrates had been a living proof of the fact. This justification of
his position is most admirably conveyed by the introduction of
Alcibiades, who insists on making a speech in praise of Socrates. The
whole tenor of this panegyric, as has often been said, is to portray
Socrates as an ἐρωτικός in action.[42] It is not, Robin points out,[43] entirely
accidental that the philosopher is at once compared with Silenus, who
was, after all, a δαίμων. It is with such purified beings that the true
philosopher belongs. Silenus is the recipient of one form of "divine
madness,"[44] that of Dionysus, Socrates of another, that of Eros.

Thus far, then, we have seen that under the inspiration of love, the
true philosopher sets out on his course of purification and study which
will culminate, when he sees the true Beauty of the Forms, in his
sharing in the divinity of the Gods. What, we may ask, is his reaction
then? Does he pass his time in contemplation freed from all emotion,
desire or action? The answer, surprisingly, and perhaps, in view of
what we have seen, illogically, is No. It is clear that for Plato the con-
templator of the Forms must, as it were, pour out his contemplation
into some kind of action. If he be a God, he will create; if he be "god-
like," he will do his best to encourage the good life among the less
fortunate mortals; the latter course may perhaps still be described as
a strictly egoistic craving for the immortality of an earthly memorial,

---

[42]Markus, "The Dialectic of Eros," 227, points out that the Ἔρως of Socrates in
the scene with Alcibiades is not a "sense of need," but rather a "completeness."
Both Socrates and Alcibiades are ἐρωτικοί (228), but the Ἔρως of each is distinct.

[43]Robin, *La Théorie platonicienne de l'Amour* 131.

[44]*Phaedrus* 244A ff., and for the whole subject see Dodds, *The Greeks* 64 ff.

but the former can hardly come under this head as Gods are already immortal.

Let us first consider the life of the Gods.[45] The essential part of it is described in the *Phaedrus*, naturally enough in mythical form. Gods, we read, are similar to men in that their souls can be likened to a charioteer and two horses. It is in the character of the horses that the difference becomes evident, for the Gods' horses are both good and obedient to the charioteer, who is the "reasoning" element (τὸ λογιστικόν), whereas the men's are inferior to a greater or lesser degree. When the souls of the Gods reach the edge of heaven and see beyond into the ὑπερουράνιος τόπος, they have no distractions from their pure contemplation. They are able, therefore, to grasp and know the Forms in completeness, and as they really are. The Forms so engrain themselves in the minds of the Gods that they need no power of ἀνάμνησις to recapture them. Form has become immanent in the Gods; we may almost say that the Gods have become *wholly* characterized by Form. They have become wholly good and just and beautiful. Since this is so, it is open blasphemy even to suggest that they could be the cause of evil, as the poets have done. This is stated explicitly in the *Republic*.[46] Socrates says: "Since God is good, he is not the cause of all . . . ; on the contrary he is responsible for only a small part of human affairs; for the larger part he is not responsible. For we have far fewer good things than bad; and we must make God the cause of the good things while we must look elsewhere for the cause of the rest, and not ascribe them to God."

When the Gods reach the ὑπερουράνιος τόπος, they come to be wholly characterized by the Forms. The Forms are immanent in them. This does not imply, of course, that they are not also transcendent, and indeed that transcendence is not their primary nature. The *Phaedrus* tells us that the Gods travel *up* to the ὑπερουράνιος τόπος in order to partake of the Forms, which have their abode there, beyond space and time and motion, as is implied. Plato is sure that the Forms have their existence outside the "being" or Νοῦς of the Gods and could continue to exist even if there were no "minds" to apprehend them. The well-known passage of the *Parmenides*[47] which insists that the Forms can

---

[45] *Phaedrus* 248. When speaking of the souls of the Gods, I include Νοῦς in my definition of soul. Similarly, when speaking of a Form-Soul dualism, I include such examples of Νοῦς *qua* Νοῦς as the Demiourgos under the general heading "Soul." Mind and Soul, though probably kept distinct, at least in the *Timaeus*, can conveniently be considered together in antithesis with the Forms.

[46] *Rep.* 2. 379C2.   [47] *Parm.* 132B.

never be equated with mere concepts is never refuted. As far as we know, the distinction between thoughts and the objects of thought always remained a cardinal point in the Platonic system.

So far we have only regarded the Gods as contemplators of the Forms. Is that, we may ask, all that their perfection allows? The *Timaeus* suggests that it is not, and this suggestion was, as will be seen, one of the most fruitful sources of the future developments of Platonism. We are told that the Demiourgos, whose outlook is that of a God even if he himself is a fiction, is the Creator of the order of the world. This idea, even in the moderate form suggested by Plato, must have sounded strange to the Greeks who heard it. And when Plato goes on to assert that he created the world because he is "good and has no envy (φθόνος),[48] thus repeating a belief he had already propounded in the *Phaedrus*,[49] he sets himself up against almost all Greek religious thinking. Pindar sums up the prevailing attitude with the words θνητὸς ὤν, θνητὰ φρόνει. To think more than mortal thoughts is to encroach on the divine prerogative, and such ὕβρις will arouse divine jealousy (φθόνος). Plato's assertion is a denial of all this. The Gods are not jealous; how can they be if they are good? On the contrary he says: "God was good and in him that is good no envy can ever arise. And since He was without envy, He desired that all things should be as like Himself as possible." Since the interpretation of this passage has aroused no little controversy, and since it is most important to our theme of the developments of Platonism, it is worth considering in more detail. We are warned by Cornford[50] against introducing "importations from later theology" and in particular against Taylor, who is said to have done so. Cornford writes:

Professor Taylor, for instance, after pointing out that Timaeus is thinking of the common Greek view that the divine (τὸ θεῖον) is grudging in its bestowal of good things, proceeds: "So just because God is good, He does not keep his blessedness selfishly to Himself. He seeks to make something else as much like Himself in goodness as possible. It is of the very nature of goodness and love to 'overflow.' This is why there is a world, and why, with all its defects it is 'very good.'" If this is intended as a paraphrase of Plato's words, it is misleading. . . . Still less is there the slightest

[48]*Tim.* 29E.

[49]*Phaedrus* 247A. φθόνος γὰρ ἔξω θείου χόρου ἵσταται. In an article in the *Classical Quarterly*, entitled "The Place of the *Timaeus* in Plato's Dialogues," G. E. L. Owen has attempted to correct the usual view of the *Timaeus* as one of Plato's latest works. Against Owen, H. Cherniss, "The Relation of the *Timaeus* to Plato's Later Dialogues," and J. M. Rist, "The Order of the Later Dialogues of Plato."

[50]Cornford, *Plato's Cosmology* 34. It will be plain that my discussion here is in complete disagreement with the view of *Timaeus* 29Eff. expressed by Goldschmidt, *La Religion de Platon* 55–56.

warrant in Greek thought of the pre-Christian centuries for the notion of "over-flowing love," or love of any kind, prompting a god to make a world. It is not fair either to Plato or to the New Testament to ascribe the most characteristic revelations of the Founder of Christianity to a pagan polytheist.

This is a damning indictment, and because it is so strong it calls for examination in detail. We may remark at once that Plotinus was certainly in a sense a polytheist, and yet the notion of "overflowing creation" occurs continually throughout his works. The word ὑπερρεῖν is frequently used to describe the "procession" of Νοῦς from the One. Whether this "overflowing" could be called "love" is a question into which we must enquire, but that it could occur at all in a "pagan polytheist" may make us suspect that Cornford has not hit upon the complete truth. Nor can we suppose a Christian source for Plotinus' doctrine. Plotinus lived in the third century A.D., but for all the influence Christianity had on his thought, he might as well have lived before Christ.

Returning to Plato, we may ask what is meant by the notion that God wanted to bring matter into an orderly form and as like himself as possible *because* he is good. Does Goodness imply this desire to *produce* perfection? Is this desire instinctive in the being that is good? If it is, then Taylor's use of the notion of "overflowing" is justified. If we do not use this word to describe the relations of the Demiourgos to the "chaos" outside, what word can we use? Beneath Cornford's attack there appears to be an unwillingness to understand what motive or nature the Demiourgos is supposed by Plato to possess.

Here it may be objected that the Demiourgos creates from motives analogous to those of a human craftsman (δημιουργός). This view is a denial of Plato's own words, for a human craftsman does not create "in order that everything may be as like himself as possible" but for ends which are both practical and, if he be a good craftsman, artistic. The man whom the Greeks call a δημιουργός is in the commercial world; at least part of his motive is to earn a living. Furthermore, he does not create "because he is good"; he may be a rogue and still be a good craftsman. The goodness of the human δημιουργός is a relative good; his moral goodness is irrelevant to his craft. The goodness of the Demiourgos in the *Timaeus*, on the other hand, is absolute good-ness. His motive for creation is that he is good, not that he is good at his job. It seems that to draw out the parallel between the human craftsman and the Demiourgos in detail is misleading. All the two have in common is the fact that they create—and from a pattern; their motives are quite different.

Taylor has used the phrase "overflowing love" of the Demiourgos. We shall discuss later the thoughts of Plato on divine love, but before doing so it is necessary to consider the notion of "overflowing" a little further. It may be objected that the application of this word to the theories of Plato is anachronistic since it suggests an emanation theory of the Neoplatonic type. However, there seems to be no reason why such a suggestion should be dismissed without a hearing. Plotinus certainly thought he found his emanation theory in Plato, and even if he read more into his Master's works than was there, it is unproven that these passages from the *Timaeus* do not to some extent fore-shadow the Neoplatonic view. As Trouillard has said of the *Symposium*:[51] "On trouverait également dans la théorie platonicienne de l'amour, qui n'est pas seulement aspiration mais générosité au sens plain, un germe de procession." We shall speak below of the connec-tion between the *Timaeus* and the theory of love in the *Symposium*, but Trouillard's view can perfectly well be accepted without assuming that the *whole* Neoplatonic theory of emanation is to be found in Plato. If this be recognized, there will appear to be no objection to Taylor's use of the word "overflowing."

In the event of its being objected that, if the Demiourgos is only a fiction, the difficulty of his motive for creation can be shown to be unreal, one must answer that it cannot, for the Demiourgos' state of mind, as a being contemplating the eternal patterns, is clearly that of the Platonic Gods in general, and few would maintain that *all* Plato's Gods, of whatever kind they be, are fictions. The mere appear-ance of the Demiourgos in the *Timaeus*, be he fiction or not, shows that Plato had thought about the nature of the Gods and had con-sidered goodness and lack of jealousy as suitable attributes.[52] This being so, we may further take into account two phrases from the *Apology* which describe Socrates as a gift from God and add that "If he be put to death, the Athenians will be allowed to pass their lives in ignorance unless God in his care for them (κηδόμενος 31A) is willing to send another gadfly to stir them up." These views may be those of Socrates, not Plato; they may be purely metaphorical, but they represent, I believe, a way of thought which is more akin to a God of "overflowing love" than Taylor's critics have allowed. It is true that

---

[51]Trouillard, *La Procession plotinienne* 60.

[52]My view of the "ontological status" of the Demiourgos is very like that of Professor Skemp (*The Theory of Motion in Plato's Later Dialogues* 110), who writes: "The ultimate ἀρχὴ κινήσεως (the Demiourgos) though hard to find . . . is as real as the Forms."

there is no formal theory here, but it does not follow from this that we can assume Plato to be using a popular mode of thinking with which he has no sympathy whatever. However unpleasant it might be to others, he would not employ it if it did not correspond to his own thoughts.

Further, if we have here a Socratic manner of thinking or speaking, since Plato was, after all, a pupil of Socrates, it is not absurd to suppose that he might have assimilated something of his master's attitude on this matter, however different from his formal theory it might be. We may surmise then that the action of God in these passages from the *Apology* bears a resemblance to the action of the Demiourgos in the *Timaeus*, for by sending Socrates into the world, God was sending an apostle of the life of reason and through him bringing order out of chaos.

Of our discussion up to this point it may fairly be said that we have demonstrated the relevance of Taylor's suggestion that Plato had a conception of God's goodness "overflowing," but that we have not shown the association of such "overflowing" with love. The nearest we have come to this is the passage from the *Apology*, and that, by itself, is not convincing. However, the passages so far mentioned do not exhaust the indications of some kind of divine love in the Platonic writings. We learn from the *Republic*[53] that only good can come from the Gods, from the *Phaedrus*[54] that Zeus "arranges all and *cares for* all," and from the *Laws*[55] that in the age of Cronos God was φιλάνθρωπος. Even if we discount the description of the Demiourgos as πατήρ,[56] as I am loath to do, evidence is not entirely lacking that Plato saw the Gods as actively beneficent and loving.

At this point we should begin to put the results attained so far into order. We have shown that the Demiourgos is without jealousy and is good; we have shown that his activities may be called "overflowing." We have seen too a little evidence that Plato was aware, elsewhere than in the *Timaeus*, of love shown by God or Gods for mankind. The question before us is: can we put all this together and conclude that Plato has, as Taylor suggested, considered the possibility of seeing God as overflowing love? There is no specific mention of God's love in the *Timaeus*; this we readily admit. The other passages about God's love for man may, though I believe should not, be dismissed as vague and inadequate. What must be accomplished, therefore, is an examination of Plato's doctrine of Ἔρως itself in the *Sym-*

[53]*Rep.* 378BC, 380C, 617E.   [54]*Phaedrus* 246E.
[55]*Laws* 713D.   [56]*Tim.* 28C, 37C.

posium and *Phaedrus!* If it can be shown that in these works there are indications of an "Ερως which is not merely appetitive, and that such "Ερως is the reward of the philosopher's quest, then it will not seem too much of a jump to attribute it to Gods as well as to philosophers, since the philosopher-king has attained likeness to God as far as he is able! Furthermore, if "Ερως in the *Symposium* and *Phaedrus* appears in any way non-appetitive, the passages about God's love for mankind will have more weight and will have to be considered more carefully! We shall then be able to say that "Ερως may be down-flowing and creative, that the Demiourgos (and therefore the Gods in general) is creative, overflowing, and good, and finally that Taylor's description of the Demiourgos as both good and loving should be considered very carefully, since the nature of "Ερως *may* coincide with the nature of the Demiourgos. As Armstrong has said:[57] "Being good for Plato means doing good." If it turns out that "Ερως may also mean "doing good," then it will look as though "Ερως and "being good" have, for Plato, similar implications. Then we may conclude that although Plato does not *say* the Demiourgos has overflowing love, he thinks of him in the same terms as he thinks of love.

Naturally, even to say that Plato thought of God in terms of over-flowing love does not necessarily imply that he held an *emanation* theory of the Neoplatonic type, since the phrase could denote other modes of creation. The point is that since the Demiourgos must have some motive for his actions, and Plato suggests that this motive is his goodness, we are justified in considering the relation of this "goodness" to similar motives for creation, if they occur, in the rest of the Platonic writings. It remains therefore to consider the *Symposium* and *Phaedrus*.

Have we not already suggested that the idea of "overflowing love" is alien to the Platonic notion of "Ερως? Does not "Ερως consist only in a *desire* for what we do not possess? Have we not found Plato saying that the Gods do not love Wisdom for they are already wise? Indeed we have, but we must further suggest that over the issue of the nature of love Plato has not worked out his thought into a fully coherent system, but left some striking contradictions which it was possible for his successors to develop. For alongside his theory of love as desire, we have his definition of its results as γέννησις καὶ τόκος ἐν τῷ καλῷ, the urge to produce a beautiful offspring as the outcome of a true association with Beauty.

When this result of the emotion of love is propounded by Diotima,[58] Socrates asks for a fuller explanation—as well he might, seeing that it

[57]Armstrong, "Platonic Eros," 109.   [58]*Symp.* 206B.

suggests that love is something more than desire. But Diotima, seeming
to hold to her principle, replies that the "begetting and bearing in the
beautiful" is man's attempt to grasp at immortality—and on this reply
may be based an objection to my thesis. The objection runs thus: "Diotima says that the desire and need for immortality is the cause of this
γέννησις καὶ τόκος ἐν τῷ καλῷ; therefore she means that creation is
simply self-perpetuation motivated by an Ἔρως which is still wholly
appetitive." This objection is answered by Markus, who reminds us
that in our admiration for the contribution of Diotima, we tend to
forget the contributions of some of the other speakers. Markus[59] points
out, for example, that when Agathon begins his speech, he "simply
ignores what Aristophanes has said" (about love as desire) and
"reaffirms what has been quite lost sight of since the first speech, that
by Phaedrus: the 'perfection' of love." As we have seen, these statements by Agathon are apparently demolished by Socrates, but they
must not be completely forgotten. Love as a "need" is not perfect,
but the love that "is desire to give rather than to receive,"[60] that is
"a kind of generosity rather than a kind of need," would fit the
eulogies of Phaedrus and Agathon much better, and Diotima herself
speaks of such love after 210A. /

We should look very closely at the passage which follows. As Cornford[61] points out, "immortality in all the three forms so far described
is immortality of the mortal creature, who may perpetuate his race,
his fame, his thoughts in another. The individual himself does not
survive; he dies, and leaves something behind. This is immortality in
time, not in an eternal world. . . . The disclosure of the other world—
the eternal realm of the Ideas—is reserved for the greater mysteries
that follow." The culmination of this latter section is the vision of
Beauty. It is certain that only the philosopher will attain this vision.
He will know the Forms, and that knowledge will carry with it the
conviction of the immortality of the soul. He will not need to crave
immortality; he will know that he already possesses it. Yet he will

[59]Markus, "The Dialectic of Eros," 222. Cf. *Symp.* 197C.

[60]*Ibid.*, 227. My attention was drawn to Markus' article by Professor Armstrong
after I had reached my own conclusions on Ἔρως. Although we differ, in that I am
more inclined than he to see a contradiction in Plato's mind on the nature of Ἔρως,
where he finds a more consistent advance in the *Symposium* towards a view of Ἔρως
as "a desire to give rather than to receive," I am glad to find confirmation of my view
that Plato is somehow expanding the meaning of Ἔρως beyond that which most
Greeks could accept.

[61]Cornford, "The Doctrine of Eros in Plato's *Symposium*," *The Unwritten Philosophy*
75.

still possess the power of τόκος ἐν τῷ καλῷ, for in 212A he is described as begetting and rearing a true virtue. What is the explanation of this paradox?

In 206E, love is said to be not of the beautiful, but of immortality. There Diotima is speaking of the less elevated kinds of love. Now, in 211–212, she is considering the higher stages—and here love is of the beautiful. (Thus in the highest Ἔρως, love is of the beautiful *as well as* being creative. This distinction is most important. Furthermore, the creativity in 212A is not the same as that in 209DE. In 209DE we hear of the "immortality" gained by lawgivers and educators—those who beget virtue according to a noble but inferior kind of Ἔρως, an Ἔρως not of the beautiful, but of immortality. In 212A, we hear of the τόκος ἐν τῷ καλῷ of the philosopher. His object of love is Beauty itself, and, since he knows the Forms, he cannot but create and beget true virtue. Love of Beauty must make the philosopher creative. His creativity is the outcome of his vision of the world of Forms; it is not *desired* for any ulterior motive of obtaining immortality. Is it then unreasonable to call such creativity "overflowing," and is not such overflowing the culmination and effect of Ἔρως? There can be no reasonable doubt that the Ἔρως of the philosopher "overflows" into creation in a way that cannot possibly be dismissed as simply appetitive. As Festugière[62] has put it: "Ainsi l'amour égoïste se transmue-t-il en un amour qui donne." Such creativity makes the philosopher dear to the Gods. Of him, if of any man, it can be said that he is immortal, since not only does he contemplate the immortal Forms and know his own immortality, but his works too must, since they derive their inspiration from what is immortal, themselves share this immortality. Yet although his works secure a finer immortality than do those of a Lycurgus, they are not accomplished for this end. They are the inevitable creations of a man given up to the love of Beauty.

Let us now turn to the *Phaedrus*. Armstrong[63] has pointed to a kind of Ἔρως in this dialogue akin to that which we have just observed in the *Symposium*. This evidence strengthens our case greatly. As Armstrong puts it:

The true lover's *eros* does not lead him to want to possess and use his beloved, physically ... or even spiritually. It leads him to try to make his beloved more god-like, to "work on him and adorn him" as if he was an image of the patron god (252D). And it is precisely in trying to make his beloved more like the god that he becomes more like the god himself (253A). Here again we find the idea that *eros* is not just a

[62]Festugière, *Contemplation* 336.
[63]Armstrong, "Platonic Eros," 108.

self-centred passion to satisfy one's own need by acquiring something good or beautiful. It is a desire of absolute good or beauty which is somehow inevitably also a desire
to increase good and beauty, to make someone else better and more beautiful.

Such are Plato's ideas in the *Symposium* and *Phaedrus* when he
formally discusses Ἔρως. It should now be clear that Ἔρως can be a
desire, as Armstrong says, "to increase good and beauty." And it is
precisely an increase in good that is the aim of the Demiourgos, who
wishes to make everything as like himself as possible. True Plato does
not *say* "the Demiourgos has Ἔρως," yet his actions are remarkably
like those of beings motivated by the down-flowing Ἔρως we have
described.

The Demiourgos acts from motives akin to, though not actually
called, Ἔρως. But surely he is not desirous of immortality! Yet he
might seem to be if a wish to produce goodness is always to be attributed to this self-centred end alone. If Ἔρως must be self-centred,
and the Demiourgos has a motive like that of Ἔρως, the dilemma is
unanswerable. Indeed even in the *Symposium*, as Markus points out,
if Ἔρως is only appetitive, then either happiness is impossible, since
desire can never be fulfilled, or Ἔρως is transcended. If this latter
alternative be accepted, then either perfect souls are motiveless, or
they possess another kind of love. It is true that the Gods are not
philosophers, that is, desirous of gaining wisdom, since they already
possess it. It does not necessarily follow that they have no other kind
of love. Our suggestion is that Plato's thought has an undercurrent
of a non-appetitive ideal which the normal usage of the word Ἔρως
tended to stifle. If the non-appetitive arose from the appetitive, this
is no more surprising than the claim that a love of beautiful bodies
can be transmuted into a love of the Beautiful itself. Armstrong has
suggested[64] that Plato declined to speak specifically of Ἔρως as an
attribute of God because he always regarded it as a human passion
and was too concerned to avoid anthropomorphism. But, as we have
demonstrated, the dispute here is about words, not things. The highest
Ἔρως, that of creation, belongs to the philosopher, the man who has
attained likeness to God as far as possible. His Ἔρως, like the rest of
his characteristics, is not merely human, but god-like. It is like the
unnamed desire of the Demiourgos to bring order into the world.

"On the other hand," we may say, "although the Demiourgos
might after all be described as overflowing with goodness and a desire
to create, as Taylor appears to suggest, surely the Platonic Guardians,
who in the knowledge of the Forms are the peers of the Gods, are not."

[64]*Ibid.* 110.

We recall the famous passage in the *Republic*[65] where the Guardians
are bidden to go back into the Cave in turns and give instruction in
wisdom to their fellow-men. If they were filled with "overflowing love"
we should expect them to be only too willing to undertake this task,
but this is very far from being the case. Plato writes: "They *must* go
back" (καταβατέον), and when Glaucon comes to agree with this
view, he says that the Guardians will obey the summons to return
because it is just, but that they will return ὡς ἐπ' ἀναγκαῖον. They will
follow the just course and become rulers in turn because it is their duty
to do so. We hear nothing of any love they may feel towards the
"lesser breeds outside the law" who are under their jurisdiction. Yet
although this going back into the Cave will cause them to live an
apparently worse life[66] than would be in their power if they were not
duty-bound, they are, by their obedience, enabled to imitate the goodness of God by helping to bring order out of chaos. To help mankind
in this way is an act of goodness, even if here Plato does not think of
it as an act of love.

The attitude of the Guardians seems to contradict both the notion
of τόκος ἐν τῷ καλῷ in the *Symposium* — for this theory would lead us
to suppose they would be delighted to have the chance to produce and
maintain an ideal society—and also the above-mentioned attitude of
the immortal Demiourgos, who though eminently able to pass his life
in contemplation chooses instead to create an ordered universe. Such
contradictions were, as we shall see, extremely fruitful for the Neoplatonists. In this case, the contradiction is not only between the life
of contemplation, where the philosopher cannot afford to waste his
time on mundane affairs, and the life of action where he is required or
compelled to do so, but also between two notions of love, that of
contemplating and absorbing into oneself, and that of giving. Some,
or indeed most, Christian writers have distinguished these two varieties
of love under the names of Ἔρως and Ἀγάπη,[67] but Origen, as we shall
see, is more in the spirit of Plato—or at least of Plato's Demiourgos—
in stating that there is nothing wrong with calling God Ἔρως,[68] which
word appears in the Rufinian translation as *Amor*.

That Plato himself was not unaware of this kind of love and of its
value is shown by his denunciations of φιλαυτία or "love of oneself" in
the fifth book of the *Laws*[69]. It would be natural to suppose that, if

[65]*Rep.* 7. 520C.   [66]See below, p. 180.
[67]Cf. Nygren, *Eros*, and later sections of this study.
[68]In the Prologue to the *Commentary on the Song of Songs*.
[69]*Laws* 5. 731D–732B.

love were solely to be regarded as desire and an attempt to grasp and possess what is good, it would be basically selfish. It would be concerned not with what is Good-in-itself but rather with the *possession* of what is Good-in-itself. This is nothing other than the love of a perfected self, and enlightened self-interest. The passage from the *Laws*, which we must now consider at length, shows that Plato had no time for such self-interest, indeed that he regarded it as the root of all sin. He writes as follows:

There is an evil, great above all others, which most men have, implanted in their souls, and which each one of them excuses in himself and makes no effort to avoid. It is the evil indicated in the saying that every man is by nature a lover of self, and that it is right that he should be such. But the truth is that the cause of all sins in every case lies in the person's excessive love of self. For the lover is blind in his view of the object loved, so that he is a bad judge of things just and good and noble, in that he deems himself bound always to value what is his own more than what is true; for the man who is to attain the title of "Great" must be devoted neither to himself nor to his own belongings, but to things just, whether they happen to be actions of his own or rather those of another man . . . . Wherefore every man must shun excessive self-love, and ever follow after him that is better than himself, allowing no shame to prevent him from so doing.

This passage, from Plato's last great work, demonstrates conclusively his view that the good man loves not himself, or his own interest, but the Good. Such love is not self-centred; considerations of self have become irrelevant. Love is therefore not necessarily a kind of grasping, for we are justified in assuming that the perfect philosopher (θεῖος ἀνήρ) or the God would not decline to love and admire perfection in *others* merely because he himself is already perfect and can grasp no more. On the contrary, as the Greeks maintained, like loves like, and therefore the good love what is good.

So we may conclude that, when speaking of the nature of Ἔρως, Plato usually tends to describe it as a passion directed *towards* the supreme Realities and as an upward movement, but that nevertheless we are justified in seeing him as the source of a second conception, that of an overflowing of love from higher to lower realities. Was Iamblichus perhaps to some extent aware of this fact when he declared that the *Timaeus* was one of the only two works of Plato that could be called vital?[70]

Finally, if for Plato Ἔρως could include some such idea as "overflowing love," we may wonder whether in this case he was unconsciously returning to the original meaning of the word, for Onians has

[70]The other work was the *Parmenides*. Proclus, in *Tim.* 1.13.15.

suggested[71] that ἐράω ("I love") is etymologically connected with ἐράω (only found in compounds), meaning "I pour out." This notion would perhaps be borne out by the famous passage in the *Phaedrus*[72] which tells us that when madness comes by divine dispensation (θείᾳ μοίρᾳ) it is a good. One form of "madness" is of course Ἔρως, and the word μοῖρα which we find related to it here is of considerable importance, for it implies a bond imposed on man constraining him to act or suffer things beyond his control.[73] It is thus an appropriate term to describe the coming of Ἔρως if Ἔρως implies etymologically any sort of physical or spiritual orgasm, a γέννησις καὶ τόκος ἐν τῷ καλῷ, or any other act which is creative rather than appetitive.

II

We have suggested that Plato would not normally call his Gods philosophers, i.e., lovers of wisdom, for they already know wisdom, and that a contradiction in his thought is implied in even applying the word to the Guardians, in so far as they are perfect Guardians. Be that as it may, there is no doubt that whatever emotions the Gods and the philosophers feel towards the Forms, they must regard them as objects outside themselves. The question is how far they are outside and whether they are all equally distant. In other words, what does Plato mean by the kinship of souls and Forms that he speaks of in the *Phaedo*, and is the Form of the Good so far beyond the other Forms that it must be regarded as of a different order of nature like the Plotinian One? We shall treat these questions in turn.

First, what does Plato say are the essential qualities of a Form? We are told painly in the *Phaedo*.[74] He writes: "Is this substance, which we describe in our questions and answers as true being, always the same or can it change? Does Absolute Equality, Absolute Beauty or any other Form . . . ever admit of any kind of change? Or rather does not each of the Absolutes, since it is uniform (μονοειδές) and exists by itself, always remain the same and never in any way admit of any change at all?" Cebes replies that it does. A little later we read: "But when the soul searches alone by itself, it goes away into the sphere of

---

[71]Onians, *Origins* 202. He suggests the possible connection of Ἔρως with ἔρση and compares such phrases as Ἔρως ὅ κατ' ὀμμάτων στάζεις πόθον. (Eur. *Hipp.* 525.)

[72]*Phaedrus* 244C.

[73]Onians, *Origins* 327, 373, 403, etc. deal with μοῖρα as a "bond."

[74]*Phaedo* 78D.

the pure, the everlasting, the immortal and the changeless, and being akin to these (ὡς συγγενὴς οὖσα) it lives with them."

These two passages provide us with several adjectives for the World of Ideas. It is pure (καθαρός), everlasting (ἀεὶ ὄν), immortal (ἀθάνατον), changeless (ὡσαύτως ἔχον), uniform (μονοειδές) and dwells by itself (αὐτὸ καθ' αὑτό). To all these qualities the soul, when it is contemplating the Forms, is "akin," so that we almost believe that Plato would regard it as the goal of human life to attain to this perfection. But, whatever he might have wished, Plato was aware that one most important difference between souls and Forms could not be ignored. This was the principle of motion, with its potentialities for good or evil, which was for him the most distinctive feature of souls.[75]

We can see from Aristotle's criticisms of the Platonic philosophy that Plato at least gave the impression of excluding motion from the "real" world. Modern historians of philosophy have been in haste to point out that this criticism is unjustified, citing passages from the *Phaedrus, Philebus, Sophist, Timaeus*, and elsewhere. Nevertheless Aristotle, for some twenty years a Platonist, must have had a good knowledge of the Master's teachings and good grounds for his remarks. This apparent contradiction can to some extent be understood if we believe that though Plato did, increasingly, admit an efficient cause as well as the Forms into the "real" world, he was not unduly interested in it, spoke little of it, and perhaps even regretted the necessity of assuming its existence at all. The passages from the *Phaedo* give a strong impression that motion is just one of the inferiorities of the world of "becoming" and thus of little interest to the philosopher. Aristotle however cannot be acquitted of ignoring a difficult and much disputed passage in the *Sophist*[76], and we should also remember that in his remarks on the lack of an efficient cause in Plato he usually thinks only of "Socrates in the *Phaedo*."[77] The statements in the *Sophist*, and in particular the outburst at the end of 248E (Τί δὲ πρὸς Διός; ὡς ἀληθῶς κίνησιν καὶ ζωὴν καὶ ψυχὴν καὶ φρόνησιν ἦ ῥᾳδίως πεισθησόμεθα

[75]If Merlan is right in maintaining that the philosophers in the Old Academy identified Soul with the objects of mathematics, as is generally admitted, and if this identification was made by Plato himself, which is a more disputed point (cf. *Tim.* 35A, Cornford, *Plato's Cosmology* 60 ff., and Robin, *La Théorie platonicienne des Idées*, then the distinction between souls and Forms is even more apparent, for if souls equal τὰ μαθηματικά, they are clearly inferior to Forms. See Merlan, *From Platonism to Neoplatonism*, esp. 8–51.

[76]*Soph.* 246A ff. See Grube, *Plato's Thought* 295, and the other discussions there cited.

[77]Arist. *Met.* A.988A 8; *de gen. et corr.*, 335B 7 ff., etc.

τῷ παντελῶς ὄντι μὴ παρεῖναι, μηδὲ ζῆν αὐτὸ μηδὲ φρονεῖν, ἀλλὰ σεμνὸν καὶ ἅγιον, νοῦν οὐκ ἔχον, ἀκίνητον ἑστὸς εἶναι), are at the very least a denial of the exclusion of soul from the most real world, since soul alone is the origin of thought and motion. Being, we remember, is defined as an active or passive potentiality.

Here, if anywhere, is a possible source of the Plotinian opinion ὅτι οὐκ ἔξω τοῦ νοῦ τὰ νοητά, and Zeller has not been alone in following the great Neoplatonist in making the Platonic Ideas into active powers. This theory, however, can only be maintained as Platonic by what Professor Grube describes as "a misunderstanding of 248D-249B and of a passage from the *Philebus*" (23C-27C). Grube's analysis[78] makes it clear that Plato teaches that the real cannot be limited to what is immobile. Therefore either the Ideas are active powers, or souls are active realities distinct from Ideas. Plato prefers the second alternative. This passage in the *Sophist* has caused interpreters a good deal of concern, and Grube has had to cut away many extraordinary interpretations to clarify its meaning. Plotinus certainly understood it wrongly[79] as teaching that the Forms possess intellection and that absolute immobility must therefore be attributed to something other than the Forms, in fact to the One which is beyond intellection. We may well suspect that Zeller was led to his conclusions precisely from a desire to tie up the views of Plato and Plotinus into an ordered whole. It will be more fruitful if, here as elsewhere, we admit that the view of Plotinus was in great part derived from a misunderstanding of Plato which brought the latter more into line with what Plotinus wished to believe.

It is possible, however, further to reconcile the passages in the *Phaedo* and *Sophist* about the relationship of souls and Forms. We should first remember that in the *Phaedo* Socrates does not attempt to draw an absolute defence of immortality from this particular argument. I should like to suggest, in the light of the *Sophist* passages, that this may have been because souls and Forms, although related (συγγενεῖς) in so far as they are both part of the "real" world, differ on the specific point that soul is an active force while the Forms can only be the indirect causes of action, that is by being παραδείγματα.

The position of Plotinus and of Zeller's Plato that Νοῦς and the

---

[78]Grube, *Plato's Thought* 295-6, 302. The phrase τὸ παντελῶς ὄν can quite correctly mean "the whole of reality." *Contra* Robin, *Rapports* 107. This is accepted by Hadot, "Etre, Vie, Pensée," 108.

[79]*Enn.* 6.7.39. Nebel, *Plotins Kategorien der Intelligiblen Welt*, also follows Plotinus in interpreting *Soph.* 248D ff. as teaching that the Ideas have motion. This view especially vitiates his discussion on "Plotin und der Platonische *Sophistes*" (49-54).

Forms are united, derives some support from the belief that in the
Sophist and elsewhere Plato posits a Form of Being. If there were such
a Form, it would plainly reduce souls and Forms to manifestations of
the same ultimate principle and thus suggest that they may well, in
some sense, be the same. It is virtually certain that Plotinus believed
that the One of the *Parmenides*[80] is fundamentally the same as his
own First Hypostasis and is thus the principle of Forms and Souls.
The Plotinian One is not a Form of Being, but "beyond Being," and
Plotinus treats Being as a "category" of the World of Forms in a
doctrine similar in some respects to that which, as we shall see, is
taught by Plato. Nevertheless, as we have already observed, he is
quite capable of misinterpreting *Sophist* 248Dff. as teaching that the
Forms are active powers, and the following passages of this very
dialogue are the source of the evidence produced by those who find a
Form of Being in Plato. We may well believe that the Being spoken
of by Plotinus in *Ennead* 6.2. is less an integral part of each Form
and more an ontological entity than Plato would have allowed.
Plotinus supposed that for Plato Being was a superior *Form* embracing
all the "real" world and thus resolving the duality of Forms and souls
into a unity. Such a belief may well have encouraged him further to
misunderstand Plato's teaching. In suggesting that there is no such
thing as a Form of Being in Plato's works as we know them, we shall
not, of course, be denying that his works contain certain contradictions
which, if expanded, might produce such a Form, nor the obvious fact
that Plotinus derived many of his own views on the One from the
writings of Plato—albeit from a misinterpretation of those writings.

The view that Plato posits a Form of Being, particularly in the
Sophist, is almost universal. It is not however supported by references
in the text to any αὐτὸ ὅ ἔστιν ὅν, which would have to be a technical
term for such a Form of Being, but rather seems to be founded on the
plainly shaky notion that in a dialogue as late as the *Sophist*, the use
of phrases such as εἶδος and ἰδέα necessarily implies the presence of
Forms. Even Sir David Ross, who has explicitly warned[81] against the
assumption that εἶδος or ἰδέα must necessarily be technical terms (e.g.
in the *Euthyphro*), seems to commit this very same mistake in his
analysis of the *Sophist*.

This belief in a Form of Being has been contradicted by Dr. Peck,[82]
who maintains that the μέγιστα γένη are not Forms at all but merely
logical expressions. Since his arguments are still a matter of contro-

[80]Cf. Dodds, "The *Parmenides*," 129–143.
[81]Ross, *Plato's Theory* 15.
[82]Peck, "Plato and the μέγιστα γένη of the *Sophist*," 32–56.

versy, I shall not use them here but turn to look again at some of the uses of τὸ ὄν and its cognates in the *Sophist*, and follow this by investigating the question whether any other parts of the Platonic writings lend support to this notion of a Form of Being.

In the *Sophist*, the first of the meanings of τὸ ὄν can be deduced plainly from a passage in 237C, where we read, 'Ἀλλ' οὖν τοῦτο γε δῆλον, ὅτι τῶν ὄντων ἐπί τι τὸ μὴ ὂν οὐκ οἰστέον, and then, immediately following, Οὐκοῦν ἐπείπερ οὐκ ἐπὶ τὸ ὄν, οὐδ' ἐπὶ τὸ τὶ φέρων ὀρθῶς ἄν τις φέροι. From this we understand that τὸ ὄν in the second of these sentences is made equivalent to τὰ ὄντα in the first, that is, used to sum up the whole realm of things that exist. Certainly we should not suppose that any notion of a Form of Being has been introduced here. As Dr. Peck points out, τὸ ὄν is used at this stage of the discussion in purely general terms. The Eleatic Visitor is soon to embark on an analysis of what various earlier thinkers (dualists, monists, etc.) have had to say about τὸ ὄν, and it would be foolish of him to expect them to be convinced by an argument which assumed a "Platonic" Form of Being at the start. When he does begin this analysis of previous thinkers, his object is to show that in whatever way a philosopher may regard τὸ ὄν, he will be led into contradictions if he treats it as any kind of entity in itself, apart from "the things that exist." Such misuse of the notion of Being would include the Parmenidean Sphere as well as the supposedly Platonic Idea of αὐτὸ τὸ ὄν. The Eleatic Visitor, then, is not concerned here with whether the monists, dualists, and the rest have a mistaken view of the world. What he is attempting to show is that the theory that τὸ ὄν is an entity in *itself* is fatal to *every* philosophical system. We see in fact that his analysis of all the systems that make this mistaken assumption about τὸ ὄν leads him to declare that both τὸ ὄν and τὸ μὴ ὄν appear lost in perplexities (250E).

At the end of 251C, the Eleatic Visitor makes sure we remember that we are still using τὸ ὄν in a general way (without necessary reference to any Form of Being and in terms acceptable to all philosophers), by suggesting that his remarks are directed towards all the theories previously considered (monism, dualism, various materialistic creeds, and the doctrines of the Friends of the Forms), and also that of Antisthenes and the others who maintained that all men can "validly" say is contained in tautologies such as "Man is man" and "Good is good." We are meant to assume therefore that the contradictions shown to be involved in these theories, including those caused by the maintainance of τὸ ὄν as an entity separable from "the things that exist," are still being upheld.

In an article opposing Peck's position, Lacey[83] has asked whether anyone who maintained Forms of Being, Same, and Other would be refuted or reduced to contradiction by anything Plato has said in the *Sophist*. He asks why, for instance, Plato should wish to defend the dualist position (p. 46). The answer is that whether Plato wishes to defend the dualist position or not is irrelevant to the point at issue. All he wishes to do is to show that *any* position which makes the tacit assumption that τὸ ὄν can be regarded as a separate entity and, as it were, abstracted or left truncated, is bound to be susceptible to attack on logical grounds.

We have seen then that in the first sense τὸ ὄν in the *Sophist* means nothing more than τὰ ὄντα. In 248A, however, this meaning is explained in a more Platonic manner. We read: καὶ σώματι μὲν ἡμᾶς γενέσει δι' αἰσθήσεως κοινωνεῖν, διὰ λογισμοῦ δὲ ψυχῇ πρὸς τὴν ὄντως οὐσίαν, ἣν ἀεὶ κατὰ ταὐτὰ ὡσαύτως ἔχειν φατέ, γένεσιν δὲ ἄλλοτε ἄλλως. This passage is directed specifically at the "Friends of the Forms" and there is little doubt that we are meant to assume that οὐσία is applied to the "real" world (the νοητά of the *Republic*) while γένεσις is the sphere of the αἰσθητά. We should observe here that Plato is not speaking of a Form οὐσία; he is only referring to his normal doctrine of the division between sensibles and intelligibles, and saying that intelligibles alone are worthy of the full value of the word οὐσία. "Being" and "Substance" here, then, are only general terms used to describe the intelligible world. It is in the light of this realization that we should examine the critical section 253D-254A.

The Eleatic Visitor begins by remarking that while engaged in a search for the sophist, he seems to have come upon the genuine philosopher or dialectician. He proceeds to describe the science of dialectic as that of divisions into definable classes which must not be confused. Then follows the account of the results a dialectician can achieve by this method, which has been regarded as proof that Plato uses a Form of Being as a normal Form, though one of larger scope than the others. Let us therefore examine the results of dialectic in turn. We are told that the dialectician can perceive:

(*a*) One Form extended through many individuals, each of which lies separate.

(*b*) Many separate Forms embraced in one greater Form.

(*c*) One Form made up of the combination of many wholes.

(*d*) That many Forms are entirely separate.

[83]Lacey, "Plato's *Sophist*," 43–52.

All this is summarized as the ability to distinguish in what general way individuals can or cannot associate with one another (ᾗ τε κοινωνεῖν ἕκαστα δύναται καὶ ὅπῃ μή). None of these observable results would be affected in any way by whether Plato believed in a Form of Being or not (though it would be interesting to discover which Forms are "entirely separate" from the Form of Being, supposing such a Form to exist). They all deal with Forms which are assumed to exist. We cannot imagine the Platonist working with "non-existent" Forms. The only question we *can* ask ourselves is whether Plato is at any time known to have posited τὸ ὄν as a "Formal Cause of the Forms," to use the Aristotelian terminology. If he did not, we are entitled to assume with Peck that in the case of the Platonic Form τὸ καλόν, for example, Being is assumed as part of the nature of the Form and does not need to be explained as the result of participation in a Form αὐτὸ τὸ ὄν. The full title of the Form τὸ καλόν, as Peck has pointed out, is αὐτὸ ὅ ἐστι καλόν. Ἐστί is included.

The phrase in 254A, stating that the true philosopher is always concerned with ἡ ἰδέα τοῦ ὄντος and that this is hard to discern because of the brightness of the real world, may appear at first a strong argument against our present position, but we should observe that there is no necessity, and indeed no justification, for affixing specific metaphysical status to this τὸ ὄν. All the phrase means, as we have seen in a similar example above (248A), is that the philosopher is concerned with the intelligible world (τὸ νοητόν) the world where Being is at its most perfect and in no way contaminated with τὸ μὴ ὄν or γένεσις. In that world each of the perfect Forms implies and includes as an integral part of itself what we may call perfect Being. The philosopher does not speak of a Form as a perfect abstraction but as a perfect existent.

As a final proof that Being is assumed as an integral part of every Form, we may cite the phrase ἕκαστον τὸ ὄν, which occurs frequently in the *Republic* and elsewhere and which can mean no more than "each Form." The Forms are each a part of that complex which is the Ideal World or the World of Realities. We may sum up by saying that the Neoplatonic view which has been upheld in recent times by Zeller and which makes the Forms active powers in the Divine Mind derives no support from the notion that the duality of Forms and souls may be reduced to a unity in the Form of Being, for Plato does not posit such a Form. We must be content with believing that both Forms and souls are realities in the Platonic sense, and that souls, in so far as they are good and filled with knowledge, have no source for this goodness and knowledge other than the Forms. In this sense, we can maintain the traditional view that for Plato the Forms are at the "head" of the Universe.

III

Must we then draw the conclusion that the highest things in the Universe are lifeless, since if the Forms are not souls nor primarily in souls, they cannot for Plato be alive? Must we even maintain that the Ideal Living Creature of the *Timaeus* is not alive? The question at once raises an issue fundamental to the student of Plato, namely: In what sense are the Forms self-predicating? To resolve this question it is necessary to look at the much discussed problem of the Third Man.

In a most important article, Professor Vlastos[84] presents the Third Man objection in the *Parmenides* as follows: If a, b, and c are F, then there exists a Form F-ness by which a, b, and c are F. This is the first step, and the second is that if a, b, c, and F-ness are all F, there must exist another Form which Vlastos calls F_1. He then calls attention to the obvious fact that this second position assumes that all the Forms are self-predicating, i.e. that F-ness is F. It is important therefore to see how far this assumption of Parmenides is justified.

Vlastos has a good deal of evidence in his favour, both from Plato's own writings and from Aristotle's. In the *Lysis*,[85] for example, we read that white hairs are of the same quality as Whiteness, in the *Protagoras*[86] that Justice is just and Holiness holy, while the *Phaedo*[87] gives the same impression in the phrase "If anything else is beautiful besides Beauty itself." In the *Nicomachean Ethics*[88] Aristotle states that for the Platonists the Form of Man is man. This looks a very imposing list, and we may assume from it that Plato's forms are self-predicating,

---

[84]Vlastos, "The Third Man Argument," 319–349. See also Sellars, "Vlastos and the Third Man," 405–437; Vlastos, "A Reply to Prof. Sellars," 438–448; Geach, "The Third Man Again," 72–82; Vlastos, "A Reply to Mr. Geach," 83–94; Bluck, "The *Parmenides* and the Third Man," 29–37; Allen, "Participation and Predication," 147–164; and especially Peck, "Plato versus Parmenides," 159–184.

[85]*Lysis* 217D.

[86]*Prot.* 330CD.

[87]*Phaedo* 100C.

[88]Aristotle *N.E.* 1096B 1. Cf. Περὶ ἰδεῶν, quoted by Alexander, *in Met.* 990B 15, where Aristotle says that if the "man" which is predicated of the Form is different from that of which it is the predicate, then the regress follows. As we have suggested, this is not necessarily the sense of self-predication that Plato employs.

but the question remains as to what meaning we give the expression "self-predicating," for Justice may be self-predicating in at least two ways. We may either say "Justice is just" or "Justice is a just thing." It is self-predication of this second kind that we find Parmenides attributing to the Forms as they are propounded by Socrates. In other words, Parmenides takes the Forms to be particular things.

Yet other passages in Plato's works show clearly that he rejected the notion that Forms are particular things. We learn from the *Republic* that God did not make two Forms of Bad, because if he had, a third Form, necessary to embrace their particularity, would automatically have come into existence. A similar argument establishes the uniqueness of the Ideal Living Creature in the *Timaeus*. Thus it is made clear that if particularity is attributed to the Forms, a regress is inevitable, and it is therefore not in the least extraordinary that Parmenides finds one.[89] To abolish the regress, we must abolish the particularity. We must not say "Largeness is a large thing" and "Justice is a just thing," but "Largeness is large" and "Justice is just." Thus Plato, while using the "self-predication assumption" attributed to him by Vlastos, does so only in a tautologous[90] sense.

Vlastos further maintains that "If the Form, Largeness, is superlatively large, while large mountains, oaks, etc. are only deficiently large, it must follow that the single word 'large' stands for two distinct predicates: (*a*) the predicate which attaches to the large particulars; (*b*) the predicate which attaches to Largeness. Call (*a*) 'large' and (*b*) 'large$_1$.'" As Bluck points out,[91] however, this method of looking at the question is erroneous, for if we say that Largeness is

[89]In a recent article in *Mind*, entitled "Regress Arguments in Plato," G. C. Nerlich suggests that the regresses of the *Republic* and *Timaeus* contain the same assumptions as do those of the *Parmenides*. These assumptions are that the objects involved in the regresses are comparable in kind. He does not make clear, however, that these regresses take place when the things compared are two identical Forms in the other two dialogues and a Form and a particular in the *Parmenides*. The *Timaeus* and *Republic* arguments show that to remove the uniqueness from a Form, even to compare it with that to which it is theoretically comparable, leads to a regress and is therefore impossible. And what Parmenides in fact does is in some sense to detract from this uniqueness.

[90]Self-predication is also suggested by the phrase "the *x*-itself" to describe a Form. Ross believes (*Plato's Theory* 88) that this suggests that Plato "treats the Idea of *x* as one *x* among others and implies an *x*-ness common to it with others," and Vlastos (*PR*[1954] 337, n.32) appears to agree with this comment. It seems however that the phrase "the *x*-itself" need only imply that the Form is *x*, whereas strictly speaking the particulars are not *x* at all.

[91]Bluck, "The *Parmenides*," 33.

large and mean anything other than a tautology, it must follow that in an ontological sense nothing else can be called large except Largeness itself. Thus Cornford's remark,[92] "The arguments of the *Republic* and the *Timaeus* indicate that Plato was not blind to the fallacy in Parmenides' assumption that Largeness is a large thing," gives rather the wrong emphasis. The real mistake of Parmenides is to neglect the uniqueness of Largeness itself. If Largeness itself were large (in any other than a tautologous sense) then nothing else could properly be called "large." Admittedly the so-called large particulars would bear more relation to the predicate "large" than to any other predicate, but ontologically they would not be large, since all but Forms are defective.[93] Thus even if the Forms are self-predicating in a non-tautological sense, Forms and particulars are incomparable not, as Cornford might have supposed, because of the nature of the Forms, but because of the inability of the particulars to admit of true predication.

With these conclusions in mind, what may we truly predicate of the Ideal Living Creature? Plainly that the Ideal Living Creature is living creature. Thus if we say that living creatures are alive, we must not say that the Ideal Living Creature is alive, for that would be to make it a particular among the other particular living creatures, though superior to them, whereas the Ideal Living Creature is incomparable.

Now, when discussing Plato's philosophy we must, to avoid confusion, use accepted terminology where possible, and in accepted terminology "living creatures are alive." Since this is so, and we are using the word "alive" to describe constituents of the world of becoming, we cannot strictly apply it to the world of Forms. We cannot therefore make the two statements "the Ideal Living Creature is living creature" and "the Ideal Living Creature is alive" synonymous. While the former is true, and an example of the self-predication assumption in the correct sense, the latter is a misleading deduction from an unconsidered interpretation of the relation between Forms and particulars.

We should therefore appear justified, since the Ideal Living Creature embraces a plurality of Forms, in excluding life from the Platonic Forms,[94] the objects of the thought of philosophers and Gods. We, as

---

[92]Cornford, *Plato and Parmenides* 90.

[93]Cf. *Phaedo* 74C, 75AB; *Rep.* 529D.

[94]In *De Anima* 1.404B20, we learn that Plato analysed αὐτὸ τὸ ζῷον, and that its (presumably abstract) components were "the One" and the primary length, breadth, and depth only.

humans, are, when aiming at our best, to be in love with the lifeless. This, we may object, is a hard task, for it is the nature of man to love "life." We may conjecture that Plato's answer would be that if a man is really a lover of Beauty, he will not regard the indwelling of life, with its concomitant γένεσις, as the thing most akin to the Good itself. Plotinus, as we shall see, finds it necessary to correct Plato on this point, but of Plato's opinion there can be no doubt.

IV

Discussion of the nature of the Good does not occur frequently in the dialogues. Plato is unwilling to describe it in the *Republic* on the ground that Glaucon and the rest of his audience will not be able to follow. He more or less contents himself with calling it μέγιστον μάθημα and with the analogy that it is the light which shines upon the intelligible objects of contemplation and thus makes them intelligible. When pressed, he feels impelled to resort to phrases like the famous ἐπέκεινα τῆς οὐσίας.[95] None of these suggestions give us much inkling of what the Good is. For that we shall derive much more help from the *Philebus*, a work devoted to that purpose. The claimants to the title of Good are Wisdom or Thought, as proposed by Socrates, and Pleasure, the ideal of Philebus and Protarchus. We are not concerned with the details of the discussion, which reveal that both the original contestants were wrong although the view of Socrates was nearer the truth. What is of importance here is that we are told that "of all possessions the first is Measure, Moderation and Appropriateness" (καίριον)[96] and, what is even more relevant, that "Beauty and Virtue always turn out to be Measure (μέτρον) and Proportion (συμμετρία)"; finally that if we want to track down the Good, we must call to our aid Beauty, Proportion, and Truth.[97] These will bring us to the threshold of a knowledge of the Good, presumably giving us what knowledge is possible of something which is in a sense "beyond Being."

Beauty, then, in the *Philebus* is identified with Measure, as we might well expect would be the doctrine of so convinced an apostle of mathematics as Plato. What makes a statue beautiful for Plato, and in this he is an exemplar of the fifth-fourth century spirit, is its harmonious arrangement. When Plotinus implies that the beauty of a statue would be inestimably enhanced if it were alive (*Enn.* 6.7.22), his remarks are straightforward evidence that the presuppositions of

[95]*Rep.* 6. 509B.   [96]*Phil.* 66A.   [97]*Phil.* 65A.

his age and of that of Plato are so radically different that to call them both classical can be very misleading.

We have suggested that the true lover, in Platonic terms, is a lover of the Forms as quasi-exemplars of mathematical perfection and reasonableness. He is a lover of something which can show no response of any kind. This is sublimation indeed, and we shall suggest that it is one of the reasons for the failure of the Platonic system in its original form to secure a hold upon the minds even of powerful thinkers. It is possible that Plato was demanding a response beyond the human range, and that by ensuring that the "love" of his Guardians was so free of contact with any physical notion and even with life itself, he also ensured that it could not inspire his successors. Speusippus was perhaps not so far from Plato when he abolished the Ideas and placed mathematical notions at the head of his system, for to anyone without the subtlety of his Master the distinction between the two cannot in practice have been very great. Aristotle's remark that philosophy has become mathematics was, we may suspect, valid in a critic's opinion against Plato himself as well as against his successor.

But was the Platonic system as mathematical and abstracted as we have suggested? Surely in the *Republic* and the *Philebus* we are told that the Good is the greatest of the Forms, while in the *Symposium* we have Beauty in a similar rôle. Both Goodness and Beauty, being "moral" or "ethical" Forms, are, we may suppose, within the scope of the emotion of love. Not, however, I would suggest, as Plato understands them. Beauty, we have already seen, has been identified with Measure and Proportion; and while Measure and Proportion can be admired and even wondered at, it seems unlikely that they can be loved, most especially since they are lifeless. What about the Good? The *Philebus* tells us that mathematical notions can only give us some idea of it, and do not exactly define it. This is true, and we can find no closer definition in the dialogues. Furthermore we can recall the passage from the *Seventh Letter*, which has already been quoted,[98] in which Plato insists that he has never written about the Good and never will. It is clear, however, that he spoke about it to his pupils in the Academy. On this subject Burnet writes:[99] "Aristoxenos said that Aristotle 'was always telling' how most of those who heard the lecture on the Good were affected. They came expecting to hear about some of the recognized good things, and when they heard of nothing but Arithmetic and Astronomy and the Limit and the One, they thought

[98] *Ep.* 7. 341C.
[99] Burnet, *Greek Philosophy* 221. Cf. Aristox., *Harm. Elem.* 2.30.

it all very strange. We know from Simplicius that Aristotle, Speusippus and Xenokrates had all published their notes of this very discourse." Aristoxenus adds that Plato declared: "ἀγαθὸν ἔστιν ἕν." As Ross admits,[100] this phrase in its context may imply that Plato claimed "that there is one Good." It seems more reasonable, however, to view it in the light of such passages as *Met.* 1091B. 13ff., where Aristotle writes: τῶν δὲ τὰς ἀκινήτους οὐσίας εἶναι λεγόντων [i.e. the Platonists], οἱ μέν φασιν αὐτὸ τὸ ἕν τὸ ἀγαθὸν αὐτὸ εἶναι. οὐσίαν μέντοι τὸ ἕν αὐτοῦ ᾤοντο εἶναι μάλιστα.[101] If this passage refers to Plato and his orthodox supporters, as many scholars suppose, we find evidence that Plato came in the end to hold that Goodness consists primarily in the imposition of Limit (as in the *Philebus*) and Unity—and we are faced with the demand that if we are to be Platonic philosophers, this is the nature of the Goodness, the μέγιστον μάθημα, that we must love.

It is necessary at this point to refer briefly to the *Parmenides*. The Neoplatonists, from Plotinus on, made frequent use of the One of the first hypothesis which they regarded as equivalent to their own Supreme Unity. We must therefore consider whether their interpretation is in any way faithful to Plato's thought. I have examined the purpose of the *Parmenides* elsewhere,[102] and it is therefore necessary here only to state my conclusions and refer the reader to my article for the argumentation. My view of the first hypothesis is this: that Plato demonstrates both that a bare Unity, such as the Parmenidean One, can admit of no predication of any kind, and that there can be no *Form* of Unity comparable with the other Forms. Unity, however, is not a non-significant abstraction, as Peck has suggested,[103] but an element that must be present in all that is real. It is for this reason that in the *Philebus*, Forms are referred to as "Henads" and "Monads," since their unity and distinctness are basic to their existence. In brief, when Plato wrote the *Parmenides*, he was coming to realize the prime importance of the unitary nature of each Form, but could not accept the view that this Unity had any semblance of reality in its own right, apart from the Forms. Unity then in the first hypothesis of the *Parmenides* has not the independent status of the Good in *Republic* VI, although later in his life Plato equated the Good and the One. A corollary of this interpretation is that Plato cannot be thinking in terms of a "negative theology of positive transcendence" in the *Parmenides*.

[100]Ross, *Plato's Theory* 224.   [101]Cf. *Met.* A, 988B 11–16.
[102]Cf. my article "The *Parmenides* Again," 1–14.
[103]Peck, "Plato's *Parmenides*."

Having considered the philosophers, the Gods, love of the Forms, and the Ideal World itself, we must now turn our attention to the status assigned by Plato to the Form of the Good which is the Sun of the Intelligible World. Could Plotinus find Platonic texts, other than those from the *Parmenides*, which might suggest that the Form of the Good is at a higher stage of reality than the other Forms? He could certainly cite the famous passage from the *Republic*:[104] Καὶ τοῖς γιγνωσκομένοις τοίνον μὴ μόνον τὸ γιγνώσκεσθαι φάναι ὑπὸ τοῦ ἀγαθοῦ παρεῖναι, ἀλλὰ καὶ τὸ εἶναί τε καὶ τὴν οὐσίαν αὐτοῖς προσεῖναι, οὐκ οὐσίας ὄντος τοῦ ἀγαθοῦ, ἀλλ' ἔτι ἐπέκεινα τῆς οὐσίας πρεσβείᾳ καὶ δυνάμει ὑπερέχοντος. Since τὰ γιγνωσκόμενα are of course the Forms, does this passage imply that the Good is not a Form but something higher, something perhaps more akin to the Plotinian One? From these words taken by themselves, we might be justified in holding that view, but the actual phrase "Form of the Good" occurs frequently in this metaphysical section of the *Republic*, in passages where it is undeniably the highest of the Forms but still a Form.[105] But how can it be both an example of τὸ ὄν, for we have seen that the Forms are frequently called ἕκαστα τὰ ὄντα, and at the same time ἐπέκεινα τῆς οὐσίας? And how can it be both a Form and the Cause of Forms as it is implied to be in 517BC (ὀφθεῖσα δὲ [ἡ ἰδέα τοῦ ἀγαθοῦ] συλλογιστέα εἶναι ὡς ἄρα πᾶσι πάντων αὕτη ὀρθῶν τε καὶ καλῶν αἰτία . . .)? There seems little doubt that Plato wished to separate the Form of the Good from the other Forms, just as the sun is separate from the objects which it illuminates, but was unwilling to deprive it of the name "Form" in the interest of raising it to a higher level.

We appear to have reached a deadlock on this matter within the dialogues and can only hope to resolve it from the Aristotelian evidence. We have already indicated support for the view that the Form of the Good was, in Plato's latest period, identified with the Form of Unity. Can we derive any help from what Aristotle has to say about this One? He writes:[106] "Since the Forms are the causes of everything else, he (Plato) thought that their elements are the elements of all things. Thus the material principle is the Great and the Small, and the substantial principle is the One; for the numbers (that is of course the Forms as Ideal Numbers) are derived from the Great and the

[104]*Rep*. 6. 509B.
[105]Cf. *Rep*. 6. 505A. ἡ τοῦ ἀγαθοῦ ἰδέα μέγιστον μάθημα. *Rep*. 7. 517BC, ἐν τῷ γνωστῷ τελευταία ἡ τοῦ ἀγαθοῦ ἰδέα καὶ μόγις ὁρᾶσθαι. For the Good as Being, see also *Rep*. 7. 518C, 532C.
[106]Arist. *Met*. A, 987B, 19ff.

Small by participation in the One." It is worth noting in passing that this analysis of the Forms does not divide each one into "Being" plus "*x*-ness in a non-existent state," i.e., Justice is not Being added to something that is "just" but non-existent, as the partisans of a Platonic Form of Being might suppose. On the contrary, we have the One and the Great and the Small, which latter is, of course, the Great-and-Small, if we discount the Aristotelian misinterpretation. Here the One is the cause of the existence of the Forms—a rôle played in *Republic* 509B by the Good.

So far, then, we may believe that Plotinus was truly interpreting his Master in believing that the One is beyond the Forms. But, we may object, Plato's analysis of each Form into its elements of the One and the Great-and-Small is only a piece of abstraction. He did not actually visualize this One as an independent reality. Furthermore, are we sure that this One, which is always linked with the Great-and-Small, is the same as the One which is identifiable with the Form of the Good?

In answer to the first point, if we accept that the division of Forms into their elements is possible in the abstract but has no relevance to ontology, are we not compelled to conclude that for Plato the Form of the Good, being as it is ἐπέκεινα τῆς οὐσίας, cannot be said to exist at all except as an abstraction in the mind of the dialectician? Plato would plainly refuse to accept this conclusion. As to whether the One-Good and the One which accompanies the Great-and-Small are the same, all we can say is that none of our texts appears to suggest that they are not. It is surely unwise to divide them if the division cannot be found either in Plato or in passages referring to his work.

On this issue of the status of the Form of the Good or of the One, as on that of Ἔρως, we appear to have reached an impasse. Try as we will, we cannot, even with the aid of development theories, reach a totally harmonious position to attribute to Plato on either of these questions. Furthermore, the developments of the system that were made later by Plotinus and others were often regarded by these thinkers as expositions of what Plato himself had actually said. And in a sense they were, for the Master's position has been shown to involve contradictions, and nowhere more plainly than in this matter of the Good; for Plato wants it to be both a Form and not a Form, both a kind of Being and "beyond Being," and even within a single work, such as the *Republic*, is unwilling to push either of these alternatives to its logical conclusion. When Plotinus takes the Platonic One or Good and puts it beyond the Intelligible World of Forms, he has grasped one side of his master's paradox. For that he can, and should, be pardoned. There is no reason why he should not have decided to choose one or other of the contradictory Platonic positions. Where he appears to have had a more misleading effect is in his belief, stated or implied, that he is necessarily interpreting the Platonic system in the way that Plato really wished. This is not true, as most scholars are agreed, though it is still not unknown for Plato to be interpreted as if he were, in all essentials, an inhabitant of Alexandria or Rome and a pupil of Ammonius Saccas.

In summarizing the effect of Plato on his successors, Burnet[107] writes as follows:

It must be admitted that Plato's immediate followers fell very far short of the ideal I have attributed to their master. Aristotle was impatient with the mathematical side of the doctrine and did not even trouble to understand it. The result was that this did not come into its rights for nearly two thousand years. Even those men who were really carrying out the work Plato began felt bound to put their results in a form which Aristotle's criticism would not touch. The *Elements* of Euclid are a monument of that position. Xenokrates confused Plato's philosophy of numbers with his philosophy of motion, and defined the soul as a "self-moving number." Speusippus held that the Good was not primary, but arose in the course of evolution. The Neoplatonists did more justice to Plato's doctrine of the Good and of the soul, but they failed to remember his warning that the detailed application of these could only be "probable tales" in the actual state of our knowledge. Yet these very failures to grasp Plato's central thought bear witness to different sides of it . . . .

All this is partially true and shows that it is no novelty to be unable to pin Plato down to a specific body of doctrine. Burnet, however, has overlooked two most important points that help to account for this continual variation in interpretation: first, that the doctrines are *not* a consistent logical whole, and secondly that some of them, for example that of the nature of philosophic love, are found by the test of experience to be impractical ideals, where Plato demands more of human nature than is within human capacity. This kind of condemnation is rarely mentioned by the Neoplatonists and perhaps was not even a conscious reaction. Nevertheless certain demands on human nature made by Plato were tacitly neglected or replaced by his successors.

[107]Burnet, *Greek Philosophy* 350.

Chapter Three

THE ONE, EROS, AND THE
PROGRESSION OF THE SOUL
IN PLOTINUS

I

THAT Plato is not the only philosopher to whom Plotinus is indebted is a commonplace. Modern scholars have devoted great pains to the demonstration of how much of his thought is derived from other sources, both Greek[1] and Oriental. It has been shown, for example, that apart from his Aristotelian borrowings Plotinus is deeply indebted at least for terminology[2] to Posidonius and to the Stoics in general, while Bréhier[3] has gone so far as to suppose that

[1] A good indication of the results of research in this matter is given by Miss C. J. de Vogel, "Neoplatonic Platonism," 43ff., who, in her attempts to prove the continuity of the Platonic tradition, reminds us that a hierarchy of Being can be found in Philo, Plutarch, Albinus, Numenius, and even Valentinus in our era, and that all these systems are to be traced in certain of their aspects to the Platonism of Speusippus and Xenocrates, and very probably of Plato himself. What Miss de Vogel's argument does not prove, however, is why these later Platonists differed in their interpretations of Plato both from each other and from Plotinus. The important point is that they may have produced different interpretations because the Platonic text admits of different interpretations. It is true that the school of Plotinus studied the texts of certain of the Middle Platonists and Neopythagoreans, but this study was for the sole purpose, we may assume, of clearing up difficulties in the Platonic text. Where the interpretations of this text differed, the work of the "commentators" began. An obvious example of this procedure is given by the treatment of the relation of the Ideas and the Divine Mind. The text of the *Timaeus*, which was a starting point, was obscure; hence the varying opinions of the commentators. For the Aristotelian, Philonic, and Albinian interpretations, see later in this essay and especially H. A. Wolfson, *The Philosophy of the Church Fathers*, 257–286. The Philonic interpretation could derive from *Rep.* 10. 597D, where the Form of Bed is said to be created by God. Thus it would appear to have two stages of existence: (1) in God's mind, (2) as an independent, transcendent entity. This view is maintained by Wolfson, *Philo* 204–210, 221–223, 229–233.

[2] See Witt, "Plotinus and Posidonius," 198ff.

[3] Bréhier, *Plotin*. For a reasoned argument against Bréhier, see Armstrong, "Plotinus and India," 22–28.

some elements of his thought can only be traced to an Indian source. Nevertheless Plotinus and his school are always referred to as Neoplatonists, not as Neo-Aristotelians, Neo-Stoics,[4] or even Neo-Buddhists, and the origin of this designation goes back to antiquity where both Plotinus' friends and opponents regarded him as a follower of Plato. We recall also that Plato is continually referred to in the *Enneads* as "He," just as the Pythagoreans spoke of their Master as αὐτός.

That Plotinus professed to follow the Platonic teachings is certain: certain too that he believed that his own written words were true Platonism.[5] But perhaps he was deceiving himself, for the history of philosophy teems with examples of those who, while professing to follow their master's doctrines, have in fact changed those doctrines radically and set them forth in an unrecognizable form. Let us therefore not trust Plotinus himself in this matter, but turn to the greatest exponent in late antiquity of a system which, though admiring certain elements in Neoplatonism, was in other ways most heartily opposed to it. It is St. Augustine who writes: "The utterance of Plato, the most pure and bright in all philosophy, scattering the clouds of error, has shone forth most of all in Plotinus, the Platonic philosopher who has been deemed so like his master that one might think them contemporaries, if the length of time between them did not compel us to say that in Plotinus, Plato lived again."[6]

Augustine is certain that fundamentally the philosophies of Plato and Plotinus are the same. Despite this we should be rash indeed to follow certain of the moderns in believing that such a claim can validly be made. We *should* be justified, however, in holding that these words of Augustine give support to the view that although "Plato's Thought" as a whole may be very different from that of his successor, yet it might be possible to interpret that thought in such a way as to make it Neoplatonic, provided the right passages were selected; further that these "right passages" might in some cases be those in which Plato's thought has already appeared self-contradictory or ambiguous. They might include his theory of Ἔρως, for example, or that of the nature of the Good.

That we are justified in speaking of "right passages" in this sense

---

[4]Porphyry had no doubts about the presence of non-platonic elements in the *Enneads*. Cf. ἐμμέμικται καὶ τὰ Στοικὰ λανθάνοντα δόγματα καὶ τὰ Περιπατητικά, *Vit. Plot.* 14.

[5]Plotinus rejects the idea that his work is a new doctrine. Cf. *Enn.* 2.9.6.

[6]St. Augustine, *Contra Academicos* 3.18.

appears plain from Plotinus' remark that the Platonic Parmenides
was a great advance on his historical prototype,[7] especially if this be
placed alongside the view of Iamblichus, that of all the Platonic
dialogues only the *Parmenides* and the *Timaeus* are absolutely vital.[8]
Of course, if there is such a thing as a "Platonic system," it makes no
difference at all that Plotinus and the Neoplatonists in general only
selected certain passages, because those passages, at the lowest estimate, at least contain nothing that is in complete discord with the
rest. If, however, the Platonic dialogues themselves contain unresolved
contradictions,[9] either explicit or implicit, then clearly by enlarging
upon certain portions of the corpus and neglecting the rest, one could
produce a system which, though more consistent than that of Plato,
would by this very consistency be open to the charge of being
unplatonic.

With these observations in mind, we can turn to some passages in
the *Enneads* where Plotinus himself describes what he regards as his
position vis-à-vis that of Plato. We read: "We must believe that some
of the blessed philosophers of old discovered the truth,"[10] and again:
"These theories are neither new nor modern, but were stated long ago,
if not stressed; our present doctrines are explanations of earlier ones
and can show the antiquity of these opinions on the testimony of
Plato himself."[11] These remarks, which could be paralleled from many
other passages, are described by Bréhier as "un peu exagérées"[12]—
but perhaps they should not be dismissed quite so lightly, unless we
are to credit both Plotinus and his contemporaries and successors with
an extraordinary blindness. While recognizing the fear of novelty
which makes itself evident in almost all the thought of the later
Empire and admitting that Plotinus may not have been free from its
effects, we can none the less hold that there are certain elements in
the thought of Plato himself which, if isolated, will turn him into a
proto-Plotinus, if any notion of a rigid Platonic system be maintained.
Bréhier's comment "Mais les problèmes qu'il [Plotinus] se pose sont
des problèmes que la philosophie grecque n'a jamais envisagés" is true
if we limit "envisagés" to its strict sense and do not imply that these

[7]Cf. *Enn.* 5.1.8 and Dodds, "The *Parmenides*," 129–143.
[8]Proclus, *in Tim.* 1.13.15. Cf. *Anon. Prolegomena* 26, Westerink ed. 47, and the discussion by J. H. Waszink is his recent edition of Calcidius (London and Leiden 1962) xcvii.
[9]Plotinus admits that Plato does not appear to be consistent at all times, and regards these inconsistencies as a challenge. *Enn.* 4.8.1. He is, of course, ignorant of any development of Plato's thought.
[10]*Enn.* 3.7.1.   [11]*Enn.* 5.1.8.   [12]Bréhier, *Plotin* 3.

problems were not only not "envisaged" but not even "implicit" in the statements, especially the apparently contradictory statements, of Plato.

The most fundamental Platonic teaching is the Theory of Forms. Plotinus naturally accepts the theory but, as an objector might point out, he transforms it radically. Before considering certain details of this transformation, however, it is worth trying to understand how Plotinus, presumably by comparing the dialogues with one another, is able to see some of the difficulties inherent in them which modern critics have also thought of importance. Most particularly is this true with regard to the question of self-predication. When treating of Plato, we remarked how much discussion this subject has aroused recently, and we should bear this in mind while we observe what Plotinus has to say on the subject.

Plotinus' own doctrine, however, presents us with a difficulty of another kind, for it appears to be contradictory. "Ἡ ποσότης αὐτὴ οὐ πόσον," he says,[13] thus appearing to concede that in some sense certain of the Forms at least (ποσότης is an εἶδος) are not self-predicating, and he goes on to explain that πόσον is not a proper predicate for Quantity itself, but for what partakes of Quantity itself. This certainly means not only that Plotinus is denying that ἡ ποσότης is material and extended,[14] but also that it is a particular quantity in the way that Parmenides, in the dialogue named after him, suggested, when he implied that Largeness is a large thing. Furthermore, by refusing to admit that πόσον can be predicted of both the Form ποσότης and the particulars that partake of it, Plotinus is refusing to allow a comparison between Forms and particulars. His refusal is in the fullest sense Platonic, for Plato always regards the unit of measure as prior to what is measured.[15] Elsewhere in the Enneads,[16] however, we find the phrase οὐ γὰρ ἀλλὸ ἀληθέστερον ἂν εὕροις τοῦ ἀληθοῦς, where Truth, a moral Form, is self-predicating, just as Plato in the Phaedo tells us that αὐτὸ τὸ καλόν and the rest are self-predicating. When discussing Plato, we found it necessary to point out that so-called "self-predication" can have one of two distinct meanings, one tautologous, such as "Justice is just," and the other particularizing, such as "Justice is a just thing." We further suggested that Plato means his Forms to be self-predicating in the former sense and not in the latter, though his

[13]Enn. 2.4.9.
[14]As Professor Armstrong reminded me in a comment on the original draft of this essay.
[15]Cf. Armstrong, Architecture 26–27.   [16]Enn. 5.5.2.

writings do not make the matter very clear and are easily misunderstood. The former of these senses would also apply to the Plotinian Form of Truth.

When Plotinus was studying the *Parmenides*, he must have come upon Parmenides' arguments directed against the Form of Largeness.[17] Parmenides asserted that a Form of Largeness involved Plato in an infinite regress, since the fact that "large" could be predicated of it reduced it to the level of a *large thing*. Plotinus was well aware that Plato did not abandon the Theory of Forms, so he must have assumed that Parmenides' understanding of the theory was incorrect, and if it was incorrect, the most obvious way to "correct" it probably seemed to be to maintain that not all the Forms were self-predicating. He may even have thought that the suggestion of Aristotle that some Platonists did not posit Forms of relative terms[18] meant that Plato himself regarded ethical Forms differently from such entities as αὐτὴ ἡ ποσότης. In any case, the difficulties that meet us in Plotinus' views on this question are evidence of the detailed consideration he gave to the Platonic text.

So far, then, we may believe that Plotinus is interpreting Platonic dogma in a way that is at least suggested by a close study of Plato himself. When we continue, however, to compare the Plotinian Form with the Platonic, we find a series of most important differences. Plato makes it clear in the *Parmenides*[19] that he rejects an interpretation of the Forms as being ἐν τῇ ψυχῇ, whereas Plotinus dedicates a whole treatise to proving a view held throughout the *Enneads*, that οὐκ ἔξω τοῦ νοῦ τὰ νοητά.[20] That this latter notion is unplatonic is clear, and we hear that its adoption by Plotinus caused considerable discussion within the school itself and was criticized by Longinus.[21] Porphyry too was originally unable to accept it and Plotinus instructed Amelius, his chief supporter, to compose a treatise which would elucidate the matter for him.[22] Porphyry was convinced and thus passed from the view of Plato to that of Plotinus.

That Plotinus was diverging from the view of Plato on this matter is certain; that he was the heir of a long line of misinterpretation is also certain.[23] Whether he was aware of the most important implication

[17] *Parm.* 130E.
[18] Arist. *Met.* A, 990B 17 ff., and see Ross, *Aristotle's Metaphysics*, 192.
[19] *Parm.* 132BC.   [20] *Enn.* 5.5.
[21] For Longinus' view, see Armstrong, "Background," 393–395.
[22] Porphyry, *Vita Plotini*, 18.
[23] For the attempt of Plotinus to defend his view by reference to *Sophist* 248A, see pp. 42–43 of this study.

of his divergence from Porphyry, and thus unwittingly from Plato, we shall never know. We shall return to this question later, but for the moment may be content with saying that the real issue was whether the Forms are inside or outside the world of life. If they are outside it, quite apart in their essence from souls, even from the souls of the Gods, as Plato held, they can only be contemplated; if, however, they are "inside," then an ascent beyond mere contemplation, a mystical union with the One, is possible, and indeed not only possible but the only worth-while τέλος of the philosophic life.

Before entering upon a discussion of these most difficult points, we must pause to ask how Plotinus came to believe that his view that "the intelligibles are not outside the Divine Mind" is to be found in Plato. First, we may recall that although there is no doubt of the dichotomy of Forms and souls in Plato, certain isolated passages may easily be interpreted as suggesting a different view. In *Republic* 10[24] Plato remarks that the Form of Bed is created by God and although, as Archer-Hind[25] has explained, this is done in order to fit harmoniously into a scheme in which a carpenter is the creator of a "particular" bed and a painter of a picture of a bed, yet it has often been interpreted as meaning that the Forms are "posterior" to God. Furthermore, the sixth and seventh books of the *Republic* subordinate the remaining Forms to the Form of the Good. If then, as has been pointed out by R. M. Jones,[26] the Form of Good was early identified with God, the misunderstanding we are considering could easily have been perpetrated.

In *Timaeus* 29A, we read that the Demiourgos fixes his eyes on an eternal model, and in 39E, a passage twice examined in detail by Plotinus,[27] Noûs is said to see the Ideas in the Ideal Living Creature. These passages, together perhaps with the description of the cosmos

---

[24]*Rep.* 10. 597D.

[25]Archer–Hind, *Timaeus* 37.

[26]Jones, "The Ideas," 324. It is not unknown, even among modern interpreters, for the Form of the Good and the Demiourgos to be identified. Cf. Mugnier, *Le Sens du mot* Θεῖος 132. In antiquity, Atticus followed the same course, according to Proclus (*Comm. in Tim.* 1.391.7), though it is impossible to say whether this was what led him to describe the Forms as τὰ τοῦ θεοῦ νοήματα (Eus. *Praep. Ev.* 15.13.815 D).

[27]*Enn.* 2.9.6; 3.9.1. The exposition of *Tim.* 39E that the intelligibles are outside Noûs is mentioned in *Enn.* 3.9.1.—which shows that Plotinus was aware of it and rejected it. Heinemann, *Plotin* 19–25, claims that this tractate is spurious, but Bréhier (*Plotin*), with more reason, believes that Plotinus is merely exposing a difficulty. Dodds has now shown ("Numenius") that in 3.9.1 Plotinus hesitantly accepts a view of Numenius which he later (2.9.6) rejects. In 3.9.1 he accepts, and in 2.9.6 rejects, a νοῦς ἐν ἡσυχίᾳ.

at 92C as εἰκὼν τοῦ νοητοῦ θεὸς αἰσθητός[28] and the theology in the supposedly Platonic *Second Epistle*, are the most likely sources of the misunderstanding, though as Miss Rich has said, "Clearly an interpretation of the Platonic Ideas as the Thoughts of God can only be elicited from the Dialogues by reading into them more than is actually there."[29]

The theory that the Forms are thoughts has been much discussed recently. I shall not attempt an account of the various ways in which it has been proposed to explain its development; instead I shall offer a summary of the results achieved and a balanced account of the way in which the doctrine came down to Plotinus, as a preliminary to an understanding of how he came to reorganize the tradition.

As we have already mentioned, Plato in the *Parmenides* rejects the notion that Forms may be ἐν τῇ ψυχῇ. Nevertheless, his near contemporary Alcimus,[30] in what appears to be a reference to this very passage, claims that the Forms for Plato *are* in the soul. Witt[31] has suggested that this statement of Alcimus is to be regarded as a serious interpretation of the Forms as Thoughts of God on the grounds that an eternal thought implies an eternal thinker. This view, though rightly rejected by Cherniss,[32] shows, if nothing else, that even in the fourth century Plato's meaning was unclear. Against it Armstrong[33] further suggests that when Alcimus described a Form as a νόημα he may merely have meant that it was immaterial. Armstrong admits, however, that this interpretation would attribute to Alcimus a hopelessly imprecise use of words, and in view of our lack of evidence that he was imprecise it can only be a surmise.

Miss Rich, following a suggestion of Cherniss,[34] provides ample evidence that the process of misunderstanding began with the interpretation of the Forms in *men's* minds. Such an interpretation most probably arose among those who wished to deny the transcendental aspect of the Forms: in particular among the Stoics.[35] Miss Rich points

---

[28]*Tim.* 92C is probably the origin of the comparison of the world to the εἰκών of God in Plutarch, *Quaest. Plat.* 1007C. Cf. Plut. *Epit.* 1.7.4 (in Diels' *Doxographi Graeci*, 299).
[29]Rich, "The Platonic Ideas," 123-133.
[30]Diog. Laert. 3.13.
[31]Witt, *Albinus* 71. Cf. Field, *Plato* 234.
[32]Cherniss, in a review of Witt's *Albinus*, *AJP* 59 (1938) 354. Cherniss was the first to suggest that the words of Alcimus, ἔστι δὲ τῶν εἰδῶν ἐν ἕκαστον αἴδιόν τε καὶ νόημα, καὶ πρὸς τούτοις ἀπαθές, are a muddled reference to the *Parmenides*.
[33]Armstrong, *Entretiens Hardt* 5, 399.
[34]Rich, "The Platonic Ideas"; Cherniss, review of Witt, 355 n.4.
[35]Cf. Zeno in Stobaeus, *Ecl.* 1.12.6; Plut., *Epit.* 1.10.11; Galen, *Hist. Phil.* 25.

out that the passages in which the Ideas are interpreted as Thoughts of God occur frequently in a "demiourgic" context. As Armstrong says:[36] "The writers who put forward the doctrine that the Ideas are the Thoughts of God seem very often to be concerned with the questions 'On what pattern did God make the world?' and 'What is the relationship between the Maker and the pattern he used in making?' " Unfortunately, however, neither Miss Rich nor Armstrong is able to find any passage of this kind in an author earlier than Philo,[37] which leaves the history of the doctrine between the early Stoics, who tried to explain away the Forms as human concepts, and the first century A.D. to be accounted for.

Philo is the first writer whom we know to have used the Ideas in a "demiourgic" context. Our problem is to try to discover how his position with regard to the Forms was inherited through earlier interpreters. To this Miss Rich has supplied a clue by comparing his statement that the Forms have no location other than the Logos[38] of God with the passage in the De Anima where Aristotle shows considerable sympathy for those philosophers who describe the soul as a τόπος εἰδῶν. Certain philosophers may well have asked the question, "Where are the Forms?," and answered, "In the human soul." Despite his occasional use of Stoic language, such an answer would be unsatisfactory to Philo. For him, the place of the Forms is τὸν θεῖον λόγον τὸν ταῦτα διακοσμήσαντα, that is, originally at least, in the mind of a transcendent God.

From thoughts in the human mind to thoughts in the mind of a transcendent God is a long step, and an intermediate stage is almost certain. Loenen[39] suggests that such a stage is an interpretation of the Forms as thoughts of an *immanent* God, such as the Divine Fire of Stoicism. This intermediate stage would complete the development of the doctrine as follows: first, Forms are explained away by early Stoics such as Zeno as concepts in the human mind; from this they become concepts in the mind of a God in the cosmos, that is the Stoic God; finally Philo and others raise them to the rôle of concepts in the mind of a transcendent God and use them primarily in a "demiourgic" context. The real difficulty arises when we attempt to discover who first adopted the intermediate stage. Theiler,[40] Luck, and Loenen

---

[36]Armstrong, *Entretiens Hardt* 5, 401.

[37]Philo, *De Op. Mund.* 4; Sen., *Ep.* 65.8 ff.; Chalcid., *Comm. in Tim.* 361.20.

[38]Rich, "The Platonic Ideas," 130. *De Anima* 429A 27.

[39]Loenen, "Albinus' Metaphysics," 44.

[40]Theiler, *Vorbereitung* 119. Luck, *Antiochus* 28–30. Loenen, "Albinus' Metaphysics," 45.

suggest Antiochus; Witt[41] in one place prefers Arius Didymus, and elsewhere joins Schmekel[42] in choosing Posidonius. Armstrong most recently has said that the study of Antiochus produced by Fräulein Lueder[43] makes it unlikely that he was the originator of the doctrine and seems to regard the question as almost insoluble. With this welter of opinion before us we may well hesitate before embarking on the question, but a re-examination of the sources can do no harm.

The most important text is to be found in Seneca's *Epistles*[44] and is not discussed by Theiler. It reads as follows:

His [the Aristotelian causes] quintam Plato adicit exemplar, quam ipse ideam vocat: hoc est enim, ad quod respiciens artifex id quod destinabat effecit. Nihil autem ad rem pertinet, utrum foris habeat exemplar ad quod referat oculos an intus, quod ibi ipse concepit et posuit. Haec exemplaria rerum omnium deus intra se habet numerosque universorum, quae agenda sunt, et modos mente complexus est: plenus his figuris est, quas Plato ideas appellat, immortales, immutabiles, infatigabiles.

In considering this passage, we should remind ourselves of what we are seeking. We are looking for the man who first understood the Forms as thoughts of an immanent God. Such a man would almost certainly be a Stoic or be influenced strongly by Stoicism. Despite Theiler,[45] the above passage of Seneca is probably derived from Posidonius. To say so much is not, of course, to show that Posidonius is the man we are seeking, but his claims should be re-examined. It is no argument against him, as Loenen[46] seems to believe, that he was apparently unknown to Albinus, in whom the doctrine of Forms as thoughts of God reappears, though it is treated very differently. If the doctrine originated with Posidonius it would have many years to permeate the philosophical milieu before the time of Albinus, to whom tradition alone could make it well known.

Witt[47] has suggested that this passage of Seneca, though probably Posidonian in origin, came to him through the mediation of Arius Didymus, but appears to have no grounds for the suggestion. He tells us that Arius "regarded the Ideas as παραδείγματα and (we may conjecture) placed them in the Mind of God." For this latter statement there is no evidence; indeed Arius, a Stoic, is not known to have had any reason for paying attention to the Platonic Forms.

[41]Witt, *Albinus* 75.

[42]Schmekel, *Die Mittlere Stoa* 430–432. Witt, "Plotinus," 198.

[43]Armstrong, *Entretiens Hardt* 5, 424 n.1. Lueder, *Die philosophische Persönlichkeit*.

[44]Seneca, *Ep.* 65.

[45]Theiler, *Vorbereitung* 34. Cf. Norden, *Agnostos Theos* 348. Jones, "The Ideas," 321, admits the passage may be Posidonian. Cf. Bickel, "Senecas Briefe," 1–20.

[46]Loenen, "*Albinus*' Metaphysics," 44–45.

[47]Witt, *Albinus* 75. Witt is in opposition to Jones, "The Ideas," 325 on Arius.

We are left with a choice between Antiochus and Posidonius as the originator of the doctrine. If, as we believe, the passage of Seneca is derived from Posidonius, this tells in his favour. What is perhaps more important, however, is that there is no doubt from certain passages in Plotinus which deal with the τόπος of the Forms that the most important text of Plato to arouse such varied interpretations was *Timaeus* 39E.[48] We know that Posidonius expounded the *Timaeus*[49] and possibly wrote a commentary on it. What is more likely than that, when he came to this passage, he transferred the Forms from the human mind— the doctrine he would have learned from his Stoic masters—to the mind of God? He may have thought that by taking them from the human mind he was following Plato correctly, as indeed he was. Then, being faced with the problem of their τόπος, he put them in the only other mind he knew, that of God, the immanent God in whom he believed. As for Antiochus, the arguments of Theiler, Luck, and Loenen suggest that he may have held the doctrine, but even if he did it seems probable that, as Armstrong says, he was not the originator of it.[50] Who that originator was can probably never be known for certain, but I believe that the evidence points towards Posidonius. As Loenen suggests, it may be necessary to distinguish between Posidonius as historian of philosophy and commentator on the *Timaeus*, and Posidonius the Stoic philosopher. For our purposes, however, this distinction can do no harm, since which of the "Posidonii" uttered the doctrine is unimportant so long as one of them did!

So far we have sketched the development of the doctrine down to Philo, and the name of Aristotle has occurred only in connection with the question "What is the τόπος of the Forms?" When we come to Albinus, however, Aristotelian influence appears in a new form. Jones was the first to suggest that the doctrine of the Forms as the Thoughts of God derived from an attempt to reconcile Platonism with Aristotle's view that the divine thought is νόησις νοήσεως, and although this is an impossible simplification of the whole history of the doctrine, it is certainly true for Albinus. The following passage, which is neglected by Loenen, from whose view of Albinus as an extremely original

---

[48]*Enn.* 2.9.6; 3.9.1; 6.2.22.
[49]Sextus Empiricus, *adv. Math.* 7.93; cf. A. D. Nock, "Posidonius," 10, n.51. According to Plutarch (*De An. Proc.* 1013B), Eudorus also commented on the *Timaeus*, and to judge from Eusebius (*Praep. Ev.* 11.23.3), Arius may also have studied it. There is little reason to suppose, however, that their teachings were original. Their views would be derived from Antiochus or Posidonius.
[50]The identification of the Ideas with Minerva mentioned by St. Augustine quoting Varro is the strongest ground for believing that Antiochus considered the Forms as Thoughts of God. Aug., *De Civ. Dei* 7.28 Cf. Theiler, *Vorbereitung* 18–19.

thinker it detracts, is most relevant. Ἐπεὶ δὲ ὁ πρῶτος νοῦς κάλλιστος, δεῖ καὶ κάλλιστον αὐτῷ νοητὸν ὑποκεῖσθαι, οὐδὲν δὲ αὐτοῦ κάλλιον· ἑαυτὸν ἂν οὖν καὶ τὰ ἑαυτοῦ νοήματα ἀεὶ νοοίη, καὶ αὕτη ἡ ἐνέργεια αὐτοῦ ἰδέα ὑπάρχει.[51] This tells us that the first Νοῦς thinks itself and its thoughts. That it thinks its thoughts (i.e., the Forms) is a version of the view of Philo in which Νοῦς stands for God. That it thinks itself is a new departure, derived beyond reasonable doubt from a close study of Aristotelian thought.[52] I cannot accept the suggestion raised tentatively by Dodds[53] that the καί between ἑαυτόν and τὰ ἑαυτοῦ νοήματα may merely introduce an "added explanation" and is equivalent to "id est." Armstrong[54] suggests that this interpretation may be strengthened by the phrase καὶ αὕτη ἡ ἐνέργεια αὐτοῦ ἰδέα ὑπάρχει. He regards this as "a somewhat clumsy way . . . of bringing the νοῦς and the νοητόν close together." There is no necessity, however, to accept this. Αὕτη ἡ ἐνέργεια could quite naturally refer to τὰ ἑαυτοῦ νοήματα and explain that the ἐνέργεια of νοῦς (not νοῦς itself) is an ἰδέα. Albinus is thus half way towards an assimilation of Aristotelian doctrine. He believes that Νοῦς thinks itself, but is still sufficiently influenced by his predecessors to add καὶ τὰ ἑαυτοῦ νοήματα.

That Albinus' Aristotelianism was not immediately accepted is natural enough. There was considerable divergence of opinion as to the merits of Aristotle among the Platonists. The Middle-Platonist Atticus shows no Aristotelian influence in his view of the Forms and was in fact a vehement opponent of those who wished to reconcile the two schools. For him, the Ideas are both universal concepts and the Thoughts of God,[55] and the new developments are of no significance.

Nevertheless they prevailed. We do not know that Plotinus read the works of Albinus. Though Porphyry does not mention his name in

[51]*Didask.* 10.
[52]Cf. *Met.*Λ. 1074B 15ff. Whether Albinus thought that Aristotle believed in the Ideas is impossible to know. That Iamblichus held that he did can be seen from Scholia *in Cat.* 26B 10.
How the Platonic school became interested in the views of Aristotle is not known. It seems not impossible that the description of Posidonius as Ἀριστοτελίζων is relevant (Strabo 2.3.8). If Posidonius introduced Aristotelian ideas into his commentary on the *Timaeus*, it would be easy to understand the renewed interest of the Platonists in the Peripatetic philosophy. However this may be, we are on surer ground when we come to Eudorus, who probably wrote a commentary on the *Metaphysics*.
We know from Alexander of Aphrodisias (*in Met.* 59.7) that he emended *Met.* 988A 10–11 by adding the words καὶ τῇ ὕλῃ.
[53]Dodds, in a discussion of Armstrong's paper, *Entretiens Hardt* 5, 416.
[54]Armstrong, *Entretiens Hardt* 5 (discussion) 423.
[55]Cf. Syrianus, *Scholia in Met.* 1078B 12; Eus., *Praep. Ev.* 15.13.815D.

the list of books used by Plotinus as texts, this is not conclusive evidence. But even if he was not read, which I think unlikely, the new Aristotelianism would be handed down in the tradition. Furthermore, it would be emphasized by the great body of works of Alexander. The subject of this latter's influence need not be discussed here. We have already shown how the Platonic Forms came to be interpreted as Thoughts of God and how Albinus introduced the Aristotelian tendency to identify God and his Thoughts, though apparently with some hesitation. By the time we come to Plotinus this hesitation has gone, and the Forms are both the Thoughts of Νοῦς and the eternal, unchanging objects which Νοῦς contemplates. This development from what we may call the Middle-Platonic to the Neoplatonic position is the final stage of a long history. Plotinus' view is both a more complete assimilation of the Aristotelian noetic and at the same time an understanding of Plato which is nearer to the Master's doctrine. For Plotinus, while holding the exteme Aristotelian view that thought and the thinker are one in actuality, has also recognized that Plato intended his Forms to be completely free of subjectivism and to be "objects in themselves."

Plotinus' interpretation of *Timaeus* 39E clearly had a long history of misunderstanding behind it, but in view of the objections of Porphyry and Longinus to the doctrine that the intelligibles are not outside Νοῦς, we may believe that if Plotinus had looked up the original passage *in its context*, instead of leaving the refutation to Amelius, he would have found that the ἰδέαι which are included in the αὐτὸ τὸ ζῷον are the Forms (*a*) of Gods, (*b*) of birds, (*c*) of creatures that live in the waters and (*d*) of those that live on dry land. He would then have realized, we may suppose, that these are only a small fragment of the whole population of the World of Forms. Where, he might have wondered, were the others? If he had considered this, he might have realized that this passage gave no support for his view that οὐκ ἔξω τοῦ νοῦ τὰ νοητά. Indeed he might have wondered whether the Ideal Living Creature was itself alive; whether, since ἡ ποσότης οὐ πόσον, if πόσον implies particularity, αὐτὸ τὸ ζῷον is ζῶν.

The system of Plato is ultimately a dualism, composed of the motionless, unchanging World of Forms on the one hand and the world of movement, potential or actual, typified at its highest by the souls of the Gods and of the θεῖοι ἄνθρωποι on the other. This "separation" which is the mark of a truly platonizing system is absent in the world-view of Plotinus where all, ultimately, is in a sense contained in the One. The substitution of monism for dualism is the direct result of putting the Forms into the Divine Mind, for although Plotinus has read the *Parmenides* carefully enough to be aware that Platonic Forms cannot simply be equated with concepts in that Mind, he decides that although they are not concepts, they can be thought of as states or activities of Νοῦς provided they be recognized in addition as the objects which Νοῦς contemplates. Thus Justice is described as οὐ νόησις δικαιοσύνης, ἀλλὰ νοῦ οἷον διάθεσις, μᾶλλον δὲ ἐνέργεια.[56] Although this definition could never have been given by Plato, yet by such an interpretation of his Master Plotinus was enabled both to meet some of the implicit inconsistencies in the Platonic teaching which we have described, and also to humanize it. By doing so he brought it within the range of larger numbers of disciples, for although Plato's own teaching has been admired by many, very few have even begun the attempt to carry it into practice. Even in Plato's own generation, all his leading pupils gave up certain fundamental propositions of their Master's thought. The discipline of Plotinus, however, by teaching that the human soul has at least the possibility of merging with the Infinite, makes less demands on human emotions. Plato demands that we love that Ideal World which we can never feel but only contemplate; Plotinus, by introducing a quasi-personal element into the Forms in the Divine Mind, has provided his followers with a link with the Good which brings the notion of love of Wisdom closer to their human capacity for love. Plato's impossible Ideal has been brought within the realms of possibility.

In order that this may become clearer, it is necessary here to give a brief exposition of the nature of the Plotinian One. During this exposition we must constantly bear in mind that it is most likely, as Dodds has shown, that we are concerned with a traditional interpretation, or rather misinterpretation, of the *Parmenides* of Plato, used to reinforce the enormous emphasis placed on that passage in the *Republic* where the Form of the Good is described as "beyond Being."[57] That in the latter point the so-called system of Plato displays one of its most important unresolved contradictions has already been shown. For the former we may rely on the words of Plotinus himself that it is relevant and may back these up by the more recent studies of Dodds,[58]

[56]*Enn.* 6.6.6. See above for the Aristotelian elements in Plotinus' theory of Νοῦς, and p. 42 for Platonic passages which may have encouraged Plotinus to persist in his erroneous interpretation. Cf. *Enn.* 6.7.39 and probably 3.6.6.

[57]*Rep.* 6. 509B. I cannot accept the view of Heinemann (*Plotin*) that Plotinus' "earlier" writings do not teach the conception of the One, since his rearranging of the chronology of the treatises has no authority.

[58]Dodds, "The *Parmenides*"; Cornford, *Plato and Parmenides*; Hardie, *A Study in Plato*.

Cornford, Hardie and others. With these considerations continually in mind, we shall pass on to the One of Plotinus which, following the method of Armstrong,[59] we shall examine briefly both in its positive and its negative aspects.

In our discussion of the Platonic Form of the Good, we came to the conclusion that it was both a Form and at the same time "beyond Being," which must imply beyond the Forms, since each one of the Forms is described as ἕκαστον τὸ ὄν. Naturally enough, a Form that is a variety of Real Being is describable in some limited sense at least, whereas what is "beyond Being" is also a fortiori beyond mere words. Since the Plotinian One is not a Form in any sense and is indeed described as ἀνείδεος, it is plain that the negative description is more relevant to it. We must follow the phrase of Trouillard:[60] "La négation est plus importante et plus révélatrice que la dialectique," because negation will make our mind more akin to the illimitable aspects of the Godhead, whereas dialectic is especially designed to speak in positive terms.

When we look at the Plotinian attempts to describe the One, we are confronted with an impressive array of superlatives. It is αἰτιώτατον (6.8.18), τελειότατον (5.1.6), δυνατώτατον (5.4.1), ἁπλούστατον (2.9.1), αὐταρκέστατος (6.9.6), ὑπέρτατος (6.8.16), ἀκρότατος (5.1.1). But these notions still tend to suggest a superior quality, though similar substance, to the other parts of the Intelligible World. So Plotinus suggests it is an activity not merely superior to that of Νοῦς, but of a different order of reality . . . . ἐνέργεια ὑπὲρ νοῦν καὶ φρόνησιν καὶ ζωήν (6.8.16). It is in fact the creator of the Forms. It is ποιητικὸν οὐσίας καὶ αὐταρκείας . . . ἐπέκεινα ταύτης (οὐσίας) καὶ ἐπέκεινα αὐταρκείας (5.3.17). It is true that the passages describing the One as "beyond Νοῦς" are usually a direct answer to the Aristotelian[61] assumption that God is Νοῦς, but even without this incentive to place it ἐπέκεινα, Plotinus would probably have described it as such since it is far superior to a knowledge which is assimilated with its object. In the ὑπερνόησις of the One, consciousness and self are the same with no qualification and no possible distinction.

The One cannot be called Beauty itself. It is rather ὑπέρκαλος καὶ ἐπέκεινα τῶν ἀρίστων (1.8.2). Plotinus refers to it as God (θεός), but since θεός might imply an Aristotelian νοῦς even this is not always satisfying. For example, he once writes ὅτε γὰρ αὐτὸν νοήσῃς οἷον νοῦν ἢ θεόν, πλέον ἐστι . . . πλέον ἐστιν ἢ θεός (6.9.6). It is possible that at

[59]Armstrong, Architecture.
[60]Trouillard, La Procession plotinienne 47.
[61]Cf. Armstrong, Entretiens Hardt 5, 410, 424.

70 EROS AND PSYCHE

such a time he would have been more satisfied with the phrase of
Pseudo-Dionysius,[62] ὑπέρθεον πνεῦμα, provided πνεῦμα had no quasi-
material implications, but even this may well have been too limited,
for the opinion of Plotinus is best expressed in passages such as 5.3.13,
where he tells us that the One is quite indescribable (ἄρρητον τῇ
ἀληθείᾳ).[63] Every description is an attempt to pin it down to some kind
of limit and it is beyond limit. To describe it is only in effect to detract
from its majestic superiority: ἡ προσθήκη ἀφαίρεσιν καὶ ἔλλειψιν ποιεῖ
(3.9.9). All we can do is to say what it is not. This does not mean,
however, that we can describe it as Erigena did, as nihil.[64] On the
contrary it is everything, or rather, beyond everything. Nor is
Pistorius[65] justified in suggesting that for Plotinus and the Neoplatonists the One does not exist in the sense that it cannot be considered
apart from Νοῦς and Soul. Pistorius believes that the One is only the
transcendent aspect of the Godhead. This, however fruitful a thought
it may be in itself, does not appear to be the position of Plotinus. For
him it would be truer to say that, whereas Νοῦς and Soul cannot be
understood without some knowledge of the One and cannot exist
without the source of their being, the One itself is quite independent
of the lower hypostases and can, in a sense, be understood apart from
them. In the unio mystica, for example, Νοῦς and Soul become irrelevant and the experience is a linking of the One in us with the One in
the cosmos.

Many passages indicate that we cannot understand the One by
merely appreciating the notion of Form or Limit. The One is rather
the cause of Form or Limit and is itself totally unspecific. In his descriptions of it, Plotinus writes: δεῖ δὲ μηδὲ τὸ ἐκεῖνο μηδὲ τὸ τοῦτο λέγειν,[66] and
again: ἀνάγκη ἀνείδεον ἐκεῖνο· Ἀνείδεον δὲ ὂν οὐκ οὐσία . . . ἐπέκεινα ἄρα
ὄντος. τὸ γὰρ ἐπέκεινα ὄντος οὐ τόδε λέγει—οὐ γὰρ τίθησιν—οὐδὲ ὄνομα

[62]Pseudo-Dionysius, Div. nom. 2, 3 and 4. For the One as God, see Rist, "Theos,"
169–180.
[63]Wolfson, in Philo (Harvard 1947) tends to refer the idea of God's being ἄρρητος
to Philo. Katz, Plotinus' Search 89 n.46, observes that many of the passages with this
idea in them are quotations from Plato's Parmenides. The truth may be that if
Plotinus knew Philo's work (either directly or indirectly), he was grateful to find
ideas akin to his own interpretation of the Parmenides. Cf. Enn. 5.5.6; 5.3.10; 6.7.38.
[64]Though not nihil, the One is the negation of all number (Enn. 5.5.6). The nearest
Plotinus comes to Erigena is his remark that οὐδὲν ὄνομα suits the One. (Enn.
6.9.5). For the importance and relevance of the idea of nothingness among the
Neoplatonists from Plotinus to Damascius, see Bréhier, "L'Idée du néant," 444–475.
[65]Pistorius, Plotinus 19.
[66]Enn. 6.9.3. Cf. Armstrong, Architecture 26.

αὐτοῦ λέγει, ἀλλὰ φέρει μόνον τὸ οὐ τοῦτο (5.5.6). Thus even the highest aspects of the lower hypostases cannot be used as terminology to describe the One. As Arnou has said:[67] "L'Un est identité pure."

However, it is plain that no philosophy can be built in negative terms alone, and Plotinus must have been aware that in some sense the Platonic Form of the Good could be described as though it were an existent, even though it is in fact "beyond Being." So the more positive terms return. We have already noticed the superlatives, but in general Plotinus describes his First Hypostasis as τὸ ἕν or τὸ πρῶτον, or more rarely τὸ ἀγαθόν, although he has said elsewhere that it transcends ordinary Goodness.[68]

This might be the furthest point we could reach if we had to philosophize about the One-in-itself. But for Plotinus we ourselves are at least partially both the results and the kinsmen of the One, and, what is more to the immediate point, the Forms in the Second Hypostasis of Νοῦς are its direct products. Now Plotinus' misunderstanding of Plato's *Timaeus*, which we have discussed, enables him to introduce the notion of the Divine Mind into the world of Forms, indeed to put these Forms into the Divine Mind itself as its thoughts, while still maintaining their reality as objects. This belief enables Plotinus to enlarge his theories of the nature of that Good which is the cause of the Forms, for he is not, like Plato, attempting to account merely for the roots of non-living beings, but also for the origin of Mind, which is the noblest form of *Life*. Because of this, it is inevitable that quasi-lifelike terms be applied to the First Hypostasis. In other words, what Plotinus has done with the Platonic Form of the Good is in a sense to anthropomorphize it. He has combined the functions of the Form of the Good with those of the Platonic Gods, who, as we suggested at the beginning, are little more than perfect Platonic philosophers. By this solution he succeeds in accounting for some of the difficulties inherent in the production of the Second Hypostasis, but he does it at the cost of introducing certain of the inherent contradictions that we noticed in the Platonic Gods into his own Supreme Principle.

This, however, is moving too fast, and the suggestion that Plotinus has personalized his Supreme Hypostasis may seem at first difficult to accept. Indeed, Plotinus himself would almost certainly have denied it, but by the side of those passages which tell against it, there are a number that operate in its favour. From this contradiction we must

[67]Arnou, *Le Désir*.
[68]*Enn.* 6.9.6.

try and find a synthesis which represents both aspects of Plotinus'
view. The problem may be stated as follows: Plotinus' awareness that
he must account for the details of the Intelligible World and not be
satisfied with negative generalities about the nature of the One leads
him on to what must be regarded as the attribution to it of quasi-
personal features. Let us then look at a few of these features, keeping
in mind as we do so that the same difficulties may arise about the
motives, if we may call them that, of the One, as arose in our scrutiny
of the motives of the Demiourgos in the *Timaeus*.

The most extreme example of the trend towards personalizing the
Supreme Hypostasis is the notion of Fatherhood which is frequently
applied to it. We find such passages as πατρὶς δὴ ἡμῖν, ὅθεν παρήλθομεν,
καὶ πατὴρ ἐκεῖ,[69] and again Ὅταν δὲ εἰς γένεσιν ἐλθοῦσα οἷον μνηστείαις
ἀπαταθῇ, ἄλλον ἀλλαξαμένη θνητὸν ἔρωτα, ἐρημία πατρὸς ὑβρίζεται· μισήσασα
δὲ πάλιν τὰς ἐνταῦθα ὕβρεις, ἀγνεύσασα τῶν τῇδε πρὸς τὸν πάτερα αὖθις
στελλομένη εὐπαθεῖ. [70] The implications of the words "Father" and
"Fatherland" in these passages are open to dispute. Henry maintains[71] that the "conception of father in Plotinus carries, it would
seem, none of the emotional or religious connotations which the
Christian world is accustomed to associate with it, but is rigorously
synonymous with such exclusively metaphysical terms as 'principle,'
'cause,' or even 'source' and 'root.' " That the One is all these things
as well as being "Father" I would readily admit and they will be
discussed later. The question we must try to answer here is whether
any of these other terms could be substituted for "Father," where
Plotinus uses "Father," without the loss of any "emotional or
religious" meaning.

Armstrong seems to follow the view of Henry, at least in as much as
he denies that the description of the One as "Father" has "any
Christian implications,"[72] but their insistence on this point seems
extraordinary in view of their expressed opinions on the nature of the
One. Armstrong again writes:[73] "I agree with Professor Paul Henry
that Plotinus too thinks of the One or Good as a personal God, pos-

[69] *Enn.* 1.6.8.
[70] *Enn.* 6.9.9.
[71] Henry, "Plotinus' Place," xlvii.
[72] Armstrong, *Plotinus* 30. Professor Armstrong informs me that he is thinking
primarily of the Christian belief in God's loving care for mankind, his children; and
this is certainly unplotinian. Yet from the fact that Plotinus does not think of the
One as Father in this sense, it does not follow that he does not think of it personally
at all.
[73] Armstrong, "Plotinus' Doctrine of the Infinite," 57.

sessed of something analogous to what we know as intellect and will in a manner proper to his transcendent unity." We have already spoken of the possible hyper-intellection of the One and the solution of this question would not necessarily bring any direct evidence to bear on Plotinus' use of the word "Father," but it is difficult to see why scholars who suggest that Plotinus regarded the One as a personal God overlook such good evidence for their position as the employment by Plotinus of the word "Father." At least it is worth considering whether it is impossible for the word "Father" to have any emotional or religious significance.

In the *Timaeus*[74] the Demiourgos is referred to as the "Father" of the cosmos, and it must be admitted that here there *may* be very little meaning in Plato's use of the word beyond that of "cause" or "creator"; but between the *Timaeus* and Plotinus Platonism passes through some strange heads, including some that believed in a personal God or gods. It is not impossible that the ideas of some of these later thinkers may have affected Plotinus' use of the word πατήρ. Philo, for example, takes over the phrase πατὴρ καὶ ποιητής from the *Timaeus* and makes continual use of it.[75] In his writings, however, there is no doubt that the word denotes more than mere causality. Philo is speaking of Jehovah and applying Plato's language to Him.

The use of the word πατήρ to describe the First νοῦς in Albinus[76] can much more easily be explained away as merely causal, but again in Numenius we are faced with the use of the word[77] by a man who was at least extremely interested in Judaism and whom Bigg and Puech have thought to have been himself Jewish. It is quite possible that Numenius' concept of a First God had in it something of Jewish personal religion, and Numenius, as we know, was read in the school of Plotinus.

We should not claim to have proved that πατήρ in any author of the period, whether or not he is a known worshipper of a personal God, *must* have a personal sense. We have, however, tried to show that the notion that Plotinus' description of the One as πατήρ contains certain emotional, religious, and even personal undertones should by no means be dismissed as easily as it has been.

---

[74]*Tim.* 28C, 37C.
[75]Cf. Billings, *Philo Judaeus* 22–23, where a very large number of passages are cited. Billings stresses the moral implications of the word πατήρ (22).
[76]Albinus, *Didask.* 10.
[77]Numenius *ap.* Proclum, *in Tim.* 1.303.27. Dodds, "Numenius," 6, seems to be correct in denying that Numenius was himself Jewish.

For Plato, the Forms are the exemplars of limit and symmetry, and symmetry is almost equivalent to Beauty. Not so for Plotinus. His One is ἀνείδεος; symmetry is irrelevant to it and thus, in a sense, irrelevant to Beauty as well. Indeed this proves to be precisely his opinion of the matter when he touches upon it in the sixth *Ennead*. He writes: Διὸ καὶ ἐνταῦθα φατέον μᾶλλον τὸ κάλλος, τὸ ἐπὶ τῇ συμμετρίᾳ ἐπιλαμπόμενον ἢ τὴν συμμετρίαν εἶναι, καὶ τοῦτο εἶναι τὸ ἐράσμιον (6.7.22). Such a conclusion, so alien in its analysis to the normal view of Plato, is another example of the logical result of putting the First Hypostasis "beyond Being." It is not symmetry but this mysterious One, which we have seen described in positive and concrete terms by the word "Father," that is the source of Beauty. We may be justified in drawing the conclusion that Beauty is the result of something much more "lifelike," if not actually alive, than the mathematical notion of symmetry.

The One is the source of life of the multiplicity-in-unity which is the Second Hypostasis, and is compared in a famous simile to the all-powerful root of an enormous tree:[78] "Therefore it has given the whole abundant life to the tree, but it remains itself not manifold but the principle of manifold life." The important thing about a root, thinks Plotinus, is that it can give of itself without in any way diminishing itself, and this nature of "undiminished giving" has long been recognized as the most striking feature of the Plotinian One. Besides the simile of the root, he uses that of a spring which he assumes will never run dry, and most of all that of the sun, which in his view suffers no diminution in any way from the fact that it is the continual source of light to the visible universe. That this metaphor of the sun is common to many thinkers in the Platonic tradition is evident, and Witt[79] is doubtless correct in emphasizing the rôle of Posidonius in spreading it, but there is no reason to assume that Plotinus needed any other source for his theory of the emanation of light than the Sixth Book of Plato's *Republic*, especially since the very foundation of his theology of the One, that is, the phrase ἐπέκεινα τῆς οὐσίας, is to be found there also.

That the creation of the hypostases of Νοῦς and Soul is the result of this "undiminished giving" by the One is, we may assume, commonly agreed by all the interpreters of Plotinus. That such giving results

[78]*Enn.* 3.8.10.
[79]Witt, "Plotinus," 198ff. But compare Armstrong, "Emanation," 61–66. Armstrong rightly points out that emanation in Posidonius is to be understood in a purely materialist sense. The intellect emanates from the divine fire.

from the "superabundance" of the One is evident,[80] and many interpreters are content to leave the matter there. Those who go on to ask
why the One "behaves" in this way almost invariably answer that it
is obliged by its nature or by some kind of necessity. Armstrong[81]
tells us that the "giving out" of the One is "necessary in the sense that
it cannot be conceived as not happening otherwise" but that "it is
also entirely spontaneous," for "there is no room for any sort of
binding or restraint, internal or external, in Plotinus' thought about
the One. The One is necessarily productive and creative because he
is perfect." Here we have an attempt to explain what sort of necessity
it is that is somehow involved in the procession of Νοῦς from the One,
and later we shall consider the study of Trouillard,[82] which has shed
much light on this problem. Before doing so, we ought to turn back to
the difficulties encountered in explaining the motives of the Demiourgos for creating the order of the world in the *Timaeus*.

In comparing the respective motives for creation of the Demiourgos
in the *Timaeus* and the One of Plotinus, I do not intend to extend the
parallel between the two, for it is certain that whereas the Demiourgos
is only the creator of order, the One is the source of Being itself. I
suggest only that similar difficulties of motive arise in the two cases,
and that Plotinus has the Demiourgos in mind when he speaks of the
One in this context.[83] The concept of a Demiourgos or creative Mind
is applicable in the context both of temporal and of eternal creation.
The Platonists disagreed as to which sense was understood by Plato,
though most of them thought that he held creation to be extra-
temporal.

With this in mind, we return to the question of what sort of motive
the Demiourgos could have had. Plato tells us that he created because
he is good, but this answer only prompts us to ask the further question
as to what kind of goodness necessitates creation, that is, what does
"goodness" mean in this context? In any case, the answer of Plato
will not exactly suit the One of Plotinus, for the One is strictly beyond
ordinary Goodness.

At this point an objection may be made to our comparison of the
Demiourgos with the First Hypostasis of Plotinus, on the grounds that

[80]On "superabundance" cf. *Enn.* 5.2.1; 5.1.6; 6.7.15, δύναμιν εἰς τὸ γεννᾶν
εἶχε παρ' ἐκείνου and Trouillard, *La Procession plotinienne* 71.
[81]Armstrong, *Plotinus* 33–34.
[82]Trouillard, *La Procession plotinienne.*
[83]*Enn.* 5.5.12. There is an allusion here to the denial of φθόνος to the Gods in *Tim.*
29E.

the Demiourgos *wills* to create the ordered world, whereas the One eternally "overflows" into the Hypostasis of Noûs. This criticism, however, is superficial, for although the Demiourgos may be said to will creation, he does not choose it as one of two alternatives. He simply wills it because he is good; being good means doing good, and the Demiourgos is thus "beyond" choice. So the dilemma in the *Timaeus* seems to bear a striking similarity to that which we now see in the system of Plotinus, and which we shall shortly investigate further. It is likely that if one of them can be solved the other will be well on the way to solution. Let us say for the moment that the One "overflows" *because* he is the One, and the Demiourgos creates because he too is what he is.

When we were considering certain aspects of the Platonic philosophy, we suggested that the dilemma about the motives of the Demiourgos might in some way be linked with that about the nature of Ἔρως. To recapitulate: the normal Platonic theory sees Ἔρως as a desire to obtain some specific end and possess it; this implies that the perfect philosopher and the Gods will no longer love the Forms when they have attained to contemplation of them and can fill and refresh their souls for ever with the perfections of reality. The notion of τόκος ἐν τῷ καλῷ in the *Symposium* may, however, be invoked to help towards an understanding of the motives for creativity. In conclusion, the root of all the difficulties is the lack of an adequate theory of Ἔρως, or rather the contradictions and impossibilities that come to light if Plato be held to maintain the view that Ἔρως is the spirit of Desire and nothing else.

Are we to avoid these dilemmas in the Plotinian system by suggesting that the Good that is the One is Love—and that kind of love which is undiminished self-giving? We should be very hesitant to do so in view of the insistence of most of the leading Plotinian scholars over this issue. Armstrong,[84] for example, writes: "Two points of great importance for the understanding of the Plotinian philosophy are first, that the production of each lower stage of Being from the higher is *not* the result of any *conscious act* on the part of the latter, but is a necessary, unconscious reflex of its primary activity of contemplation . . . ," and Arnou[85] has bluntly described the undiminished giving of the One as "une bonté sans amour."

These decisive views seem at first sight to be justified by several passages from Plotinus himself. In the ninth tractate of the Second

[84]Armstrong, *Architecture* 111.
[85]Arnou, *Le Désir* 226 ff. Cf. Trouillard, *La Purification plotinienne* 127.

Ennead[86] he writes that "It is of the essence of things that each gives
of its being to another; without this communication, the Good would
not be the Good, nor the Νοῦς a Νοῦς, nor will Soul itself be what it is."
Again, in the Third *Ennead*,[87] we find that "The world is a product of
Necessity, not of deliberate purpose." It would appear that Armstrong
is right to insist that the coming-to-be of the Second Hypostasis from
the One is not the result of any conscious act. This we may admit, but
we are not bound to accept Armstrong's conclusion that it is therefore
an *unconscious* reflex. The One is neither conscious nor unconscious:
οὐκ ἔστιν οἷον ἀναίσθητον.[88]

We have already seen how Armstrong modifies his description of
the procession from the One as unconscious by his use of the word
"spontaneous." Trouillard rightly goes further in this direction by
elucidating the Plotinian distinction between the "hyper-will" of the
One and the free will of other "conditioned" realities. Speaking of
"procession," he tells us that[89] "Ce n'est pas œuvre de libre arbitre,
délibération et sélection, production artisanale . . . le générateur pro-
duit par la volonté fondamentale en laquelle il se pose lui-même."
Having explained that Plotinus prefers to describe "procession" in
terms of works of nature rather than works of art,[90] since the latter
are not spontaneous, he defines the "necessity" of procession from the
One as "l'expression d'un *vouloir* inconditionné."[91] While we may
believe that Trouillard's remark that the "engendering" of the Forms
reveals them as "la seule 'grâce' qui nous soit offerte, mais néces-
sairement offerte,"[92] even when the word "grâce" is put between
inverted commas, is going too far, he is certainly right in insisting that

---

[86]*Enn.* 2.9.3.

[87]*Enn.* 3.2.3.

[88]*Enn.* 5.4.2. Cf. Trouillard, *La Procession plotinienne* 79. Plotinus frequently
denies συναίσθησις (5.3.13.21; 6.7.41.26; 5.6.5.4) and τὸ παρακολουθοῦν ἑαυτῷ
(3.9.9.18) to the One because they seem to involve duality and are more appropriate
to Νοῦς. But he seems to express qualms at the idea of the One's being ἀναίσθητον
ἑαυτοῦ καὶ οὐδὲ παρακολουθοῦν ἑαυτῷ at 5.3.13.1. In 5.4.2.17 he speaks of ἡ
κατανόησις αὐτοῦ [the One] οἱονεὶ συναισθήσει οὖσα and in 5.1.7.12 we find the phrase
οἷον συναίσθησιν τῆς δυνάμεως. It appears that, while to apply the word συναίσθησις directly must involve duality and is therefore impossible, Plotinus finds the notion
of the One's being ἀναίσθητον intolerable even if it is ἀναίσθητον ἑαυτοῦ. Hence
οὐκ ἔστι οἷον ἀναίσθητον and οἷον συναίσθητον. The οἷον appears to suggest that
the One is conscious without being conscious of any *thing* or in the way of consciousness appropriate to lesser hypostases. Cf. Schwyzer, "Bewusst und Unbewusst,"
374–5.

[89]Trouillard, *La Procession plotinienne* 62.   [90]*Ibid.* 73.

[91]*Ibid.* 50.   [92]*Ibid.* 51.

78 EROS AND PSYCHE

Plotinus often thinks of the One in voluntarist terms.[93] He renders Plotinus' ἡ βούλησις αὐτός by "La volonté de l'Un c'est lui-même." We recall that Arnou maintains that not only is procession "of necessity" but that it is quite unconnected with love. We may well believe, however, that difficulties have arisen in commenting on Plotinus through the confusion of the notion of "a will to give" with that of a certain kind of unwilled or perhaps "hyper-willed" love which results in undiminished giving.

Let us consider the matter again. It is certain that the One is beyond Will, if Will means merely the faculty of choosing. There is too a concept of love that is beyond Will, the love that gives without counting the cost, the love that is spontaneous in its overflowing. Such is the highest love of the philosopher in the *Symposium*. There is then at least a similarity between a particular kind of love and the One that is beyond Will in that they are both spontaneous and that they both create. Furthermore, the One does not create mechanically, nor is it bound by necessity to do so, for we have already observed how Plotinus thinks of it in voluntarist and quasi-personal terms. One might suppose that the logical conclusion would have been for him to say that the One loves all things, but he refuses to take this step. We must now investigate this refusal and try to understand the precise relationship of the One to Ἔρως, together with the significance of that relationship.

The most important passage for our present purposes runs as follows:[94] καὶ ἐράσμιον καὶ ἔρως ὁ αὐτὸς καὶ αὐτοῦ ἔρως, ἅτε οὐκ ἄλλως καλὸς ἢ παρ' αὐτοῦ καὶ ἐν αὐτῷ.... ταὐτὸ ἡ ἔφεσις καὶ ἡ οὐσία. Insufficient notice has been taken of this passage. Ἔρως has perhaps been regarded as just one more of those names which give us some inkling of the First Hypostasis but which, if treated as accurate descriptions, are more of a hindrance than a help. This supposition may be correct, and we accept that Plotinus would insist that to say "The One is good" or "The One is beautiful" is to give a very inadequate description of it. To attribute "Goodness" or "Beauty" to the One is to attribute qualities to it, and the One is above qualities. But Ἔρως, in the ordinary Platonic or Plotinian view, is not a quality but a δαίμων, that is, a substance. Thus to say that the One is Ἔρως is not

[93] *Ibid.* 77. *Enn.* 6.8.21.

[94] *Enn.* 6.8.15. Armstrong (*Architecture* 6) maintains that the connection between *Enn.* 6.8 and Arist. *Met.*Λ is very strong. There is, however, no notion of God as "Love loving itself" in the Aristotelian passages. In Aristotle, God moves as an object of love, but is not himself love. And, in general, Armstrong seems to over-emphasize the Aristotelian elements in the One by insufficiently distiguishing it from the First Mind of the more Aristotelianized systems of Albinus and Numenius.

to attribute qualities to it; it may even be to utter a tautology, for
it is possible that Plotinus regarded Ἔρως as an all-embracing term.
At this point we are confronted by the opposition of Nygren.
Nygren insists[95] that at all costs we must avoid attributing to Ἔρως,
as used by the Platonic and Neoplatonic philosophers, the attributes
of the Christian concept of Ἀγάπη. The two, says Nygren, are oppo-
sites. Ἔρως is always a fundamentally selfish desire to grasp what is
good for oneself. It is an upward-looking, self-seeking emotion, and
has no connection with the downward-moving procession of the
hypostases, which is merely a "cosmological process" (p. 196). His use,
however, of the phrase "cosmological process" instead of the less
clinical "process of creation" is very nearly an implication that some
sort of necessity constrains the One to overflow mechanically, an idea
which others as well as I have shown to be erroneous. Turning to
Ἀγάπη, Nygren speaks of it as the "Love that seeketh not its own,"
that is, a love which is glad to give of itself without any considerations
of gain, or of what certain theologians call Eudaimonism. Nygren
hammers home his point by the words:[96] "There cannot actually be
any doubt that Ἔρως and Ἀγάπη belong originally to two entirely
separate spiritual worlds, between which no direct communication is
possible," and appeals to the formidable name of Wilamowitz[97] for
support.

If we abide by the letter of the formal analysis of the nature of
Ἔρως in the fifth tract of the Third *Ennead*, we must admit that Nygren
is partially right, but even here there is an important distinction
which he overlooks. Armstrong[98] has called attention to the fact that
in 3.5.4 Plotinus separates two kinds of Ἔρως—the Eros-God and the
Eros-Daemon. The former alone links the Soul with the Divine. This
Eros-God is specifically stated in 3.5.2 to be the medium between the
object who desires and the object desired (τὸ εἶναι ἐν τούτῳ ἔχουσα
μεταξὺ ὥσπερ ποθοῦντος καὶ ποθουμένου). It is compared not to the desirer,
but to the eye through which the desirer sees the object desired. Here,
even in Plotinus' formal treatise on love, is an Ἔρως which is not
appetitive. We should further recall that, when speaking of Ἔρως and
the motives for the actions of the Gods in Plato, we found indications
that Plato had a second view of love, a view perhaps partly contradictory to his appetitive theory. We suggested that the Demiourgos

[95]Nygren, *Eros*.
[96]*Ibid*. 31.
[97]Wilamowitz-Moellendorf, *Platon*² I, 384.
[98]Armstrong, "Platonic Eros," 113.

might create out of a motive somewhat more akin to that of the
Christian 'Αγάπη than Nygren, and perhaps Plato himself, would care
to admit. Later, when we consider how Origen is willing to interchange
the words "Ερως and 'Αγάπη, we shall suggest that his investigations
of the Platonic systems have led him to the conclusion that the two
notions have more similarity than Nygren would allow them.

Nygren's view of the complete separation that should be maintained
between "Ερως and 'Αγάπη assumes, rightly, that the whole Christian
concept of Love implies a gulf between creature and Creator. This is
true, but such a gulf is also present in Neoplatonism between the One
and the others. It has been suggested to me[99] that the giving of self
implies "otherness" in the object and that such giving is impossible
for the Plotinian One since it bestows itself on what is simply an
emanation of itself. There is a limited sense, as we shall see, in which
the One is present to the others, but in whatever manner this be understood, it must not lead to any neglect of those statements of Plotinus
which stress the extreme transcendence of the One and the "otherness"
of the Second Hypostasis. We read that the One made all things and
left them to their own being (ἐφ' ἑαυτῶν εἶναι)[100] and again that after
constructing being (οὐσία), he left it *outside* himself (ποιήσας ταύτην ἔξω
εἴασεν ἑαυτοῦ).[101] Elsewhere we find that in order that the Divine Mind
may come into existence, "otherness" must be involved.[102]

But there is a sense in which Plotinus thinks of the One as immanent
as well as transcendent. In general, this has been made clear by
Arnou,[103] but since I would wish to express the matter a little differently, a few words should be said about it at this point. As Arnou
puts it (p. 162): "Il y a dans les Ennéades une corrélation frappante
entre les formules ἐν ἄλλῳ et ὑπ' ἄλλου, entre l'idée d'immanence et
celle d'origine, 'être dans' et 'venir de.'" It is well known that for
Plotinus the effect is said to be *in* its cause (ἅτε γὰρ γενόμενον ὑπ'
ἄλλου . . . διόπερ καὶ ἐν ἄλλῳ).[104] Thus Soul is *in* Νοῦς and Νοῦς *in* the
One. Thus, as Arnou points out, it is correct to say that all things are
immanent in the One rather than that the One is immanent in all
things.[105] If we may say that all things are in the One, what can we

[99]By Miss A. N. M. Rich in a comment on the original draft of this essay.
[100]*Enn.* 5.5.12.
[101]*Enn.* 6.8.19. Cf. 6.7.37. Armstrong ("Platonic Eros," 114) rightly stresses that
the One's transcendence implies that he cannot love all things.
[102]*Enn.* 6.7.39. For this discussion, compare Trouillard, *La Procession plotinienne*
49, 63–64.
[103]Arnou, *Le Désir* 162–181.   [104]*Enn.* 5.5.9.   [105]*Enn.* 5.5.6.

say is the relation of the One to all things? The expression Plotinus favours is "presence" and it is in *Enneads* 6.4 and 6.5 that the best account of the doctrine can be found. There, especially in 6.4.3, we find that Plotinus, in opposition to many thinkers of his day, held that the One is directly present, not merely present through intermediaries.[106] He affirms its presence with the word συνεῖναι (6.9.7), and denies its absence with οὐκ ἄπεστιν (6.9.4). There are many passages (such as 6.4.2.20ff.) where he speaks of the higher being "in" the lower, a rather pantheistic concept if taken out of context, but in view of his more normal thought, we should understand "in" in the sense of "present with." This presence is the presence of the cause "in" its effects. It does not, in Plotinus' view, limit transcendence in any way: ἔστι γὰρ καὶ παρεῖναι χωρὶς ὄν.[107]

It is in his doctrine of man that Plotinus shows most clearly his view of the transcendence and "immanence" of the One. In 6.9.7, he says that "we read that God is outside of none, that he is present with all, though they do not know it. For men flee outside him, or rather outside themselves. . . . The man who has learned himself will know his origin." Here Plotinus is certainly speaking of the "immanence" of the One in mankind, and probably, though less certainly, of its presence in the universe as a whole. In the following essay he continues: "Thus the Supreme as containing no otherness is ever present with us, we with it when we put otherness away. It is not that the Supreme reaches out to us seeking our communion: we reach towards the Supreme; it is we that become present. We are always before it: but we do not always look. . . . We are ever before the Supreme—cut off is utter dissolution. . . ." (Trans. MacKenna-Page.)

This belief in the presence of the One with man leads into the doctrine of the "infinite self"—the idea that the One is the absolute self (πρώτως αὐτὸς καὶ ὑπερόντως αὐτός).[108] It is probable too that we should link the close association of the self with the One—a proximity that does not exclude the chance of the removal of all barriers between them and the rejection of all "otherness"—with the theory that part of the soul never "descends," but always remains pure in the intellectual realm.[109] This part of the soul is linked to the One that is ever present.

In concluding these remarks on the relationship between the One and the others, we may state the case as follows. The others are *in* the One, since they are caused by the One. This causation enables Plotinus

106Arnou, *Le Désir* 173–4.   107*Enn.* 6.4.11.
108*Enn.* 6.8.14.   109*Enn.* 4.8.8; 5.1.10.

to say further that the One is always present with the others and to believe that the progression of the human soul towards union is the way back from effect to cause, to the final breaking down of barriers between the ever-present One and the others with which it is present. It is only man that can enjoy the mystic union to the fullest extent, and it is only man who has part of himself always "above." We may say then that there is something of the One present *with* all things, a something which holds them in existence, and that this presence is the most strongly felt in the case of man. Nevertheless, despite this presence, Armstrong[110] is right to insist that the transcendence of the One precludes him from a love of creation or love of mankind. What then is the meaning and sense of the description of him as Ἔρως?

Plotinus speaks of the One in 6.8.15 not only as Ἔρως but as Ἔρως αὐτοῦ. This provides the solution to the problem, for since the One is love of itself, it must love not only "itself in itself," but "itself as present with its effects." Furthermore, in the mystic union, at the time the soul is restored to unity with the One, it must itself be the object of the One's love, since the One loves itself, and the elevated soul *is* the One's self. Thus it is fair to say that by loving itself the One is in effect loving created things in so far as they are itself and has no care for them in so far as they are not. In the mystic union, then, the One loves the soul, since the soul is no longer soul.

Thus it is true to say that although there are indications that Plotinus conceived of the One as in a sense personal, although he saw it as "giving" to the rest of creation, he did not conceive of this giving as a love of other things. At first sight this appears a step back from Plato, whose Demiourgos, as we recall, though not said to have Ἔρως for the created world, accomplishes his function of bringing order into the universe from a kind of goodness, which, like the highest Ἔρως of the *Symposium* and *Phaedrus*, desires to make others as good as possible. Armstrong[111] has pointed out how Plotinus' interpretation of a passage in the *Phaedrus* shows that the idea of creativity in the form of directly doing good to others has dropped out of Plotinus' account of the ascent of Ἔρως, and this, together with the emphasis on the One's transcendence, accounts for the fact that the One does not care for the others, even in the sense that the Demiourgos does when he wishes them to be as like himself as possible. Yet the presence of the One *with* the others—a doctrine that has nothing to do with the

[110]Armstrong, "Platonic Eros," 114.
[111]Armstrong, "Platonic Eros," 112; *Phaedrus* 252D; *Enn.* 1.6.9.

Demiourgos—enables Plotinus to rectify the balance, for although the One's Ἔρως looks to itself, that very self is the ever-present cause of Being to the rest of creation.

We may conclude this discussion with the remark that the mere description of the One as Ἔρως is an objection to Nygren's view. The Ἔρως of the One cannot be an upward motion, for it has nowhere to which it could ascend. It must be conceded that the Ἔρως of the One is concerned with itself; yet that does not make it appetitive, since it is by nature perfect and without needs. Furthermore, all things are in the One. Ἔρως looks to the One in itself and to the One present with its effects. As this presence is the very cause of the existence of the others, it is clear that Plotinus is not far from equating Ἔρως with the power of creation, the undiminished giving, that the One possesses. The One is the cause of the other hypostases; it is also love of itself. Therefore the One's love of itself, with its contemplation of itself, must be the cause of the other hypostases. Thus although the One's Ἔρως is directed neither upwards nor downwards, it is the cause of a movement directed downwards, though admittedly indirectly so.

Miss Rich[112] has reminded me that in *Ennead* 3.5.3, Plotinus suggests that the derivation of Ἔρως is from ὅρασις. She holds that the phrase Ἔρως αὐτοῦ means that the One is simply the object of its own vision. I do not think, however, that the word "object" has meaning in discussions of the One. The derivation from ὅρασις may shed light on the Plotinian use of the word Ἔρως on some occasions, but not in the case of the One. The Ἔρως of the One must have nothing to do with any distinction between subject and object, for in the One no such distinctions exist. As Plotinus[113] says in a description of the mystic union: "The vision (of the One) floods the eyes with light, but it is not a light showing some other object; the light itself is the vision." We should only employ the analogy of seeing with great care when speaking of the One.

Father Henry[114] aptly reminds us that in accounts of the mystic union Plotinus, though sometimes speaking of "vision" and "contemplation," prefers terms "deriving from the theme of unity or those which indicate presence and contact." Ὅρασις may be a suitable word to describe what the προκόπτων can "see" of the One *before* he has attained to union, but in the moment of ecstasy it is not a question

[112]In a comment on the original draft of this essay.
[113]*Enn.* 6.7.36.
[114]Henry, "Plotinus' Place," 49.

of seeing but of being the One.[115] Thus the term ὅρασις is appropriate to the soul in ecstasy only with strict reservations, and is a misleading description of the One itself. The One does not see itself, is not the *object* of its own vision; rather it is itself, cause of itself and of all things. Ὅρασις is transcended though Ἔρως is not. The phrase Ἔρως αὐτοῦ must then be a tautologous description of the One's nature— a nature which, as we have seen, overflows.

At this point we may with profit consider how Plotinus, who is unwilling to agree with Aristotle that the Supreme Hypostasis knows itself, is able to maintain that it is love of itself. Plotinus holds that the One cannot have intellection only of itself, as an Aristotelian might expect, since intellection of itself must include intellection of all things.[116] He who has a complete knowledge of causes must have a complete knowledge of effects. But with love the matter is different. Since the One loves only itself, if it loved all things, all things would be itself, and Plotinus would be a pantheist. Therefore to preserve the One's transcendence and at the same time show how the One, which is Ἔρως, is the cause of the others, he holds that the One loves itself as something present to the others.

What then are we to conclude about the One? We have found it described as Source, Root, Father and as Ἔρως, where the word must be stretched far beyond its normal Platonic and Plotinian meaning. Plato, we remember, was at one stage of the *Symposium* unwilling to describe the Gods as *lovers* of Wisdom, for they already possessed Wisdom, and love (Ἔρως) could only be of that which is not yet possessed. That Plotinus accepted this aspect of Platonic theory is beyond doubt. In describing the birth of Ἔρως, following the *Symposium*, he describes the union of Poros and Penia and its fruit as follows:[117] Λόγος οὖν γενόμενος ἐν οὐ λόγῳ, ἀορίστῳ δὲ ἐφέσει καὶ ὑποστάσει ἀμυδρᾷ, ἐποίησε τὸ γενόμενον οὐ τέλεον οὐδὲ ἱκανόν, ἐλλιπὲς δέ, ἅτε ἐξ ἐφέσεως ἀορίστου καὶ λόγου ἱκανοῦ γεγενημένον. "Imperfect," "inadequate," "deficient": these are the words to describe Ἔρως. Can we possibly believe that Plotinus would apply them to the One and that such an idea would not strike him as almost blasphemous? Is it not much more feasible to suppose that, like Plato, and partially under Plato's influence, Plotinus has been led to see more in Ἔρως than mere self-

---

[115]Cf. the remark of Schwyzer, "Bewusst und Unbewusst," 376: "Die beiden Ausdrücke σύνεσις und συναίσθησις bezeichnen hier die tiefste Verinnerlichung; der Ausdruck ὅρασις wird in dieser Stelle als zu wenig angemessen, als zu plump, als zu sinnlich empfunden."

[116]*Enn.* 6.7.39.   [117]*Enn.* 3.5.7.

seeking and desire? In terms of mere statistics Nygren is undoubtedly correct to hold that both Plato and Plotinus say more about appetitive Ἔρως than about any other variety, but both of them have refined their concept of love in the direction of Ἀγάπη to a degree far greater than Nygren has admitted. It might perhaps be supposed that if Plotinus—who lived in a society where Christian beliefs were far from unknown, and who, in his youth, had been the pupil of a philosopher (Ammonius Saccas) said at one time to have been a Christian—had been fully aware of any non-appetitive theory of Ἔρως, he would have spoken out clearly in favour of a view that was of increasing significance among his contemporaries. The fact that he did not do so can be accounted for by his desire to depart from the "system" of Plato as little as possible.

At this point it should be emphasized that, whatever cosmological or metaphysical significance be allowed to the One as Ἔρως, Nygren is quite right to insist that Plotinus never thinks in terms of Salvation.[118] This is particularly clear from *Ennead* 3.2.[119] There we read that "It is not right that the wicked should think that their prayers should make others sacrifice themselves as saviours for their sakes, or that Gods should lay aside their own life to rule over their daily affairs, or that good men who are living a different life, one superior to power among men, should become their rulers." Armstrong has suggested[120] that this passage refers to "the general belief of unthinkingly religious persons that their gods ought to help them out of the troubles they have become involved in through their own bad conduct," rather than to any kind of doctrine of salvation in the eschatological sense. I am inclined to agree with this view against that which believes that Plotinus is referring here specifically to Gnostic teachings, because from the beginning of this section he has been speaking against the Stoic view of Providence as immanent *in this world*, and not in any after-life. He has noted that the good will enjoy a good life both here and hereafter, but the "hereafter" is not strictly relevant to the tenor of the passage, which insists that the wicked have no right to expect divine intervention in their *daily* life (cf. τὰ καθέκαστα). In any case, whether the passage refers to this life or to a later one, Plotinus' main point, that God will not intervene to "save" mankind, is clear. It is up to man to save himself by becoming as like God as possible— which means, if our interpretation is correct, as like Ἔρως as possible.

καὶ τοίνυν ψυχὴ λαβοῦσα εἰς αὐτὴν ἀπορροὴν κινεῖται, καὶ ἀναβακχεύεται,

[118]Nygren, *Eros* 196.   [119]*Enn.* 3.2.9.
[120]In a comment on the original draft of this essay.

EROS AND PSYCHE

καὶ οἴστρων πίμπλαται καὶ ἔρως γίνεται.''[121] This Ἔρως will not show itself in granting Salvation; it is rather the creative force of "undiminished giving."

"It is not the One that seeks to be present with us, but we who seek to be present with the One," says Plotinus,[122] "for we are always with it, but we do not look at it." There is then no ἐπιστροφή of the One towards us;[123] there is no reason for there to be, since the One is always present. The effort must come from us. Nor is this affected by the fact that the highest state of man is beyond effort and willing, for although all living things, reasoning and unreasoning, are striving for the mystic union as far as they are able,[124] in the case of man the desired end is best achieved as the result of a long process of purifications involving deliberate intellectual and moral discipline. The One is certainly beyond all effort and willing in the human sense, and to attain to union with it a similar simplicity must be achieved by the philosopher. Yet according to Plotinus we reach our highest state beyond Will and beyond Νοῦς by using the very aids we shall somehow transcend. Our will and intellect can raise us to the hypostasis of the Divine Mind, and once there we are *prepared* for the vision of the One. The preparation must not be omitted.

Armstrong, in the introduction to his book of selections from Plotinus, tells us that "Plotinus sometimes calls the One the Father, (but without any Christian implications)."[125] By this he presumably means that it would be wrong to describe the First Hypostasis as personal, and no doubt this is correct. Yet it would be even worse to describe it as impersonal. Plotinus likes the "Father" metaphor, and using his terminology we are justified in describing his One as οἶον πατήρ. If the "Father" is Ἔρως, it is justifiable to believe that it is suprapersonal rather than impersonal. Plotinus seems to stand midway between Plato and the Christian Platonists. His Absolute is not the

[121]*Enn.* 6.7.22.   [122]*Enn.* 6.9.8.

[123]The One can neither "turn" to its origin, since it has no origin, nor to the other hypostases, in that it is somehow always before them. Aubin ("L'image," 376) wishes, wrongly, to attribute to it ἐπιστροφή towards itself on the basis of *Enn.* 5.1.6.18 and 5.1.7.5. For a correct interpretation of these passages, see Henry, *Entretiens Hardt* 5, 387.

[124]*Enn.* 3.8.1.

[125]Armstrong, *Plotinus* introd. 30. It is worth recalling again that the Neopythagorean Numenius described his First God as "father" (*ap.* Proclum *in Tim.* 1.303.27). He also supposed that in order to contemplate (νοεῖν), the First God made use of the Second (ἐν προσχρήσει τοῦ δευτέρου). This view may have helped towards the formulation of a downward-flowing motion from the highest Reality. Cf. Procl. *in Tim.* 3.103.28–32.

Platonic motionless, lifeless Form (his misinterpretation of the *Timaeus* has ensured that it is not lifeless), nor is it simply a personal God with a Will expressed in the outpouring of divine grace. Plotinus appears to attempt to have the best of both worlds; he believes his One to be beyond Will and conscious thought but still wishes to describe it in semi-personal terms. Some believe that this leaves him between two stools, having failed to attain either the objective reality of Plato or the appeal of a personal God. Dean Inge,[126] for example, writes: "There is therefore in Plotinian Mysticism none of that deep personal loyalty, none of that intimate dialogue between soul and soul, none of that passion of love—resembling often too closely the earthly love of the sexes—which is so prominent a feature in later mystical literature."

That there is no *personal* loyalty and intimate dialogue is perhaps true, for in the Plotinian view the element of personality is transcended; that there is none of the passion of love is more doubtful. We have already seen how the One is a kind of Ἔρως. That being so, it is hard to see how union with it could be free from the passion of love, especially since, in the Platonic view, love implies a going beyond the limits of one's normal self in a kind of madness.[127]

II

We have at our disposal yet another method of learning about the One. We can discover what effect the *unio mystica* has on individual souls, and in what condition the souls must be to enable this union to take place. This will involve an investigation of the πορεία or journey of the philosopher towards his goal of union, and to that we may proceed. Before so doing, however, we may claim to have shown that the remark of Arnou[128] that the procession or emanation from the One is "une bonté sans amour" gives a misleading impression of the Plotinian system.[129]

[126]Inge, *Plotinus* II. 162.
[127]*Phaedrus* 244A. νῦν δὲ τὰ μέγιστα τῶν ἀγαθῶν ἡμῖν γίγνεται διὰ μανίας, θείᾳ μέντοι δόσει διδομένης.
[128]Cf. n.85.
[129]For an account of what can be predicated of God, see the important article by Wolfson, "Albinus and Plotinus," 115–134. Wolfson maintains that Plotinus enumerates three methods that lead to a knowledge of God (ἐπιστήμη or νόησις), as distinct from a vision (θέαμα) of Him. These are as follows:
    (1) By negations (ἀφαιρέσεις); and he points out that the Plotinian (and Albinian) use of this word makes it equivalent to the Aristotelian term ἀπόφασις, "which is

What is the nature of the philosopher's journey? Plotinus sees it as arduous and difficult, as did Plato. Dodds[130] has aptly written that "What makes him (Plotinus) exceptional in the Third Century is his resolute objection to every short cut to wisdom proffered by Gnostics or Theurgists, Mithraists or Christians." This is true, but we must also bear in mind that Plotinus was always sure that, given due effort, the necessary vision of God was within his reach. Since every man has something divine within him, he can be sure that by his own efforts he can attain the goal of mystic union. We may well conclude that Plotinus has no notion of Divine Grace precisely because he never considers it necessary. Man, inasmuch as he contains the element of Divinity, is of himself capable of the highest things.

The aim of education for Plotinus is to experience union with the One, which, as we have seen, is partially to be understood in terms of two somewhat contradictory notions of the Form of the Good. It is both Being and "Beyond Being"—and we suggested that though formally Plotinus has removed *his* One "beyond Being," it still retains certain of the elements of existents and even of a personal existent. Since, then, it has two different aspects, it is likely enough that the training necessary to reach it will take two forms at least partially distinct. In fact this proves to be the case, for the philosopher's path

---

used by Aristotle in the technical sense of 'negation' in a logical proposition," and is thus sharply distinguished from στέρησις. Wolfson cites *NE* 7, 1045A 25–27 as a precursor of the Neoplatonic use of negations to describe the Godhead. In this passage Aristotle claims that to apply the term "virtue" to a God is an irrelevancy. This, in Wolfson's view, means that God is "above Virtue," as the Neoplatonists would phrase it. (Cf. Alb. *Didask.* 10.5.)

(2) By analogy (*Enn.* 6.7.36 and *Didask.* 10.5).

(3) By grades of perfection (*Didask.* 10.6; *Enn.* 6.7.36 and *Symp.* 210A ff.).

Wolfson later reduces methods (2) and (3) above to "actions" (p. 125), by which he means statements of the causal relationship between the One and the remaining hypostases. This schematic arrangement is implicit in the *Enneads*, as we have shown, but by relegating the various analogies to a somewhat subsidiary rôle, Wolfson appears to overlook the relationship between the ways of reaching God by knowledge and the mystic vision. This seems surprising, in view of the fact that he points out (p. 127) that the vision of God in Plotinus is a culmination of the progress towards Him by knowledge, whereas in Philo it is only attained by revelation and Grace. The importance of the way of analogy will appear to be that it gives the philosopher an idea of the sort of being or super-being with which he strives to obtain ὁμοίωσις. I have therefore concentrated upon it as being the most important road for the Plotinian philosopher to follow. The *via negativa* tells him of the dross he must strip off; the way of analogy can lead him to become an incarnation of Ἔρως, that is, to be at one with the First Hypostasis as far as he can (Cf. Wolfson, 128).

[130]Dodds, "The Parmenides of Plato," 143.

consists both of a positive collection of knowledge, in the Platonic sense of the word, and also of a *via negativa*. Is it not at least possible that the *via negativa* is to be regarded as an approach towards the Good *qua* "beyond Being," while the positive training is a result of the survival of the Platonic doctrine that τὸ ἀγαθόν, though the highest entity in the intelligible world, is none the less still a Form and to be approached in the same way as Beauty, Truth, and the rest: that is, by dialectic?

Plotinus, like Plato, believes that we must resemble God:[131] that is, as he interprets it, the World-Soul, or rather that element in the World-Soul which is not Soul, but Νοῦς. This latter stage is not quite the position to which Plato would bring us, for when Plotinus bids us become like Νοῦς, he means that we are to become Νοῦς as he understands it; and he has adopted the Aristotelian view that mind in act is the same as the object of its thought. Thus when we are "assimilated" to the World of Νοῦς, we become assimilated to the Forms, for οὐκ ἔξω τοῦ νοῦ τὰ νοητά. Plotinus has lost that distinction between the transcendent Form and whatever is characterized by Form that Plato insists upon in the *Phaedo*.[132] This loss, if we may again sum up a conclusion we have already stated, is a result of the misunderstanding of the famous passage in the *Timaeus*.

So we are not so much to resemble as to become Gods. The process, carried out under the motivation of a desire ("Ερως) given[133] to us by the Good, is one of purification which will make us ἀπαθεῖς.[134] We must practice the virtues as καθάρσεις, again in the manner that Socrates recommends in the *Phaedo*.[135] The aim of this purification is to make us ἀπλοῖ, for the One is eminently uniform and free from all notion of Difference (ἑτερότης). Πᾶν γὰρ τὸ οὐ πρῶτον οὐχ ἀπλοῦν.[136] These purifications are to be accompanied by prayer,[137] presumably because Plotinus believes this will involve thinking thoughts similar to those

---

[131]*Enn.* 1.2.1. Plato, *Theaet.* 176AB.

[132]*Phaedo* 102B ff. Cf. Hackforth, *Plato's Phaedo* 153.

[133]For the relevance of the power of "Ερως as something "God-given," cf. *Enn.* 6.7.31 and Armstrong, "Platonic Eros," 113.

[134]*Enn.* 1.2.5. Cf. Daniélou, *Platonisme* 100. Merki, 'ΟΜΟΙΩΣΙΣ 20, suggests that whereas Plato is only urging us to become like God, Plotinus proposes "eine Vergöttlichung, eine Rückkehr zur Göttlichkeit." This is an exaggeration. The real difference is that involved in Plotinus' accepting the view that Νοῦς, which we are to resemble, is both the Platonic God *and* the Forms. That Plotinus proposes "eine Vergöttlichung" is true, but not entirely unplatonic. Cf. *Enn.* 1.2.5 and 6.

[135]For Plotinus' views on the "civic virtues," Cf. *Enn.* 1.2.1.

[136]*Enn.* 2.9.1.   [137]*Enn.* 5.1.6.

of the Divine Mind and will thus help the soul to attain to that state of mystic love that is the goal of the philosophic life.

The so-called civic virtues are only preliminary. True, the man who practices them is to some extent worthy of the name "godlike," but he achieves assimilation with Divinity only in a very imperfect sense. When he has mastered them, he must go on to more difficult disciplines if he will be perfect. Of those who do not take this next step Plotinus is critical, and he insists that they cannot completely fulfil the aspirations of their own divinity. τούτους γοῦν καὶ θείους ἡ φήμη λέγει καὶ λεκτέον ἀμήγεπῃ ὡμοιῶσθαι, κατὰ δὲ τὰς μείζους τὴν ὁμοίωσιν εἶναι.[138] Nevertheless the civic virtues are necessary, and the possession of the higher degrees of excellence implies the possession of the lower, at least potentially.[139]

Three kinds of men are most likely, in Plotinus' view, to be able to attain to the world of Νοῦς and the Forms: the lover, the music-lover[140] and the lover of wisdom or philosopher. Here we come upon yet another contradiction, for theoretically at least all men are supposed to be able to attain to the highest things. It is merely, Plotinus often implies, a question of γνῶθι σεαυτόν and of bringing out the divine element that every man has within him. If we can close the eye of our body, he tells us, we can resurrect another kind of vision, which all of us possess but few are able to use.[141] When he comes to describing how we can begin to use this vision, however, we find that the necessary training and mental abilities must limit it to the few. It is true that Plotinus does not put as much emphasis as Plato on the exact sciences, but he still insists that they are necessary. For even the philosopher, who is further advanced towards the Intelligible World than the other candidates, has still to study τὰ μαθήματα[142]—presumably the Platonic sciences of arithmetic and the rest—before being allowed to go on to dialectic. So although all possess the divine spark, only those, after all, who have mathematical ability are able to bring it to perfection. In view of the general tone of Plotinus' work and of the age in which he lived, we can attribute this continued interest in mathematics solely to Plotinus' unwillingness to diverge from the Platonic method as he knew it. That the reason for the insistence on mathematics was its magical importance and the unphilosophic rôle it played in Neopy-

---

[138]*Enn.* 1.2.1. For further discussion of civic virtue, see below, pp. 168–169.

[139]*Enn.* 1.2.7.

[140]*Enn.* 1.3. For this rarer sense of μουσικός as "musician," cf. *Rep.* 10. 620A and Athen. 4.176E.

[141]*Enn.* 1.6.8.　　　　　　　　　　[142]*Enn.* 1.3.3.

thagorean and Chaldaean systems is unlikely, in view of the almost total disregard of such aberrations that the whole of the *Enneads* displays.

After mathematics the Plotinian philosopher proceeds to dialectic and apparently spends the rest of his life perfecting himself in this in the hope that one day he will be rewarded by the mystic vision. There is no talk of returning to the Cave. Plotinus has no doubt of the superiority of the contemplative life to the life of action, as it is normally understood.[143]

The philosophic goal of the historical Plato is to contemplate the Forms, but that of the Plato of Plotinus is to become a Form, to be at one with the Divine Mind and thus to be able to receive the vision of God when it presents itself. Καὶ ἡ σπουδὴ οὐκ ἔξω ἁμαρτίας εἶναι, ἀλλὰ θεὸν εἶναι.[144] The highest stage we can be sure of reaching is that of Νοῦς, the Divine Mind, but we must at least prepare ourselves for the Good, though we have no guarantee that we shall ever see it. A part of the method advocated by Plotinus is the *via negativa*, which many thinkers believe totally unplatonic. Caird, for example, writes as follows: "They (the Neoplatonists) did not observe that Plato reaches his conception of it (the Good) not by abstraction, but by synthesis, not by turning away from all the special principles of knowledge but by thinking them together, that is, by finding the one principle which shall determine the place and relations of all the others. Nor did they attach sufficient weight to the passages in which the good is spoken of as a unity which is always presupposed, though never distinctly reflected upon in our ordinary consciousness of the word."[145] This criticism is harsh on Plotinus, but in a sense justified. It depends on such passages in the *Republic* as ὁ μὲν γὰρ συνοπτικὸς διαλεκτικός, ὁ δὲ μὴ οὔ,[146] where the synthesis of knowledge of which Caird speaks is important. But it overlooks an important contradiction in Plato himself which we have already had occasion to mention. This is the duality inherent in his manner of describing the Good now as a Form, now as beyond the Forms since it is "beyond Being." In general, we suggest, Platonic dialectic is designed to enable the philosopher to contemplate the World of Forms as a whole: in Plotinian terms, to attain to the Divine Hypostasis of Νοῦς. When Plato speaks of the Form of the Good it is only by analogy. We are, in other words, supposed to grasp at its nature from its implications in the rest of the Ideal World. Dialectic can tell us about the Good *qua* Form, but the

[143]This is discussed further on pp. 170–171.   [144]*Enn.* 1.2.6.
[145]Caird, *Evolution* 165.   [146]*Rep.* 537A 7.

Good *qua* "beyond Being" must be grasped by an intuition, albeit an intuition which only the dialectician can hope to possess.

The real difference between Plato and Plotinus here is that although Plato describes the Good as "beyond Being" and thus apparently puts it in a different category from the other Forms, in practice when speaking of dialectic, he tends to forget this distinction. Plotinus does not, and by thus seizing upon one aspect of a Platonic paradox he succeeds in producing a theory which is more coherent than, and distinct from, that of his Master. Plato usually regards the Form of the Good as a Form rather than as something "beyond Being," and this means that it is perfectly limited and defined. Accordingly, the soul that wishes to become a god through obtaining the immanent character of the Good, must concern itself with what Caird describes as a synthesis of the special sciences. Plotinus, on the other hand, realizes that such a synthesis will not make the philosopher "like" the One which is "beyond Being" and which, as we have already seen, is frequently described in negative terms.

If we are to be satisfied with the merely moral virtues, then the ordinary purifications which, we must remember, are themselves denials and negations of *bodily* preoccupations, are sufficient. Soul, for Plotinus, is a descent from Νοῦς, and even to begin to make the ascent back, we must strip off the bodily trappings: ἀποδυομένοις ἃ καταβαίνοντες ἠμφιέσμεθα.[147] We must practice for death, as the *Phaedo* recommends,[148] and separate our soul from its wretched body as far as we can, that it may be able to concentrate upon the divine element,[149] the Νοῦς, that it contains within itself. Indeed, death should be most welcome to the follower of Plotinus, for, like his Master, he can then merge what is divine in himself with what is divine in the Universe.[150]

It must be remembered, however, firstly that Plotinus himself, by dissuading his disciple Porphyry from suicide, showed himself a true follower of Plato and of the Socrates of the *Phaedo*, and secondly that just as death, though perhaps desirable in itself, is not to be anticipated by suicide, so the mystic vision is to be awaited in calmness, without any of the artificial stimulation by which more materialistic mystics have attempted to take heaven by storm. Bréhier appears to have supposed that this calmness and hope of divine favour was the cause of Plotinus' confidence when he delivered his celebrated rebuke to his follower Amelius. Amelius had developed an enthusiasm for the outward forms of worship and was frequently to be seen paying his

[147] *Enn.* 1.6.7. [148] *Phaedo* 64Aff.
[149] *Enn.* 1.2.5 and elsewhere. [150] Porphyry, *Vita Plotini* 2.

respects in the temples of the Gods. Indeed, he became so self-righteous about his devotions that he asked Plotinus why he did not do the same; to which the philosopher replied that it was for the Gods to come to him, not he to them. Bréhier believes that in this passage Plotinus is alluding to his confidence in attaining to that mystical union with the One which, according to Porphyry, he enjoyed four times.[151] This interpretation, however, is not the most obvious deduction from Porphyry's account. Porphyry says that the words of Plotinus were ἐκείνους δεῖ πρὸς ἐμὲ ἔρχεσθαι, οὐκ ἐμὲ πρὸς ἐκείνους.[152] In view of the language used throughout the *Enneads* when Plotinus is speaking of the One, it seems unlikely that the plural would be suitable or that Plotinus would use it of the One which is totally free of multiplicity. Furthermore, it is difficult not to feel that in this sharp rebuff there is a more arrogant tone than Plotinus would use, if, as Bréhier believes, he were speaking of the One.

These words, then, almost certainly refer to gods or δαίμονες far lower and far less important than the One. Merlan[153] supposes that Plotinus is alluding to his power to compel such lesser divinities to come to him by the use of theurgy. This solution again appears to contradict the spirit of the *Enneads*, where theurgy is unknown. Armstrong[154] seems to be right in believing that the ἐκείνους "refers to the crowd of lower gods who are to be found at sacrifices" and that Plotinus expresses "not an assertion of theurgic power over them, but at least a sense of social superiority." To support this "sense of social superiority," Armstrong points to a most relevant passage of the *De Abstinentia*[155] where Porphyry inveighs against men who lay claim to philosophy but patronize the popular worship. He tells us further that the "gods" that are present at sacrifices are δαίμονες, and if, as seems clear, the passage reveals an attitude held by Plotinus himself, namely, that though δαίμονες exist, their cult is unworthy of the philosopher, whose gaze is turned on far higher spiritual things, then we can the more readily understand why Plotinus rejected the invitation of Amelius.

It appears then that we cannot use these famous words of Plotinus to exemplify his calmness in awaiting the mystic vision, and his absolute refusal to attempt those gross magical acts by which, for

---

[151]*Ibid.* 23.   [152]*Ibid.* 10.
[153]Merlan, "Plotinus and Magic," 341–348.
[154]Armstrong, "Was Plotinus a Magician?," 77–78. Armstrong here agrees with Henry, "Dernière Parole," 115.
[155]Porphyry, *De Abstinentia* 2, 34–43.

example, Proclus "was granted the sight of luminous phantoms sent by Hecate."[156] We can, however, insist that throughout the *Enneads* there is no mention of such aberrations. Indeed, if there had been, it seems unlikely that Plotinus would have succeeded in attaining that union with the One which he sought. Proclus, the adept in "Chaldaean purifications," failed to attain the mystic vision; Plotinus, on the other hand, was rewarded for his practice and devotion on at least four occasions.

We are travelling too fast, and we must return to what Plotinus thinks of dialectic and how he believes he is expounding the true thought of Plato. In the seventh tractate of the Sixth *Ennead* he defines the position as follows:[157] Ἔστι μὲν γὰρ ἡ τοῦ ἀγαθοῦ εἴτε γνῶσις εἴτε ἐπαφὴ μέγιστον καὶ μέγιστον φησι (i.e., Plato) τοῦτο εἶναι μάθημα, οὐ τὸ πρὸς αὐτὸ ἰδεῖν μάθημα λέγων, ἀλλὰ περὶ αὐτοῦ μαθεῖν τι πρότερον. Plotinus understands Plato to mean that we can contemplate the Form of the Good by dialectic; that is, that we can learn *about* it, but we cannot merge ourselves with it by thought alone. Union, according to Plotinus, is attained by another process, that of simplification, the stripping off of those trappings of "form" and "limit" which are necessary for our attaining to the Hypostasis of Noûs, but not to that of the One, which is formless.

Plotinus is still following the Platonic principle of ὅμοιος ὁμοίῳ and it leads him further than Plato has gone. In Plato, we remember, the aim was to obtain ὁμοίωσις θεῷ (*Theaet.* 176A) and thus to contemplate the Forms, which, however, were still separated from the Gods by the barrier of lifelessness. In Plotinus, as we have seen, no such barrier exists between the One, Noûs, and the Forms that are within Noûs; they are all the result of a single system. Since there is no Platonic dualism of Forms and souls, we are free to apply the principle of ὅμοιος ὁμοίῳ to the supreme ambition of the philosophic Ἔρως, that of union with the One, the source and Father of all, that is "beyond Being." And, to do this, we must leave everything behind, even the Forms and the World of Noûs Ἀποτίθεται πᾶσαν ἣν ἔχει μορφήν. τὸ νοητὸν πᾶν ἀφεὶς θεάσεται· ὁμοιοῦσθαι γὰρ δεῖ.[158] Everything, even dialectic, is irrelevant and we are commanded to cast it all away. Ἄφελε πάντα.[159]

---

[156]Cf. below, p. 95 and n.160.

[157]*Enn.* 6.7.36. [158]*Enn.* 6.7.34.

[159]*Enn.* 5.3.17. I do not think that Plotinus' basic position that Noûs is transcended in the union with the One is seriously modified by the passage 6.7.35, which speaks of Noûs as being beyond itself ἐρῶν. The union of the soul with the One is in Noûs and with Noûs—but also beyond Noûs.

We set out with the intention of examining what Plotinus means by his One, and since we now know that the soul becomes like the One, or rather becomes merged with it, during the mystic vision, we may hope, therefore, greatly to increase our understanding of it by observing what Plotinus has to say about that moment when it can be truly known, that is, the moment of the mystic union itself. Plotinus, as we have noted, was rewarded with this experience on at least four occasions, and Porphyry claimed to have enjoyed it once. None of the other Neoplatonists are recorded to have experienced it, and Dodds, writing of Proclus, the greatest of them, thinks that when he speaks of it he is referring to something that he knows of only in connection with the great men of the past,[160] and with the literary tradition. Let us see, then, what conclusions Plotinus himself reaches about it, and while doing so let us remember his warnings that his descriptions will never be able to do justice to the truth. During the experience itself, he says, a man is unable to speak, and afterwards is compelled to use terms about it which can never be a truly adequate description.[161]

Suddenly, says Plotinus, the vision is present. One is not aware of its coming and cannot detain it for longer than the short time that is all one can hope for on any occasion. The philosopher always longs for its presence (This is the philosophic Ἔρως of the *Symposium* and *Phaedrus*); but he must wait until he is duly prepared for the vision. "Therefore we should not pursue it, but wait quietly until it appears, preparing ourselves to view it, as the eye awaits the rising of the sun." Dean Inge has justly remarked on the comparative rarity of the visions of the Neoplatonists as compared with the later mystics of the cloister, adducing the parallel that "Just as young people in some Protestant sects experience sudden conversion at the age of adolescence, while in other Christian churches this is almost unknown or regarded as a rare phenomenon, so visions and trances come often when they are looked for, and seldom when they are not expected."[162]

But when the vision arrives, what is it and what does it tell us about the One? All experiences which may be called mystical in the vulgar sense are, as is well known, of two kinds: one is characterized

[160]Dodds, *Elements*. In his introduction, p. xxiii, he writes: "It is significant that Marinus never claims for his hero (Proclus) that he enjoyed direct union with God, as Plotinus and on one occasion Porphyry had done; instead he tells us that he was an expert in weather-magic, and in the techniques of evocation, and that while practising 'the Chaldean purifications' he was vouchsafed personal visions of luminous phantoms sent by Hecate." Marinus, *Vita Procli* 27.
[161]*Enn.* 5.3.17.
[162]Inge, *Plotinus* 2, 154. *Enn.* 5.5.8.

by wild excitement and a loss of control and will, often manifesting itself in forms of frenzied dancing and bacchanalian revelry; the other is calm, but intense. This latter kind is the aim of Plotinus. It is described as a simplification (ἅπλωσις), an absolute trust in Divinity and a total merger of the Self within it. But most frequently it is described in terms that suggest the intoxication of passionate love. Let us examine two famous passages. The first is in the seventh essay of the Sixth *Ennead*, where we read as follows:[163] "Intellectual-Principle, thus, has two powers, first that of grasping intellectively its own content, the second that of an advancing and receiving whereby to know its transcendent; at first it sees, later by that seeing it takes possession of Intellectual-Principle, becoming one only thing with that: the first seeing is that of Intellect knowing, the second that of Intellect loving (νοῦς ἐρῶν); stripped of its wisdom in the intoxication of the nectar, it comes to love (ἐρῶν γίνεται); by this excess it is made simpler and is happy; and to be drunken is better for it than to be too staid for these revels." (Trans. MacKenna.)

Here are two prominent features: the emphasis on love and the resulting state of being ἄφρων. We may wonder why it is right for the philosopher to become "witless"; and indeed such a question is at the bottom of many objections to the *via negativa*, both from Caird and others like him who regard it as unplatonic, and from others who regard it as inhuman. But must we not admit that Plato's teachings are equally "inhuman," if we are to define as "inhuman" anything which demands a degree of restraint and discipline? We must remember that Plotinus does not insist that the philosopher should be ignorant; that would be unplatonic. On the contrary, he demands the same exacting and rigorous training as his Master has demanded. He goes beyond his Master, however, in his clearer recognition that such a training is not adequate in itself. At times even dialectic must be laid aside, though this in no way detracts from its value as a necessary preliminary. The one thing that we must not lay aside, however, is that Ἔρως which will in a special way make us "drunken" and "witless." And the reason this should not be laid aside is clearly that it is the only quality in us that is truly akin to the One. It is the bond of union of the negative and positive approaches to divinity.

When speaking of the One, we found that Plotinus sometimes uses the quasi-personal term πατήρ and is very fond of describing its nature as that of a spring or source or principle of existence. If we keep these descriptions in our minds when we turn to those passages

[163] *Enn.* 6.7.35.

which make the One equal to Ἔρως and Ἔρως αὐτοῦ, we shall understand that the reason why the one thing the *via negativa* cannot deny
is our own Ἔρως, is that in some sense Ἔρως is the One that we seek.

The second passage that we must examine in this connection is also
in *Ennead* 6,[164] and here too we must observe carefully what Plotinus
has to say about the intoxication of love and the transcendence of the
will it involves. "That light known, then indeed we are stirred towards
those Beings in longing and rejoicing over the radiance about them. . . .
Every one of those Beings exists for itself but becomes an object of
desire by the colour cast upon it from the Good, source of those graces
and of the love they evoke. The soul taking that outflow from the
divine is stirred, seized with a Bacchic passion, goaded by these goads,
it becomes Love" (Trans. MacKenna). When the soul sees the Forms
illuminated by the Good, it rejoices (εὐφραίνεται), is stirred (κινεῖται),
and goes into uncontrolled ecstasies (ἀναβακχεύεται). No will can chain
the Bacchant and nothing can reach the mind of the goaded creature
except the continual consciousness of the goad. The soul, as Plotinus
says, becomes single, or as we might say, single-minded. It is nothing
but Ἔρως; it is nothing but the One.

We have found in Plato two contradictory notions of Ἔρως: the
one that of simple desire, and the other something more akin to giving,
perhaps even to creation, though Plato never follows up this aspect
of his thoughts to its logical conclusion. In Plotinus, too, it is not only
possible to observe these two contradictory notions of Ἔρως, but to
see how the former, inferior variety can be transformed into the latter.
The key to this change is that it is caused by the actual vision of the
One; the soul translates its feelings of desire into those of worship.
Let us consider the following passage:[165]

Therefore we must ascend again to the Good, the desired of every Soul. Anyone that
has seen this, knows what I intend when I say that it is beautiful. Even the desire of
it is to be desired as a Good. To attain it is for those that will take the upward path,
who will set all their forces towards it, who will divest themselves of all that we have
put on in our descent: so, to those that approach the Holy Celebrations of the Mysteries, there are appointed purifications and the laying aside of the garments worn
before, and the entry in nakedness—until, passing, on the upward way, all that is
other than the God, each in solitude of himself shall behold that solitary dwelling
Existence, the Apart, the Unmingled, the Pure [cf. *Symp.* 211C], that from which all
things depend, for which all look and live and act and know, the Source of Life and of
Intellection and of Being.
     And One that shall know this vision—with what passion of love shall he not be
seized, with what pang of desire, what longing to be molten into one with This,

---

[164] *Enn.* 6.7.22.   [165] *Enn.* 1.6.7.

what wondering delight! If he that has never seen this Being must hunger for It as for all his welfare, he that has known must love and reverence It as the very Beauty; he will be flooded with awe and gladness, stricken by a salutary terror; he loves with a veritable love, with sharp desire; all other loves than this he must despise, and disdain all that once seemed fair (Trans. MacKenna-Page).

The most significant fact about this passage is that the man who has not yet been rewarded with a vision of the One still desires it, as a "good" that he may possess. Plotinus uses the word ὀρέγεσθαι. The man who has seen it, however, though admittedly gripped by δριμεῖς πόθους for a recurrence of the vision, is now filled with the joy and wonder of a true love (ἀληθὴς ἔρως).[166] The feeling of amazement is repeated twice (ἄγασθαι, θάμβους πιμπλᾶσθαι, ἐκπλήττεσθαι). This is the overwhelming sensation of "true love" when it has seen what was once purely the object of desire. Desire gives way to adoration, though the word used to describe the state of the soul is still the same, that is Ἔρως. Indeed, what other word is possible? Not, surely, Φιλία, for the culmination of ecstatic Ἔρως;[167] Φιλία is too unemotional a word for Plotinus to be able to use in this context, where nothing that might suggest a merely rational relationship would suffice. The word Φιλία suggests the association of *two* equal or unequal partners working together out of mutual respect and trust, but, for all their faith in one another, φίλοι remain two. Plotinus wants to describe a state where the two (the One and the purified soul) become *one*. Φιλία would have sounded to the Greeks inappropriate for this notion of fusion; it insists too much on the importance of the individual personality, and in any case "friendship" between man and God was usually regarded as out of the question. Plotinus might have made use of the word Ἀγάπη for his descriptions of the joy and wonder aroused by the sight and realization of the One, as he uses it to describe the One itself in the Sixth *Ennead*. Here we find:[168] Ὅδ' εἰς τὸ εἴσω οἷον φέρεται αὐτοῦ, οἷον ἑαυτὸν ἀγαπήσας αὐγὴν καθαράν, αὐτὸς ὢν τοῦτο, ὅπερ ἠγάπησε — — τοῦτο δ'ἐστὶν ὑποστήσας αὐτόν, εἴπερ ἐνέργεια μένουσα καὶ τὸ ἀγαπητότατον οἷον νοῦς. The feelings of the One towards itself, and thus, we can assume, of the "soul enraptured" towards the One are here described

---

[166]Since the first draft of this essay, Professor Armstrong has commented on this passage and offered an explanation similar to my own. Cf. "Platonic Eros," 113.

[167]In *Laws* 8, 837A, Plato describes Ἔρως as the intense form of Φιλία. It is true that Albinus insists that Ἔρως must be watered down into Φιλία (*Didask.* 23, τέλος δὲ αὐτοῖς τὸ ἀντὶ ἐραστοῦ καὶ ἐρωμένου γενέσθαι φίλους), but as Witt points out (*Albinus* 10), this is based on Aristotle's *Nicomachean Ethics* rather than on Plato. Cf. Plutarch, *Amatorius* 758C, 759D.

[168]*Enn.* 6.8.16.

in terms of 'Αγάπη. Previously we have seen them described as "Ερως and αὐτοῦ "Ερως.

Plotinus, then, makes little distinction between the two terms and makes no attempt to clarify the difficulty caused by the two senses of "Ερως: that of desire and that of joyful union with the self-sufficient creativeness of the One. He might have used 'Αγάπη for the latter idea, as the above passage shows. Why he did not do so we shall never be certain, but it is not beyond the bounds of possibility that he knew the word in its Christian connotation and therefore refused to have truck with it. We have seen how little satisfied he was with the Gnostics and how he despised those who, as he thought, demanded a saviour to help them out of the difficulties in which they had involved themselves. It is quite possible that among these latter he included Christians and, if so, the dislike that he must have felt for them would probably have precluded him from the use of 'Αγάπη, their peculiar term for love.[169]

'Αγάπη, then, is neglected by Plotinus, though it was a term that might have been employed for one of the two senses of "Ερως, and we have suggested a possible reason for this neglect. There is a further reason also: one which Plotinus would have regarded as of the utmost importance. The two kinds of "Ερως are not entirely separate; rather the higher is the logical and best possible result of the lower. The "Ερως of the mystic union is the actuality of the "Ερως which, as mere potency, is still at the stage of desire. Nevertheless, there is no short cut to the higher state. There is only one path to the union with God, and that is the one we have described, motivated by the lower and normal Platonic variety of "Ερως.

Plotinus deliberately compares this transference of emotion, this fulfilment of desire in joy and self-surrender, to physical love. He writes that the soul suddenly realizes its unity with the One:[170] "She (the soul) has seen that presence suddenly manifesting within her, for there is nothing between: Love is no longer a duality but a two in one; for, so long as the presence holds, all distinction fades: it is as lover and beloved here, in a copy of that union, long to blend; the soul has now no further awareness of being in body and will give herself no foreign name, not man, not living being, not being, not all." (Trans. Mac-Kenna-Page.)

---

[169]I do not mean to suggest that Plotinus would necessarily have understood or appreciated the specifically Christian *meaning* of the word 'Αγάπη, only that he probably knew that it was in current use among Christians. For this subject, cf. Nygren, *Eros*, D'Arcy, *Mind and Heart*, and De Rougement, *Passion and Society*.
[170]*Enn.* 6.7.34.

The physical imagery is not forgotten. Plotinus realizes as well as Plato that what he is demanding is a sublimation of Aphrodite Pandemos, but his demands are much more within the realms of possibility than are those of his Master. By postulating that the Good is the source both of the Intelligible World of Forms, themselves now alive, and of the world of Soul which includes our own individual souls, and by offering us a quasi-personalized representation of the First Hypostasis with which we must merge ourselves in the mystic union, Plotinus is presenting his followers with a goal at least within the powers of the human emotion of love to attain. Plato, in asking us to love the lifeless Forms which are always separate from us and which can only be experienced as immanent characteristics, asked, we suggested, what might seem noble but impossible. Plotinus, by avoiding the dualism of Forms and souls, and by asking us to love *his* version of the Good, has shown that if he misunderstood the meaning of his Master's teachings, it was because he better understood the nature of the human spirit in love (νοῦς ἐρῶν).

That Plotinus recognized the physical basis of Ἔρως and made his demands on human nature more modest does not imply that he was any more lax than Plato towards the perversions to which his doctrine was and always will be prone. Indeed, to our eyes, he may seem more enlightened in that he speaks of Ἔρως in a context which may imply heterosexual rather than homosexual love. This is, indeed, only a conjecture, for many passages can be cited where he speaks of the ἐραστής and his ἐρώμενος in the usual homosexual manner, and Harder's suggestion that he shared the specifically *Roman* dislike of Ἔρως παιδικός must remain only a surmise. Yet the use of language drawn from the mystery religions may have led him to believe that heterosexual relations were as likely to lead to the "philosophic" Ἔρως as those between man and boy. Indeed, Plato in his old age may have led the way to this conclusion too, for perhaps Plotinus had more understanding of that mysterious phrase in the *Laws*, so tantalizing to the commentators, which briefly expresses the hope that some relation of φιλία can exist between men and their wives.[171] However that may be, there is no doubt that the phrase ἱερὸς γάμος was used in discussions of the mystic union within the school of Plotinus. For this we have the express testimony of Porphyry[172] who tells us how, when he read a poem with this title, certain other members of the school thought him

[171]*Laws* 8, 839B. Grube, *Plato's Thought* 118. For Harder's suggestion on Ἔρως παιδικός cf. *Entretiens Hardt* 5, 90.
[172]Porphyry, *Vita Plotini* 15.

THE ONE, EROS, AND THE PROGRESSION OF THE SOUL 101

demented, but Plotinus himself hailed him as poet, hierophant and philosopher.

On the positive side, then, we see Plotinus showing interest in discussion of the ἱερὸς γάμος, which, even if it involved relations that were physical rather than sublime—as the Christians, probably unjustly, alleged—was at least concerned with the male-female relationship. Even the most ardent pederasts of the ancient world would rarely have described their affairs in terms of a marriage! Furthermore, we know that Plotinus' physical imagery was not intended to support any relaxation of that strict self-control that Socrates displays in the *Symposium*. Immediately after the passage describing his poem on the ἱερὸς γάμος, Porphyry mentions the reaction of his Master to the behaviour of a certain rhetor, Diophanes by name, who made so bold as to defend the conduct of Alcibiades in aiming at physical relations with Socrates, on the ground that the pupil must be all things to his Master, provided that he is able to derive the virtue that is knowledge from him. Plotinus was indignant at the idea and could hardly restrain himself from leaving the room; afterwards, however, he instructed Porphyry to write an answer to Diophanes and was, we are told, delighted when it was read out to him.

That Plotinus had more time for women in his private affairs than had Plato is good evidence that he was more likely to count them capable of attaining to the philosophic Ἔρως; and whereas it is a commonplace that women play almost no part in the life of Plato and that, except for his mother, they are hardly even mentioned in any connection with him, this is very far from being the case with Plotinus. The invaluable Porphyry recounts how many women were devoted to him, and how some of these even engaged in philosophic pursuits.[173] This sounds rather different from what we know of the Platonic Academy, where one of the only two women members is reported to have worn men's clothes, presumably because it was thought that, since the work she was doing was best done by men, she should resemble a man as far as she was able.[174]

Plotinus' more moderate attitude finds support within the Platonic tradition itself in Plutarch's *Amatorius*. Here Plato's explicit attack[175] on physical homosexual relations is repeated,[176] and heterosexual love,

[173]*Ibid.* 9.
[174]Cf. the opinion of Plato that men who had lived unworthily would be reincarnated as women.
[175]See the passage on love in *Laws* 836B–842A.
[176]Plutarch, *Amatorius* 751E ff.

culminating in marriage,[177] is defended at great length against its traducers, whose chief spokesman is appropriately named Protogenes. Although, as we have seen, Plutarch's suggestion that Φιλία must eventually replace Ἔρως is unsuitable in a context of a mystic's love of the One, the new doctrine, derived from a hint in the *Laws* about men's being "friendly" with their wives, and placing especial emphasis on marriage, must have done much to help the Platonists to an understanding of the most natural direction in which the emotion of love can be channelled. Plutarch is insistent that those who claim that inspiration can only come from love for boys are mere voluptuaries seeking to cloak their immorality beneath the garb of philosophy. From the point of view of inspiration, he says, the sex of the beloved is irrelevant.[178]

Reverting to Plotinus, we may say in brief that although he explained his *unio mystica* in terms that betray more understanding of the impulse of love and of its capabilities, we should be unjustified in believing that this implied any slackening of the high standards in human relationships and self-control that his Master Plato had set up. Indeed, his interest in heterosexual relationships, however slight it may have been, can only be regarded as a great advance, even if one fraught with very great dangers. But to that subject and to precursors of the new view in Plato himself we shall return when we speak of the more explicit contributions made by Origen. For the moment we must look once more at the following passage from the *Enneads*, which describes the physical analogies inherent in Ἔρως, be it of the lower or the higher form, as we have distinguished them. We read as follows:[179]

The soul in its nature loves God and longs to be at one with Him in the noble love of a daughter for a noble father; but coming to human birth and lured by the courtships of this sphere, she takes up with another love, a mortal, leaves her father and falls. But one day coming to hate her shame, she puts away the evil of earth, once more seeks the father, and finds her peace. Those to whom all this experience is strange may understand by way of our earthly longings and the joy we have in winning to what we most desire—remembering always that here what we love is perishable, hurtful, that our loving is of mimicries and turns awry because all was a mistake, our good was not here, this was not what we sought; There only is our veritable love and There we may unite with it, not holding it in some fleshly embrace but possessing it in all its verity. (Trans. MacKenna-Page.)

The soul is likened to a maiden yearning with a noble love. This in itself is a little strange, since, according to the more usual theory of

[177]*Ibid.* 767DE.   [178]*Ibid.* 766EF.   [179]*Enn.* 6.9.9.

Platonic Ἔρως, love is an emotion between two men seeking to grasp the philosophic life together. Clarification is given in a famous passage in which Plotinus describes the rival loves of the Good and the Beautiful.[180] He points out that the Good is gentle and agreeable and tender, and that it is with us whenever we wish, whereas Beauty, the inferior love, involves excessive amazement, and in the enjoyment of it we find pain as well as pleasure. Plotinus links excessive desire with the pursuit of Beauty, thinks this pursuit can even distract the soul from the Good, and finds the desire for the Good more spiritual, since it is ἀναίσθητος. Perhaps he associates Ἔρως as male desire with the pursuit of Beauty, whereas when he speaks of love of the Good, he thinks rather of the Ἔρως of a "noble maiden"—a love which involves both desire and a peaceful union with God the "father" which transcends desire. In conclusion, Ἔρως as desire unfulfilled and nothing more is not the Ἔρως of the "philosophic lover" and is transcended; we have already seen that it is not the Ἔρως of the One.

With these preliminary matters clear, we can now proceed without fear of misinterpretation to Plotinus' description of the mystical union itself, in so far as he feels himself able to describe it at all. He plainly expects his readers to have some preliminary notion of it as a kind of vision or contemplation (θέαμα),[181] but rejects this as inadequate. It is rather, he explains, another kind of vision, a "being out of oneself" (ἔκστασις), "an act of self-surrender" (ἐπίδοσις αὐτοῦ), "a simplification" (ἅπλωσις), "a kind of sustained thought directed towards conformity" (περινόησις πρὸς ἐφαρμογήν). These expressions are certainly not purely visual images, and indeed it would be most surprising if they were, for we have been taught to suppose that the experience is not one of the admiration of something inexpressibly beautiful but distant (like the Platonic Forms, which are χωριστά), but rather a total submergence of the Self in the Ἔρως of the One. Accordingly we find a tactual image (ἐφαρμογή) used in the comparison[182] (as is fitting, since Plotinus regards the transports of love as the only possible analogy) and beside it one of a superior variety of thought: thought that is not only above mere ratiocination, but even beyond intuition where intuition is of something outside the Self. For in the *unio mystica* nothing is outside the Self, since the Self, by giving itself up, has become both the whole

[180]*Enn* 5.5.12. Cf. Plato, *Phaedrus* 250 and Armstrong, "Platonic Eros," 108. Kristeller shows, in *Der Begriff der Seele* 65, how important this passage is for the relation of the Soul to Νοῦς and the One respectively.
[181]For what follows cf. *Enn*. 6.9.11.
[182]For terms of "contact" cf. *Enn*. 5.3.10 θῖξις καὶ οἷον ἐπαφή; 6.7.39.

and the part of the One. It is "the whole" of the One by having no qualitative ἑτερότης, although, since Plotinus is not a pantheist, it still remains numerically distinct.[183]

For the mystic, led on by the Ἔρως that is desire to win happiness for the Self, the end of the journey is to realize that the Self, the individual personality, is to be abandoned. We have already seen how the One is beyond Personality, though spoken of in quasi-personal terms, and we decided that, strictly speaking, the only element of Personality it may be said to possess is its Ἔρως, which shows itself in spontaneous creation. Accordingly, when the mystic succeeds in becoming merged with the Absolute, this Ἔρως is all that will remain of his personality.

It is a temptation, as we have seen, to regard the Plotinian Absolute as totally "determined." Plotinus, far from concluding this, holds that, on the contrary, both the Absolute and the philosopher who is at one with it are "beyond freedom" (πλέον ἢ ἐλεύθεροι, καὶ πλέον ἢ αὐτεξούσιοι).[184] By this he means that mere mortals have some degree of choice, yet if they are good their goodness makes them *bound* to choose the Good, even though the possibility of evil is always before them; the Absolute, on the other hand, is its own guarantee that it will react in the form of undiminished giving. Any other activity would be unthinkable for it. There is no extrinsic factor which compels the One to make this choice; it is its "nature" to do so, and Plotinus attempts to describe such a "nature" by such phrases as πλέον ἢ αὐτεξουσία.

It is the discarding of Self or of Personality, that the critics of Plotinus have regarded as his primary unplatonic feature, and for which they have sought parallels from the exotic cults of the Near East. These cults were of great influence in Plotinus' day and, as an inhabitant of Egypt,[185] if not an Egyptian, he cannot but have been well aware of them. Bréhier, as we have already noticed, has even discovered traces of the effects of Indian thought in the "depersonalization" of the soul in ecstasy in Plotinus, and he has not been alone in doing so. In this matter, however, as in some of the others that have already come under review, it may be shown that the difficulty of understanding how Plotinus could have derived his theories from Greek origins, and especially from Plato, is not as great as is sometimes

[183]For ἑτερότης cf. *Enn.* 6.9.8 and Arnou, *Le Désir* 246.
[184]*Enn.* 6.8.15. Cf. Henry, "Le Problème," and Clark, "Empirical Responsibility," 16–31.
[185]According to Eunapius, Plotinus came from "Lyco." This is generally supposed to be Lycopolis in Upper Egypt.

supposed. It is quite possible to "discover" most of the essential features of the Plotinian system within Plato's works, and that without necessarily assuming that Plato's outlook was the same as Plotinus'. To make this latter deduction would be as unreasonable as to maintain that because Calvin draws heavily on St. Augustine in certain specific departments of thought, therefore his general theological outlook is necessarily similar.

Plato's views on the immortality of the soul have always posed considerable problems for his interpreters. In the *Apology*, where he is probably giving the view of Socrates rather than his own, he is not prepared to state categorically that the soul is immortal, though we may well believe that Socrates thought it to be so. In the *Phaedo*, he produces three (or four) arguments to prove an immortality of which he seems convinced, whereas in the *Symposium* (206C–208C) he does not formally mention it at all. His silence here is perhaps partly to be explained by the problems he finds himself compelled to face as a result of his new theory of the tripartite soul. In the *Phaedo* (78C), immortality is seen to depend on the singleness of the soul's nature, since all composite objects are liable to destruction. This is admirably suited to what Plato says of the soul in the *Phaedo*, but when we come to the fully-fledged theory of the tripartite soul which is presented in book four of the *Republic*, we have the right to ask whether the "simplicity" of the soul has been abandoned, and, if so, what are Plato's thoughts at this stage about immortality.

Plato himself is well aware of the difficulty. He tells us in book ten[186] that it is difficult for anything that is composite (as the tripartite soul appears to be) to be eternal. Nevertheless, he explains, our regarding the soul as full of ποικιλία, ἀνομοιότης and διαφορά is the result of our only seeing it when harmed by the body. We ought rather to look at it when it is pure, and then we shall realize that it is akin to what is divine, immortal, and everlasting.[187] If we do this, we shall see whether its real nature is simple or manifold (τὴν ἀληθῆ φύσιν εἴτε πολυειδὴς εἴτε μονοειδής).

Professor Guthrie[188] has re-emphasized that "the only reasonable conclusion from all this is that the soul for Plato is still in essence simple and only appears composite as the result of its association with the body." If this is so, then the introduction of the theory of the tripartite

---

[186]*Rep.* 10. 611A ff.

[187]συγγενὴς οὖσα τῷ τε θείῳ καὶ ἀθανάτῳ καὶ τῷ ἀεὶ ὄντι. Cf. *Phaedo* 79D.

[188]Guthrie, "Plato's Views on the Immortality of the Soul," 4–22. The references to Guthrie that follow in the text are to this article.

soul makes no difference to the Platonic view of immortality, for if the two lower elements are not ψυχή in essence, but only accretions due to the association of the soul with the body, then it is evident that the higher part (τὸ λογιστικόν) is the equivalent of the whole soul in the *Phaedo* and is the only part which is immortal. This interpretation is supported by the doctrine of the *Timaeus*, where in 72D immortality is restricted to reason. This element alone is the creation of the Demiourgos; the lesser elements are the work of the lesser gods and apparently perish with the body.[189]

The *Phaedrus* and the tenth book of the *Laws*, however, pose more difficult problems, and Hackforth[190] sees here one of those contradictions in Plato's thought to which we have referred so frequently in this essay. "Plato wavers to the end between the religious, Orphic-Pythagorean conception of a divine soul essentially ('in its true nature') divorced from all physical functions, all 'lower' activities, and a more secular and scientific conception of soul as essentially a source of motion both to itself and to τὰ ἄλλα." This latter view implies that "it can only move the body in virtue of itself possessing 'motions' over and above the reason which contemplates the eternal Forms." Hackforth believes that these "motions over and above the reason" are implied in the myth of the *Phaedrus*, where souls *still in heaven* are already composite, their three parts being likened to a charioteer and two horses, one of which is obedient while the other is not. To deny Hackforth's view of this passage, there is no need for us to follow Wilamowitz and Taylor[191] in assuming that Plato's poetic talent has outrun his metaphysics, since Guthrie has proposed a less despairing and perfectly reasonable solution. His view is that Plato's eschatology is in origin that of Empedocles and of the tradition sometimes known as Orphic. "For one who holds these beliefs, the essential contrast is not between an incarnate and a discarnate soul. . . . The essential difference is that between a soul that is in, or destined for, the κύκλος βαρυπένθης (i.e., due for reincarnation) and one that has escaped from it and returned εἰς τὸ αὐτὸ ὅθεν ἥκει.[192]

[189]It is unimportant in this connection whether we believe the Demiourgos to be merely a useful mythical device or whether we regard Plato in the *Timaeus* as attempting a more exact and literal account of the ordering of the Universe. It is at least clear that Plato wishes his readers to consider the rôle of the Demiourgos of more importance than that of the lesser Gods. This distinction serves to emphasize the difference between the immortal and mortal parts of the soul.

[190]Hackforth, *Plato's Phaedrus* 76.

[191]Von Wilamowitz-Moellendorf, *Platon* I, 467; Taylor, *Plato* 307.

[192]Guthrie, "Plato's Views," 11–12.

This suggestion clears up the difficulties seen by Hackforth in the interpretation of the "charioteer" myth. When Plato speaks of the two lower parts of the soul existing when the soul is outside the body, he is not speaking of souls that have escaped the wheel of rebirth, but only of those that are rid of a *particular* body. Indeed, as Guthrie reminds us, indications of this doctrine of the survival of bodily aspects of the soul are present in the *Gorgias*[193] and, more important, in the *Phaedo*[194] itself, the dialogue where the *simplicity* of the immortal soul in its true nature is most stressed.

Hackforth,[195] however, maintains that according to the *Phaedrus* even the souls of the Gods are composite. This, as Guthrie shows, is a misinterpretation. It is true that they too are likened to a charioteer and his horses, but Hackforth does not enough consider the fact that the charioteer and both his horses are wholly good (246A). This is clear evidence that the souls of the Gods and of philosophic men who have attained to knowledge of the Forms and freedom from the body are not composite but simple in goodness.

Hackforth claims that a passage in the tenth book of the *Laws*[196] supports his interpretation of the *Phaedrus* passages discussed above. We hear there, he says, of an "attribution to the world-soul (and by inference to the individual soul 'in its true nature') of much besides reason, viz., 'affection, reflection, forethought, counsel, opinion true and false, joy, grief, confidence, fear, hate, love, and all the motions akin to these." Hackforth's translation, however, is seriously misleading. First of all, it is very doubtful whether Plato is referring to the world-soul. What he has said from 896D onwards that is relevant here is that "the things of soul ($\tau\grave{a}$ $\psi v \chi \hat{\eta}s$)," in which he includes the dispositions and emotions mentioned above, are prior to those of body, that soul is the cause of things good and bad since it is the cause of all things, and that involved in the movement and government of the universe there are at least two souls, one beneficent and the other capable of causing what is the opposite of beneficent. It is clear that when Plato speaks of "soul" here, he means not the world-soul but souls in the world.[197] It is absurd to suppose that the world-soul can

---

[193]*Gorg.* 524DE.   [194]*Phaedo* 81A.
[195]Hackforth, *Plato's Phaedrus* 76.
[196]*Laws* 10. 897A. Hackforth, *Plato's Phaedrus* 75.
[197]The bad soul in this passage has resemblances to the evil $\pi a \rho \acute{a} \delta \epsilon \iota \gamma \mu a$ of *Theaet.* 176E, and the $a \grave{\iota} \tau \acute{\iota} a$ $\delta \iota a \kappa \rho \acute{\iota} \sigma \epsilon \omega s$ of *Phil.* 23DE which Protarchus wishes to introduce. It is a soul which forgets its divine origin *and* associates with the $\grave{a} \nu a \gamma \kappa \acute{\eta}$ of the *Timaeus.* Though its force may be cosmic, it is wholly wrong to speak of it in the *Laws* as a bad *world*-soul. Cf. Gaye, *The Platonic Conception of Immortality* 187.

108   EROS AND PSYCHE

"associate with folly" (ἀνοίᾳ ξυγγενομένη 897B), but quite in accord with Plato's normal view that an ordinary soul may do so. Obversely, there is no question of the world-soul's "adding νοῦς to itself" (νοῦν προσλαβοῦσα) since it is already a soul filled with νοῦς.

Hackforth's view that Plato is here speaking not only of the world-soul but by inference of the individual soul in its true nature is even more surprising, and has rightly been rejected by Guthrie.[198] Guthrie explains that Plato is here describing the behaviour of souls in this world, not of the souls of the Gods or of purified philosophers. In addition to Guthrie's evidence, we can point to the fact that "soul" in 897A is described as having "hatred" as one of its "motions," but that the Gods are once more described as ἀγαθοὶ καὶ ἄριστοι in 901E. It is impossible that souls that are ἀγαθοὶ καὶ ἄριστοι can have anything to do with hatred since "all soul that is good is beneficial by nature" (904B).

The conclusion is clear that Hackforth is unjustified in attributing to Plato a duality of thought on this issue. For him the νοῦς, the δαίμων in man, alone is immortal. The other "parts" of the soul are excrescences which derive from the contamination of νοῦς by the wheel of rebirth. When the philosopher is free from that wheel and truly godlike, they cease to be. We return to Plotinus.

Plotinus probably held that there is no essential difference between the state of the soul in the *unio mystica* and that of a philosophic soul after death.[199] If, therefore, we show that Plato believed that the element of Self or Personality could be transcended at death, we can be sure that Plotinus, since he taught that in union with the One self-identity is lost, could easily have believed that this doctrine was in accordance with his Master's thought. For Plato the rational element of the soul, situated in the head,[200] is the sole part that can

[198]Guthrie, "Plato's Views," 15–16.

[199]Inge (*Phil. of Plotinus* 2, 33) and Pistorius (*Plotinus* 98–99) deny that Plotinus accepted the Platonic theory of reincarnation. That their denials are unwarranted is conclusively shown by Rich, "Reincarnation," 232–238. The most important passages in the *Enneads* are 3.4 and 4.3.8. Plotinus refers to *Phaedo* 82A and *Tim.* 91 on this matter. Miss Rich further shows that not only reincarnation but the transmigration of human souls into animal bodies is Plotinian doctrine. For Plato's view of transmigration, see Hackforth, *Plato's Phaedrus* 88–91. Naturally, for Plotinus as well as for Plato, the philosopher can clear himself from the cycle of reincarnations (*Enn.* 3.2.5, Rich, "Reincarnation," 234). It is then only for those souls still bound to the wheel that we should accept Henry's statement, "Plotinus clings firmly to the *personal* [my italics] individuality of souls and their survival after death (Henry, "Plotinus' Place," xlii).

[200]For the importance of this, see Onians, *Origins*, esp. 118ff.

concern itself with the Forms. The other two elements are only a hindrance to the faculty that can gain ἐπιστήμη; they are, as we have seen, the unfortunate result of our mortal state, which, however, can by diligent training be put to good purpose, and of which we shall be rid at death. Then, if we are philosophers, we shall consist of the rational element alone and be filled with the immanent character of the Forms. Since, however, these Forms are always the same, unchanging and eternal, all the knowledge that will characterize the rational souls of men will be the same, and since our souls will contain nothing but the truth, we must suppose that they will all be the same. The element of variety in the human soul is thus, for Plato, introduced by the two lower elements, and when we are rid of these elements we shall be rid, he supposes, of the inferiorities which are inherent in what we call personality. As Grube writes:[201] "We must remember that from first to last the aim of the Platonic philosopher is to live on the universal plane, to *lose himself* [his italics] more and more in the contemplation of truth, so that the perfect ψυχή would, it seems, lose itself completely in the universal mind, the world-psyche. Hence it remains individual only in so far as it is imperfect, and personal immortality is not something to aim at, but something to outgrow." If this estimate of the teachings of the *Timaeus* is justified, we have no grounds on which to charge Plotinus with deviation from Plato if we find him teaching the transcendence of the self. Our only criticism can be that perhaps he is more optimistic than Plato in his belief that such a divine state can be attained during this life.

Here let us consider a possible objection, that to assert with Bréhier and Heinemann that self-identity is lost in the union with the One and to conclude that this means that Plotinus places little value on the human personality is to misread the doctrine of the *Enneads*: that Plotinus would not posit Forms of individuals if he believed, with Plato, that the highest state of man is one where he has "outgrown" his personality. There is no doubt that Plotinus posited Forms of individuals,[202] and it is legitimate to deduce from this that he placed a higher value on personality than had Plato. For Plotinus, the Form of the individual constitutes the real personality of which the ἔμψυχον ζῷον living in the spatio-temporal world is only an image, but this must not make us forget that even the Forms are not, for Plotinus, the highest of the hypostases nor the final goal of the soul's quest. Doubtless it is true that the soul must always seek its true self in the World of Forms, but once "there" it is not at the end of its journey, only at the place of repose where it can await the mystic vision in which, as Plotinus himself tells us, "there is neither reason nor intellection nor self (οὐδὲ λόγος οὐδέ τις νόησις οὐδ' ὅλως αὐτός).²⁰³

It may be advisable at this stage briefly to summarize the discussion so far, and to review the comparative positions of Plato and Plotinus on the questions we have been considering. First of all, for Plato the Good is both Being and "beyond Being," while for Plotinus it is entirely "beyond Being" in theory, although some qualities derived from the Platonic Form regarded as τὸ ὄν still occur in certain parts of the *Enneads*. Secondly, Plotinus is more rigorous than Plato in applying the Platonic purifications, for whereas Plato only employs his principle of ὅμοιος ὁμοίῳ to making the soul like to the Good *qua* Being, Plotinus, by his *via negativa*, makes it resemble its Source *qua* "beyond Being" as well. Thirdly, when the soul, according to Plato, is purified and has become θεῖος, it is able to look *out* upon the World of Forms which is the object of its contemplation, but essentially outside itself; for Plotinus, however, the soul, being fused with the One, is itself the cause of the Forms, which are thus in a sense *inside* itself and are a lower hypostasis. In brief, the Platonic dualism has been replaced by a Plotinian unity, and that almost entirely by the aid of texts drawn from Plato's writings.

Of all the points of comparison between Plato and Plotinus, of the greatest import is that which concerns the nature of the One and its relationship with Ἔρως. Both had a low opinion of the ultimate value of the individual human personality and were hesitant about making it prominent in their systems. In the Platonic World of Forms it is neglected altogether, and we have already observed that what makes the original Platonic system so difficult to accept is the impersonality and the lifelessness of the Ideal World. Even Aristotle, whose views of the active element in the human personality are such as to weigh against personal survival, insisted at least on the necessity for a cause of *motion* and criticized Plato for not providing one. Perhaps this attack is unjustified, as most modern writers on the subject believe, but Plato's continual emphasis on the Forms, which are quite remote from motion and life, is at least an indication that his introduction of a separate cause of motion was rather the result of an honest appreciation of hard fact than a fulfilment of his philosophical ideals.

The position of Plato on this matter is simple, if inhuman. That of Plotinus is more complicated but an advance, at least in the eyes of

²⁰³*Enn.* 6.9.11.

those who favour a personal religion. His Good may be described as both "supra-personal" and "quasi-personal," but never as personal. By supra-personal I imply that to speak of conscious love and the Will of God in connection with the One of Plotinus could be totally unjustified. The One is above Will and above conscious thought. Yet he contains, or rather he is, something we should regard as personal, and that is Ἔρως, which, however, ordinary mortals possess only when in some way aroused or awakened out of themselves into what is beyond themselves by what Plato in the *Phaedrus* describes as a "divine madness." In order to see what Plotinus has to say about this awakening, let us turn to a relevant passage of *Ennead* Four,[204] where in a description of the ascent of the soul to the hypostasis of Νοῦς we read as follows: "Many times it has happened: lifted out of the body into myself; becoming external to all other things, and self-encentred; beholding a marvellous beauty; then, more than ever, assured of community with the loftiest order, enacting the noblest life, acquiring identity with the divine; stationing within It by having attained that activity; poised above whatsoever within the intellectual is less than the Supreme." (Trans. MacKenna-Page.) This awakening is the result of the perpetual yearning of the soul to regain its "Fatherland Yonder," as Plotinus says, and in brief, the philosophic Ἔρως in the soul is at its fullest development when the soul is nearest to losing its individuality and personality in the universal perfection of the Divine Mind. Thus when we say that the Plotinian One is Ἔρως and Ἔρως αὐτοῦ, we must not deceive ourselves that this implies personality as the word is normally understood. On the contrary, it implies a trans-cendence of personality, and we have thus designated the One as supra-personal.

But the One is also Father, and Heaven is our Fatherland, and Ἔρως itself is not impersonal but supra-personal. The One is thus aptly described as quasi-personal as well as supra-personal, for analogies to it are continually drawn from the world of life and from parent-children relationships. Plotinus, we may conclude, is thus considerably nearer having a personal God as his First Principle than is Plato, for the Demiourgos, even if we allow him to be the symbol of a high God rather than merely a useful contrivance, is still far from being supreme in the Cosmos and possesses a status immeasurably inferior to that of the Forms and the Good, which are his models when he strives to bring order to the world.

Plotinus, then, took a step towards personalizing certain theories of

[204] *Enn.* 4.8.1.

Plato, but his changes were insufficient for many of the new "Platonists," for Platonism had attracted the attention of certain devotees
of religions that accepted a completely personal God. Philo the Jew
attempted a synthesis of Platonic theory with the Old Testament,
though there is little trace of mysticism in his writings. Several of the
Alexandrian Christians were deeply impressed by the Middle Platonist
writers of their day and attempted to incorporate as much of their
work as possible into their own teachings, though often making use
of the idea we can find in the neo-Pythagorean Numenius that Plato
was Moses talking Attic. These thinkers chose Platonism not because
it was the only philosophical system with which they were acquainted
—for Christians such as Tertullian tended to prefer Stoicism and to
teach the corporeal nature of the soul[205]—but, as St. Augustine says,[206]
because many of them found that it could be fitted into a Christian
framework with a minimum of alterations.

[205]Tertullian regrets that Plato is the unwitting cause of all the heresies ("Doleo
bona fide Platonem omnium haereticorum condimentarium factum." *De anima* 23),
and is not alone in this opinion. See below, pp. 179–180.

[206]"Itaque si hanc vitam illi viri nobiscum sursum agere potuissent, viderent pro-
fecto cuius auctoritate facilius consuleretur hominibus, et paucis mutatis verbis
atque sententiis christiani fierent, sicut plerique recentiorum nostrorumque temporum
Platonici fecerunt." Aug., *Epist.* 118.

PART TWO

Chapter One

KNOWING HOW AND
KNOWING THAT

THE Socrates of Plato's dialogues, whether he be historical or not, is said to have held that Virtue (ἀρετή) is Knowledge (ἐπιστήμη). It has been generally recognized, and more especially in recent years, that the proposition "Virtue is Knowledge" may cause a different mental reaction in the hearer from ἡ ἀρετή ἐστιν ἐπιστήμη; in other words, that the expressions "Virtue" and "Knowledge" as translations of these two key Greek terms are so misleading that they can prevent the doctrine being understood at all.

The ambiguities of the translation "Virtue" have been more readily perceived, especially perhaps by those disciplined to recognize that the Latin word "virtus" is not as simply rendered in English as the unsuspecting might believe. "Knowledge," however, has been, until quite recently, regarded as self-evident. In broad terms, the theory has been understood to mean that if a man is good he can *do* good deeds, and that "to be good" means to be able to distinguish between good and evil, to *know*, in fact, what good and evil are. As Cornford put it:[1] "Socrates had been convinced that all men . . . cannot be just until they know what Justice is." Other interpreters might have found fault with the capital J, but in the main they accepted this definition.

This interpretation is of long standing and is supported by the authority of Aristotle, who writes in the *Eudemian Ethics* (1216B 2ff.) that "Socrates held it to be the aim to know what ἀρετή is. . . . He believed that all the moral virtues were forms of knowledge, in such a way that when one knew what justice was, it followed that one would be just." From Aristotle's day, this interpretation, in all essentials, has been held until 1955, when Mr. J. Gould, in a book entitled *The Development of Plato's Ethics*, produced a certain amount of evidence designed to show that it was erroneous.[2] Gould points out that the

[1]Cornford, *Principium Sapientiae* 47.
[2]All further references to this book will be to *"Gould."*

accepted view implies that ἐπιστήμη in Plato means knowledge of facts, or as he puts it, that it "is the 'bit of theory' which precedes the 'bit of practice.' " (p. 5) Making use of Ryle's[3] distinction between "knowing that" and "knowing how," Gould suggests that ἐπιστήμη is knowledge of the latter kind, that it is an ability to act morally to which Plato is referring. This suggestion, if true, is a great advance in our study of Plato, and even if false is useful in showing how ancient modes of thought differ from our own.

Helped by the pioneer studies of Bruno Snell,[4] Gould has accumulated a considerable amount of evidence to show that the meaning of ἐπίστασθαι, in the pre-Platonic writers, is predominantly "to have the ability to perform some action," in other words "to know how." The meaning "to know that" occurs as early as the *Odyssey*,[5] as Gould points out, but this is the rarer sense and clearly not the original. As with ἐπίστασθαι, so with ἐπιστήμη itself, the meaning "knowing how" or "skill" is the more frequent. 'Επιστήμη is, in a passage of Bacchylides, clearly the equivalent of τέχνη.[6]

The most interesting evidence produced by Gould is that which leads to his affirmation (p. 10) that in Herodotus ἐπίστασθαι denotes not "an awareness of (objective) facts" but "merely a subjective feeling, which we should have to translate by certainty or conviction." This meaning is found by Gould fourteen times in Herodotus and compared with a fragment of Heraclitus[7] which has been given a similar interpretation by Snell. In brief, as Gould later puts it, (p. 15): "since ἐπιστήμη does not act, it remains a purely subjective 'faith.' It retains this characteristic . . . in Plato's early dialogues."

Gould's evidence on the pre-Platonic writers is unexceptionable, and a yet stronger point in his favour is that the words ἐπιστήμη and ἐπίστασθαι do not occur in the extant fragments of Parmenides. If Parmenides recognized their normal sense as "knowing how" rather than "knowing that," it is plain he would have no use for them, at least in his account of the Real, where action, and therefore "ability to act," have no place. The only objection so far, and it may turn out to be one based on the prejudices induced by a traditional training, is that if ἐπιστήμη is subjective in the way that Gould suggests, it would

---

[3]Ryle, *The Concept of Mind* 25–61.
[4]Snell, "Ausdrücke" and *Die Entdeckung des Geistes*[2] (Hamburg 1948), translated by T. G. Rosenmeyer as *The Discovery of the Mind*.
[5]*Odyssey* 21, 406; 9, 49; 13, 207, 213. *Gould* 9.
[6]Bacchylides 10, 38 (Snell). Cf. *Gould*, 13–14; Schaerer, 'Επιστήμη et Τέχνη 5.
[7]Heraclitus, fr. 57 (DK). Snell, "Ausdrücke," 83.

appear not to admit of a λόγος. To give a concrete example, if a man knows *how* to cure diseases, he cannot, if Gould interprets ἐπιστήμη correctly, explain the rationale of his treatment in other terms than by saying "That's how it's done. I know it is." If someone were to ask "Why do you do it this way?," he could only answer "Because that is the right way. I know it is, because it works." If this was the sense of ἐπιστήμη understood by the Platonic Socrates, then he was not a very energetic enquirer, but one who was content to overlook the cloudy meaning of the word "right."

Before proceeding further, we must look at some of the evidence for ἐπιστήμη as "knowing how." Gould supplies little, since he assumes that "knowing how" is the rule and that it is only the few apparent cases of "knowing that" that require an explanation. But perhaps it is better to document "knowing how" first and then examine how far this meaning, if it occurs, covers the sum total of occurrences of the word ἐπιστήμη in the early dialogues.

The use of the *verb* ἐπίστασθαι with the meaning of knowing *how* is common throughout the dialogues. Three examples will therefore suffice to prove the point. In the *Euthyphro*, Socrates speaks of knowing how to look after horses as being the mark of the ἱππικός (13A) and of knowing how to look after dogs as that of the huntsman. In the *Gorgias*, he asks Callicles (511C) if he thinks there is anything of note in knowing how to swim. In the *First Alcibiades*, he speaks of knowing *how* to speak Greek (111C). A glance at the section on ἐπίστασθαι in the majority of lexicons will show that this usage is primary, and there is, therefore, no need to linger on it.

When we pass from ἐπίστασθαι to ἐπιστήμη, the meaning is often harder to distinguish, but there are certainly several passages which bear out Gould's interpretation. One of these is *Apology* 22DE, where Socrates is recounting his experience of the knowledge of the hand-workers (χειροτέχναι). He says that they know many fine things (πολλὰ καὶ καλὰ ἐπισταμένους)—which looks at first sight perhaps like "knowing that," but it appears that this knowledge of theirs consists only in "practising their art well" (τὸ τὴν τέχνην καλῶς ἐξεργάζεσθαι). If there is "knowing that" in this passage, it is certainly subordinate to "knowing how."

Similarly in the *Laches*, when Nicias breaks in upon the discussion between Laches and Socrates on the nature of courage, he declares (194D) that he has often heard Socrates say that every man is good in that in which he is wise (ἅπερ σοφός) and bad in that in which he is unlearned. Socrates understands this as a suggestion that courage is a kind of knowledge (ἐπιστήμη) or wisdom (σοφία).[8] He asks what kind of knowledge it is, whether it is that of flute-playing or harping. It is clear that by this he does not mean the knowledge that a certain combination of notes on a flute or harp produce a tune, but primarily the knowledge of how to produce that tune on a flute or harp. At this point the emphasis on "knowing how" as the predominant aspect of the knowledge of these τέχναι is certain. Later on we shall return to this passage to see if this usage is continued, but for the moment we may assume that the meaning of "knowing how" can be attached to ἐπιστήμη.

In the next stage of the enquiry, we must look at the relation between τέχνη and ἐπιστήμη in somewhat more detail. It is generally agreed that before Plato's time the two were often almost synonymous.[9] Their use as virtual equivalents was adopted but not invented by Plato. The innovation made by the latter (or by Socrates) was to extend the use of the word ἐπιστήμη into the realm of morals, and thus to involve τέχνη also in that realm. Before Plato, ἐπιστήμη meant predominantly "knowing how," and clearly τέχνη, to an unsophisticated age, would have a similar meaning. Such a meaning would almost justify the use of the word "technique" (whose relevant sense is given by the Oxford English Dictionary as "a mechanical skill in art") as a translation for τέχνη, and if Plato had applied the analogy between moral virtue and τέχνη without limitation, one might be able to say that he regarded ἀρετή as a technique. In fact, the application of the analogy is limited in several important ways, even in the early dialogues with which we are concerned here. This limitation has been discussed fully by several scholars, and there is no need to do more here than to quote H. W. B. Joseph's remark that "[conduct] differs [from the τέχναι] in not having, as every art has, a special field or subject-matter."[10] It is sufficient to say that if for Plato ἐπιστήμη means "knowing how," τέχνη must have a similar meaning, but that if it ever means "knowing that," then τέχνη too may involve more than "knowing how." In short, if there are aspects of τέχνη, as understood by Socrates, which are inconsistent with the notion of "knowing how," they may be of service in formulating a correct understanding of ἐπιστήμη. Two such aspects must now be investigated: that the τέχνη looks to the good of its object and that it can give an account (λόγος).

In the Euthyphro (12E), after pointing out that the art of a horse-

[8]For the association of σοφία and ἐπιστήμη, see Snell, "Ausdrücke," 86ff.
[9]Cf. Schaerer, Ἐπιστήμη et Τέχνη 5; Thuc. 2.87.4.
[10]Joseph, Essays 9. Cf. Gould, 31–46; Moreau, Construction.

man looks after horses, that of hunting looks after dogs, while the oxherd, by his art, looks after his oxen, Socrates rams home his investigation of τέχνη as θεραπεία by saying that the object of every art is looked after in the same way (12C). Similarly, in the *Gorgias*, a distinction is drawn (464–5)[11] between arts properly so called and their images, which latter are not τέχναι but the products of mere ἐμπειρία or τριβή. The distinction between these classes is that a τέχνη knows what is best for its object, whereas its "image" looks only to what gives pleasure. The true arts, such as politics, medicine, and gymnastic, know what is best for their objects and prescribe it, while their "images," rhetoric, ὀψοποιϊκή,[12] and self-adornment, are careless of the good, or, to put it more bluntly, are immoral deceivers.

This looking to the good of the object is hardly reconcilable to "knowing how." A man who knew how to cure an illness might or might not exercise his ability to do so. It is hard to see how the mere "knowing how" could exercise a moral force, but could the possessor of the τέχνη of medicine not look to the good of his patient? As Socrates would perhaps have put it: could a doctor, in so far as he is a doctor, look to the good of anything except his patient? *Qua* doctor, he would be obliged to treat the sick. If he did not, let us suppose for some mercenary motive, he would temporarily be acting not *qua* doctor (i.e., *qua* practitioner of the art of medicine) but *qua* money-maker (i.e., with the help of the art of money-making). The true τεχνικός is morally obliged in so far as he is a τεχνικός to look to the good of the object of his τέχνη; the man who merely "knows how" is under no such obligation.

The second feature of τέχναι that we should consider here is also prominent in *Gorgias* 465. Socrates says that he refuses to give the title τέχνη to anything which is ἄλογος. A proper art must be able to give a λόγος of whatever it applies. The λόγος must explain the nature (φύσις) of what is presented by the art as well as the reason (αἰτία) for its presentation. If it cannot do so, it is not an art at all.

We have already noticed the fact that "knowing how" cannot give this kind of account. To know how to make a public speech is not necessarily to have the ability to give a λόγος of the suggestions— which, though pleasing, may be harmful—which that speech contains.

---

[11]Cf. *Gorgias* 500AB. For τέχνη as θεραπεία, see also *Rep.* 342A, 346E3.

[12]The usual translation of ὀψοποιϊκή as "cookery" seems in this context to be incorrect. True cookery might well be an art designed to further the good condition of the body, whereas ὀψοποιϊκή must mean the ability to prepare luxurious dishes which will be attractive to the palate but harmful to the constitution.

Still less does "knowing how" imply knowledge of an αἰτία. To "know how" is, in fact, to possess a technique—a mechanical skill in art—which one can employ in a given circumstance if the time seems ripe. Τέχναι are something much more than this. The man who "knows how" *qua* "knowing how" cannot give a λόγος of his acts; the τεχνικός must be able to do so.

To sum up the position so far, we may say that a τέχνη, as understood by the Platonic Socrates, is something superior to a mere "knowing how." It is rational and has some kind of built-in moral force. Even if it is some sort of ability, it is, when strictly defined, very different from what we might call "know-how" or from a technique. Both the features described above might suggest that it involves a "knowing that," since to seek someone's good is to know what is good for him, and a λόγος is clearly a fact. But this will become clearer later.

At this stage we may pause to wonder in what terms, if any, a Greek might conceive of the distinction between "knowing how" and "knowing that." The difference between the average Greek modes of thought and that of Plato on this subject, as far as it is relevant to morality, has been clearly demonstrated by Tuckey in the final section of his book on the *Charmides*.[18] Tuckey points out that in this dialogue there are two definitions of σωφροσύνη given which contain the word "good," and that neither of them is specifically rejected. The two are "doing good things" (ἡ τῶν ἀγαθῶν πρᾶξις), suggested by Critias at 163E, and "knowledge of good and evil" (ἐπιστήμη ἀγαθοῦ τε καὶ κακοῦ), suggested at 174B. As Tuckey points out, it is likely that a final definition of σωφροσύνη must embrace both these suggestions, and thus be that σωφροσύνη is "doing what is good with the knowledge that it is good." "Doing what is good" is a practical virtue and must imply a "knowing how." Gould would presumably assert that this is *all* that Critias meant by his suggestion, that "doing what is good" refers only to the ability to do good. Let this pass, for it may well be correct that Critias was thinking in this unintellectualized manner—a manner and attitude to morality which he had learned from the poets. Tuckey perhaps agrees with Gould over this; but it is clear that he understands the phrase "with knowledge that it is good" in an intellectualized sense. If this is right, he is pointing to a distinction between "knowing how" and "knowing that" which was intelligible to Plato. "Doing what is good" would involve "knowing how;" "knowledge that is it good" is "knowing that."

18Tuckey, *Plato's Charmides* 91.

Tuckey's view of the *Charmides*, however, might be rejected on the ground that ἐπιστήμη ἀγαθοῦ τε καὶ κακοῦ means not "knowledge of good and evil" but "knowing how to do good and evil." This perhaps seems an absurd objection, but it must be allowed to stand until we have further investigated the uses of ἐπιστήμη. Before leaving the point, however, we should consider whether any light is shed by two passages of the *Euthydemus*. In 280-281, Socrates and Cleinias are discussing the difference between the possession of a skill such as carpentry and the use of it. Only the use, they agree, is any benefit to the carpenter. Clearly both the possession and the use of the skill of a carpenter are ἐπιστήμη—and Plato speaks in 281A of ἐπιστήμη ἡ τεκτονική. Clearly too they both involve "knowing how"—although there is the possibility that this is not the whole story. What is important here is the difference between "possession" and "use," for it bears on the interpretation of the *Charmides* given by Tuckey. Σωφροσύνη was there described as an ἐπιστήμη ἀγαθοῦ τε καὶ κακοῦ together with a πρᾶξις τῶν ἀγαθῶν. Here there is the distinction between the possession and the use of what is good. Only the two in combination, as we see from the *Euthydemus*, are beneficial, and σωφροσύνη, which every Greek would regard as beneficial, must therefore be this combination. The question is whether we have a combination of ability with use of ability or whether σωφροσύνη may more rightly be described as a combination of the knowledge of what is good with the ability, which must inevitably be exercised, to put that knowledge into practice. If knowledge is a τέχνη in the sense we noticed in the *Gorgias*, then moral knowledge will be some kind of categorical imperative.

Finally, and before leaving this question of the possession and use of skills, we should look at one further passage of the *Euthydemus*, the section in which Socrates and Cleinias discuss the βασιλικὴ τέχνη. In 290CD, they agree that certain of the τέχναι, such as hunting, are only concerned with the acquisition of goods, not with their use. The huntsmen, as they say, hand over their catch to the cooks, and similarly geometricians, astronomers, and arithmeticians hand theirs over to the dialecticians. The "royal art" is agreed to be one concerned both with acquisition and with use. It acquires the products of the other arts and uses them to make its subjects better men (292C). The phrase "better men" leads to difficulties in the argument which Socrates ironically asks the "heavenly twins" Euthydemus and Dionysodorus, to unravel, but this does not concern us at the present. What is important for our purposes is that the distinction between the possession and the use of goods is clearly revealed. The possessor of "the royal art" knows *that* the products of the inferior arts are good. He possesses this knowledge as well as the ability to use those products for the good of his subjects.

Let us return to "knowing how." If "Virtue is Knowledge" means that ἀρετή is the ability to do good deeds—assuming for the moment that "ability" involves inclination—then morality consists in knowing how to do good deeds and in doing them. But here a difficulty arises. Is it possible to do good deeds without knowing that they are good? Is it possible *to be able* to do good deeds without knowing that they are good? If ἀρετή is "knowing how," understood in this sense, then the man who does good deeds through his ἐπιστήμη is good because he acts well even if he has no intellectual grasp of what is good and what is bad. Such a man's "knowledge of good and bad" is, as we have already seen, a purely subjective faith that he is right, grounded on no principles whatever. In other words, it is in the action itself that the moral quality lies, both the motives of the doer and the question of the recognition and understanding that certain things are good in themselves being irrelevant.

The *Euthyphro* is undoubtedly an early dialogue, yet even there Socrates believes that what is holy is not holy because the gods love it, but that the gods love what is holy because it is holy (10A-11B). What is holy is holy in some objective sense, and thus we may say that if a man does what is holy, the holiness is not entirely in the *action* but in the recognition by the doer that there is some *thing* which may be called "holy." Yet despite all this, the theory that ἀρετή is "knowing how" seems to neglect the possibility for Plato of the good man's recognizing that there is some *thing* which may be called good, if not to deny this possibility altogether.

I have used the word "thing" advisedly, for it is Plato's own. In the *Protagoras* (330C), shortly after Protagoras has finished his opening harangue, Socrates addresses him as follows: "Come now, let us consider together what kind of thing each of them is . . . Is justice some thing (πρᾶγμα) or not a thing (οὐδὲν πρᾶγμα)? I think it is. What do you think?" To this Protagoras agrees without demur, and Socrates, as if to tell us that he has not used the word πρᾶγμα inadvertently, adds: "Suppose someone were to put a question to you and me; O Protagoras and Socrates, tell me, this *thing* (πρᾶγμα) you named just now, justice, is it just or unjust?"

In a note discussing the "moral facts" which the traditional theory of the meaning of ἐπιστήμη takes as the objects of knowledge, Gould writes (p. 4 n. 1) that "if 'right' and 'wrong' are taken as applying to individual actions, not only would this involve a peculiar sort of mental feat, but it would run counter to the whole of Book One of the *Republic*. If, on the other hand, the moral facts are those of the nature of Right and Wrong, this would seem to involve a metaphysical theory of the object which few would attribute to Socrates." It is quite certain that the Platonic Socrates no more regards his remarks about τὸ ὅσιον in the *Euthyphro* as concerned with "holy" and "unholy" as applying to individual actions than he does in similar passages in the *Republic* and elsewhere. As Joseph[14] has commented, in a passage noted by Gould, the "false assumptions (in the argument with Polemarchus) are so many forms of a simple error, that of supposing that the practice of justice (or righteousness) consists in the performance of specifiable acts." Nor is the Socrates of the *Euthyphro* referring to Holiness and Unholiness in a metaphysical sense if by this is meant an existence as entities in themselves *outside the realm of particulars*. What he appears to imply is that "the holy" could be grasped as a universal seen in a series of particulars but not existing apart from them. The phrase τὸ ὅσιον is a shorthand device for naming all the things which are holy by referring to what they have in common. In the *Protagoras* passage, the word πρᾶγμα perhaps indicates that the common element in all just acts which we call justice is beginning to emerge as an element in its own right. This may be an advance on the position of the *Euthyphro* in the direction of what afterwards became the Theory of Forms. Thus, in the light of the passage from the *Protagoras*, Gould may even be wrong to imply that a metaphysical theory of the object should not be attributed to the Socrates of these dialogues. This theory is not the Theory of Forms, and may be merely the recognition that there is some kind of object of ἐπιστήμη, without the understanding of its nature. There have been many men in the past who have been convinced that they know that such a thing as goodness exists, without their knowing precisely what kind of entity it is. The man who led the way to the Theory of Forms almost certainly passed through this stage of mental development.

I have already suggested that the theory that ἀρετή is "knowing how" seems to neglect the possibility of the good man's *recognizing* that there is some *thing* which may be called good. Gould attempts to avoid this problem (p. 17) by suggesting that "we could say of an intelligent practioner in any field that he recognized the object of his activity for what it was: all still depends [he adds] on whether we regard this as an *explanation* [his italics] of his activity and its excel-

14Joseph, *Essays* 6.

lence." As we shall demonstrate later, this explanation is inadequate; let us for the present content ourselves with noticing that even if ἐπιστήμη is primarily "knowing how," it must, in the hands of the "intelligent practitioner," be accompanied by some form of "knowing that." The human mind is such that if a man knows *how* to swim, he also knows *that* he is swimming at the time he is doing so. He may also be said to know that in some sense "swimming exists."

Furthermore, if we consider briefly the man who is unable to swim, we should recognize that his knowledge *that* there are people who know *how* to swim is a considerable, indeed a necessary motive for his having himself taught. If a man did not know *that* his fellow humans were capable of swimming, he might well have serious doubts as to whether it was possible for him to learn to swim.

We must now return to the question of whether these early dialogues contain anything approaching what has been described as a theory of the object, and whether the evidence of the dialogues themselves can be cross-checked by the accounts of Socrates given by other writers. And this brings us to the question of definitions. In his account of Socrates' place in the history of philosophy, Aristotle[15] says that his interests were ethical, and that one of his main contributions was the introduction of general definitions. Aristotle's value as an historian of philosophy has been under continual attack in recent years,[16] and this may perhaps lead us to give his remarks less credence than they deserve. In this case, however, he is certainly borne out by the Socrates of the early Platonic dialogues. In the *Euthyphro* the speakers are seeking a definition of Holiness, in the *Laches* of Courage, in the *Charmides* of σωφροσύνη, and in *Republic* I of Justice. Frequently the first definition offered by an interlocutor is proof that its propounder does not understand what Socrates requires in a definition. Thus Euthyphro defines τὸ ὅσιον as "what I am doing now" (5D), Laches, mistaking "bravery" for a brave act, says that it is found when "a man is willing to remain at his post and face the enemy and not fly the field" (190E), and Charmides' first attempt to define σωφροσύνη is that it is "doing everything in an orderly fashion and quietly, both walking in the streets and talking and doing everything else in the same way." It is worth noticing that all these "definitions" are in terms of action, as though the virtues were purely practical matters, and that all of them are unsatisfactory to Socrates. He does not want to know how to act σωφρόνως but what σωφροσύνη is, not how to act bravely, but

[15] *Met.* M. 1078B 28.
[16] Cf. Cherniss, *Riddle* and *Aristotle's Criticism.*

the nature of courage. Thus we may say that even the most casual glance at the Platonic Socrates of these dialogues is enough to show that Aristotle was right in suggesting that Socrates was interested in general definitions, if—as is surely the case—he meant by Socrates the Socrates he met in the writings of Plato. Indeed in this connection we should remember the well-known reference to "the Socrates of the *Phaedo*."[17] We may conclude that Aristotle's reading of the Platonic dialogues could not but have given him the idea that Socrates was interested in definitions, and that the kind of definition he required was a far more "intellectualized" one than that of τὸ ὅσιον first given by Euthyphro. Presumably Euthyphro thought he knew how to be holy when he defined holiness as "what I am doing now." Presumably Socrates wanted to find out whether that "knowing how" was firmly based on a "knowing what" τὸ ὅσιον is.

I am not competent to dogmatize on the question of whether the *Hippias Major* is a genuine work of Plato.[18] Since the commentary of Professor Tarrant appeared, there has perhaps been a tendency to accept it as genuine. Ross,[19] who does so, thinks that it is most likely that it should be dated after the *Euthyphro*. But whether a genuine work of Plato or not, it can be admitted as valid evidence for the views of the Platonic Socrates. Its main object is thoroughly in line with the approach of the *Euthyphro*, *Laches*, and *Charmides*, for it is a discussion of the nature of beauty. In the course of the discussion, as Ross[20] points out, one may find a hint of the reason for Socrates' interest in definitions. Ross assumes, as is right, that such an interest is present in all the early works. The passage in question is 286C5, where Socrates says: "Recently when I was finding fault with some things in certain speeches as ugly and praising others as beautiful, a man threw me into confusion by asking me, in some such way as this, and very insolently too, 'Socrates, how do you find out what sort of things are beautiful and ugly? Come now, could you say what the beautiful is?'" At this, Socrates, so it is said, was angry with himself and wanted to go and question wise men on the matter.

This incident gives a clear impression of what led Socrates to an interest in definitions and to an interest in "things in themselves"

---

[17] *De Gen. et Corr.* 335B 11.

[18] For a discussion of the views of authorities before 1928, see Professor Tarrant's edition (Cambridge 1928) ix-xvii. For the authenticity of the dialogue, see Grube, "Authenticity," 134–148, and "Logic and Language," 369–375.

[19] Ross, *Plato's Theory* 4.

[20] *Ibid.* 16.

viewed in abstraction from particulars. Such an interest is plainly likely to lead to a theory of what these definitions refer to, of what nature these "things in themselves" are, a theory of the object. Finally, to ram the point home from the dialogues, we can turn once again to the *Euthydemus*, this time to 300E. Dionysodorus is questioning Socrates, and the debate runs as follows:

> DIONYSODORUS: Socrates, have you ever seen a fine thing?
> SOCRATES: Certainly I have, many of them.
> DIONYSODORUS: Did you find them different from the beautiful, or the same as the beautiful?

At this point Socrates says that he was baffled and felt that he had received his deserts for interrupting the conversation, but replied that he thought that beautiful things were different from the beautiful, though some beauty was present (πάρεστι) in each of them. This answer is mocked by Dionysodorus, or rather used as a peg on which to hang a preposterous piece of logic-chopping, but it reveals Socrates' attitude clearly. When forced by an opponent in debate, he has to admit that he recognizes a thing in itself, "the beautiful," apart from beautiful objects. The whole section, as Taylor points out,[21] employs the "technical language of the so-called 'ideal theory,'" but there is no need to assume that the Platonic Socrates held the theory at the time of this dialogue. The truth would rather seem to be that Socrates' impulse to define, to speak of "things by themselves," to attempt to built up a theory of the object, was the precursor of the fully-fledged theory of transcendent Ideas.

The passage of the *Euthydemus* discussed above leads us to a most important topic which can only be treated briefly here. Socrates distinguishes between a series of things that are beautiful and the beautiful itself. In the *Gorgias* (474D), he suggests that beautiful objects often receive the appellation "beautiful" in virtue of their use for some particular purpose. Thus the beautiful may well be useful, and if something is useful it is good for a particular purpose. Thus, in conclusion, it may be said that beautiful objects are in a sense good.

Now as there are a series of beautiful objects apart from the beautiful itself, there must likewise be a series of good objects (i.e., objects that are good for something) as well as the good itself. As well as objects that are "good for" there are, of course, people who are "good at." Indeed, being good at something is often the meaning of "possessing ἀρετή" itself. In *Apology* 18A, the ἀρετή of a judge is his

21Taylor, *Plato* 100.

ability to distinguish what is just and what is not. We have, then, a
distinction between things beautiful and the beautiful, between things
good for (or people good at) and the good. A question which must
have puzzled Socrates when he was asked, in the *Hippias Major*,
about the beautiful, is "What use is the beautiful?" Does it have a
use, or is it entirely valued for the sake of pleasure? Surely not the
latter, for if so, it must be a mere form of flattery, as are rhetoric and
self-adornment and ὀψοποιϊκή in the *Gorgias* (464–5).

We can think of the Socratic progress to a theory of definitions and
of objects in the following manner. First, in his conversations, he
speaks of justice as good, courage as good, and so on. At this stage he
probably means that these virtues are good for the well-being of the
state or the individual citizen. He fails to see that it is pointless to
re-define a virtue in terms of another still undefined, and possibly
undefinable entity. He could, admittedly, speak of the virtues as being
"good for" the individual, meaning that they are useful to him, but a
persistent enquirer would soon run into the problem of what is really
useful and what only seems so. Thus, in the *Gorgias*, Polus thinks it is
useful to have power, but Socrates wants to know what benefit such
power is to the tyrant Archelaus, and is then led on to his paradox
that it is better to suffer evil than to do it (474B).

The next stage in the Socratic progress is that represented by the
Hippias Major and the *Euthydemus*, where Socrates is compelled to
turn to the beautiful itself and ask what it is. Similarly, he wants to
know what is justice, piety, and the rest. The result is the search for
definitions in the early dialogues. As is well known, and as we shall
later investigate, this search led to the re-defining of these "things in
themselves" in terms of knowledge and Goodness. Hence the search
for a clearer understanding of these things, which leads, via the
doctrine of the unity of the virtues, to the theory of the Good as the
ἀρχή of the Forms, and of knowledge as the motive force of the philosopher-kings in the *Republic*. But this must be left aside for the present
in order that once more we may concentrate on the earlier form of the
theory of the object of knowledge. Socrates had to discover that there
is a good before fully understanding what it is. Hence the definitions
of the virtues in terms of knowledge and good lead to a theory of
the good itself.

In the *Charmides*, as has already been noticed, no formal solution
is offered for the problem of the nature of σωφροσύνη. It is likely enough
that Tuckey's suggestion that σωφροσύνη is to be defined by a combination of the definitions ἡ τῶν ἀγαθῶν πρᾶξις and ἡ ἐπιστήμη

ἀγαθοῦ καὶ κακοῦ is what Plato intended, but the problem then arises: Why did Plato not draw this conclusion himself? To this there can be only one answer, that is: Because Plato was aware that to define in this way is merely to replace one unknown by another. Σωφροσύνη, he believes, can perhaps be restated in various ways, but until one can discover the meaning of the word "good," the meaning of σωφροσύνη, defined in terms of what is good, is still obscure.

The sort of puzzle that lack of clarity about the good would have posed for Socrates can easily be seen. In the first book of the *Republic*, he refers to Autolycus (334B) as a man who excelled all others in lying and perjury. In other words, Autolycus was good at lying and perjury. In other words, to the unthinking, Autolycus was good. Socrates plainly could not agree to this. In a similar vein, Thucydides, in the eighth book of his history, says that Antiphon was the best of his contemporaries in ἀρετή.[22] Of this ἀρετή Bury writes: "Thucydides has used ἀρετή in his notice of the oligarch Antiphon, to express the intelligence, dexterity and will-power of a competent statesman, in sharp contradistinction to the conventional ἀρετή of the popular conception. The only appropriate equivalent by which we can render in a modern language this Thucydidean ἀρετή is a key-word in Machiavelli's system, *virtù*, a quality possessed by men like Francesco Sforza and Cesare Borgia."[23] Ἀρετή then certainly need not not be moral, but amoral ἀρετή was of no real interest to Socrates. In his investigation of the nature of the good he was looking for a good which could by no means be morally bad.

Thus once more we find it likely that Socrates was interested in what we should call a theory of the object, though so sophisticated a term would hardly have satisfied him. Theories of the object, definitions, and "knowledge that" are all connected. As a final confirmation of the previously cited view of Aristotle, that one of the main contributions to philosophy made by Socrates was his search for general definitions, we may turn to the *Memorabilia* of Xenophon. In 3.9.5 we find Xenophon offering us his version of Socratic definitions. Socrates is said to have seen that justice, and every other virtue, is wisdom (σοφία). Similarly in 3.9.8 he is seen to be "considering what Envy is," and in 3.9.9 investigating the nature of Leisure. The parallel between these facts and what we have already seen in Plato and Aristotle is clear. We may be justified, therefore, if, before returning

---

[22]*Thuc.* 8.68.
[23]Bury, *Greek Historians* 145. For ἀρετή as *virtù*, see also Murray, *Literature of Ancient Greece* 198.

to the Platonic dialogues in our investigation of whether ἐπιστήμη means primarily "knowledge that," we look more specifically at the nature of knowledge in the *Memorabilia*.

In a discussion on the nature of piety in 4.6.1ff., Socrates asks Euthydemus what it is, and receives the answer that the sort of man who is pious is one who worships the gods. In other words, the unthinking first reply given by Euthydemus is a definition of piety in terms of action. This is probably the typical Greek view; we have seen it represented in the *Laches*, *Charmides*, and *Euthyphro*. Socrates (as in the Platonic works) is not satisfied, and eventually the disputants conclude that the pious man is he who knows what is lawful concerning the Gods (ὁ τὰ περὶ τοὺς θεοὺς νόμιμα εἰδώς). It is agreed by both that the man who has this knowledge will certainly worship the Gods lawfully. Perhaps one might quibble that here ἀρετή (for piety is certainly a virtue) is not associated with the verb ἐπίστασθαι but with εἰδέναι, and that the original significance of the two words was distinct. However, though εἰδέναι is used in this passage, what matters at this stage is that, whatever word is used to describe the process, piety is some kind of "knowing that."

Similarly in 4.6.6, after a discussion of justice and just men, it is decided that just men are those who know what is lawful in human affairs. Again εἰδέναι is the verb employed. In order to put the debate between "knowing how" and "knowing that" in the clearest possible light, we must now look at 4.6.2-3, where we read as follows:

Socrates: Is it possible for a man to worship the Gods in whatever way he wishes?

Euthydemus: No, there are laws in accordance with which one must worship the Gods.

Socrates: Then will he who *knows these laws know how* (εἰδείη ἄν, ὡς) he must worship the Gods?

To this Euthydemus agrees, making it common ground between the parties that "knowing how" is subordinate to and derived from "knowing that."

It can be seen from these passages and others that the distinction between "knowing how" and "knowing that" is clear if an ancient author uses the verb εἰδέναι. Here the addition of the conjunction ὡς makes all the difference either way. But Plato never uses a noun formed from the word εἰδέναι to express "knowledge." Εἴδησις occurs first in Aristotle, and even there is most infrequent.[24] Although it may have existed in his day, Plato seems to have preferred other terms,

[24]Cf. Schwyzer, "Bewusst und Unbewusst," 353.

including ἐπιστήμη, to express both "knowing how" and "knowing that."

That Xenophon at least was prepared to switch readily from εἰδέναι to ἐπίστασθαι in the sense of "knowing that" is clear from Memorabilia 3.9.4. He speaks first of recognizing the good and the bad (τὰ μὲν κακά τε κἀγαθὰ γιγνώσκοντα), then of the man who knows the ugly (τὸν τὰ αἰσχρὰ εἰδότα) and finally of those who know what they ought to do (ἐπισταμένους μὲν ἃ δεῖ πράττειν). That all these three words, γιγνώσκοντα, εἰδότα, and ἐπισταμένους mean some form of knowing which is not "knowing how" seems undeniable. Furthermore, if ἐπίστασθαι can have this sense, when εἰδέναι could well have been used instead, why should not ἐπιστήμη follow suit—especially as εἴδησις was extremely rare?

Similar to the above passage is a sentence from 3.9.5: καὶ οὔτ' ἂν τοὺς ταῦτα εἰδότας ἄλλο ἀντὶ τούτων οὐδὲν προελέσθαι οὔτε τοὺς μὴ ἐπισταμένους δύνασθαι πράττειν. It is very difficult to translate τοὺς ταῦτα εἰδότας and τοὺς μὴ ἐπισταμένους in any other way than as "those who know these things" and "those who do not know them." Ἐιδέναι and ἐπίστασθαι are undoubtedly synonymous, whatever be the distinction between them in earlier writers. Our general conclusion from the evidence of Xenophon must therefore be that the various uses of ἐπίστασθαι, εἰδέναι, etc. tell against Gould's thesis, and in particular against his view that no kind of theory of the object is to be attributed to Socrates and that "knowing how" is prior to "knowing that." Perhaps all this Xenophonic evidence must be dismissed as irrelevant to the Platonic Socrates, who is, after all, the object of Gould's enquiry. If, however—as does Gould—we are to admit philological enquiries into the uses of certain key terms for "knowing" in writers from Homer to Herodotus, Thucydides, and the tragedians, the evidence of Xenophon—particularly when it refers to Socrates himself—is not lightly to be dismissed. As for the question of definitions, it simply confirms what is amply clear from the Platonic dialogues and repeated by Aristotle.

Finally, before considering in greater detail various passages from the dialogues most relevant to the issue, it is worth pointing out that Gould's position about "knowing how" does not prevent him from making a number of interpretations of the dialogues which, on principle, he ought not to admit. Thus on p. 42, in a correct analysis of a section of the Hippias Minor, he writes as follows: "Socrates questions Hippias on the merits of the characters of Achilles and Odysseus, and Hippias replies that Achilles is the finer character, being straightforward and upright where Odysseus is wily and resourceful. Yet it is the latter, as Socrates points out, who relies on knowledge for his ability to deceive; only knowledge could give a would-be deceiver the certainty of achieving his purpose. This is clearly true, for example, in the case of arithmetic: we cannot be sure of giving the wrong answer to a sum without knowing what the right one is. Socrates declares this to be the case with all techniques." Had Gould written "we cannot give the wrong answer, even if we know how to give a wrong answer (i.e., by lying), without knowing *what* is the right one (in this case), and therefore presumably the wrong one also," he might have wondered more about his general position.

Again, on p. 29, during a discussion of *Laches* 194, the same ambivalence arises. Gould writes as follows: "Courage is *like* (his italics) knowing how to play the flute or the harp, but it is only like these: its sphere of action is different. It is defined as 'knowing what one must fear and what one may venture' (τὴν τῶν δεινῶν καὶ θαρραλέων ἐπιστήμην). At this point we seem to pass abruptly from a description of knowing *how* to one of knowing *that*, and it is noticeable that in the following discussion the word γιγνώσκειν appears several times: ... A doctor can know what is to be feared, *from a medical viewpoint* (his italics), but whether health is worth venturing upon at all is beyond his awareness, as a doctor." Gould continues by suggesting that the distinction between "knowing how" and "knowing that" may well "not fit exactly." Nevertheless, had he not attempted to make it fit, he would have interpreted this passage better. The brave man, according to Nicias, does not know primarily *how* to face dangers, as the harpist knows *how* to play the harp. Rather he knows what is in reality to be feared and what is not. Courage is not only different from the recognized τέχναι (assuming a τέχνη really is only "knowing how") in scope, but also in kind. We have already seen, however, that a τέχνη, for Plato, is more than a mere "knowing how."

Finally, we must look at Gould's interpretation (pp. 16–17) of *Protagoras* 352A 8ff. Socrates enquires of Protagoras whether he regards knowledge (ἐπιστήμη) as do the majority of men, as something which can very easily lose its control over a man in the face of the temptations of pleasure and pain. In 352C 2, he says: "Is your opinion of it something of this kind or do you think that knowledge is something fine and able to rule a man, and that whoever recognizes good things and bad (γιγνώσκῃ τἀγαθὰ καὶ τὰ κακά) cannot be mastered by anything else so as to act otherwise than knowledge bids (κελεύῃ)?" Of this passage Gould writes: "It seems to imply that ἐπιστήμη has the connotations of knowing *that*; yet clearly we could say of an intelligent practitioner in any field that he recognized the object of his activity for what it was: all still depends on whether we regard this as an *explanation* of his activity and its excellence." This last remark is true and apposite, but Socrates clearly means that the recognition of "the goods and bads" will have such a hold over the knower that he will not be mastered by pleasure and will only act *as knowledge bids*. "Knowledge how" cannot bid in matters of morals, as we have seen, for it has no moral force, and in any case the passage refers not to knowledge of how to do "the goods and bads" but to knowledge of what they are. Socrates' view is that knowledge is strong (ἰσχυρός), a leader (ἡγεμονικός), and like a ruler (ἀρχικός) who gives out his commands. This "knowledge that," seen as a commanding force, is the *explanation* of action and its excellence.

The three passages from Gould discussed above are of course not his only evidence for the "Platonic" use of ἐπιστήμη as "knowing how." That Plato on occasions admits this use we have already shown. That Gould has failed to prove its priority on several occasions has been our conclusion so far. Where Gould sees the matter in doubt, as in the *Protagoras* passage, we regard the evidence as telling against him. It is time now to examine those passages of the Platonic corpus which show clearly how Plato's attitude to definitions and to his so-called "theory of the object" is reinforced by his belief in the efficacy of "knowing that," that inevitable "bit of theory" which precedes the "bit of practice." As this discussion will have to be related to the problem of what is the knowledge that the good man has, and later to the more refined point of the possible difference between "knowing that" and "knowing what," it will be necessary to make some preliminary remarks on a topic which recurs with monotonous regularity in the early dialogues, namely that of the unity of the Virtues. We can observe this as a particularly Socratic idea in the *Memorabilia* (3.9.5). What can we understand of its relevance in the Platonic dialogues? Finally, what relation has it to the analogy of ἐπιστήμη with τέχνη?

In the *Charmides*, after a number of failures to secure the definition of σωφροσύνη, the last suggestion made (174C) is that it is knowledge concerned with good and evil (περὶ τὸ ἀγαθόν τε καὶ κακόν).[25] In the *Laches* (199C), the final definition proposed for courage is that it must be a knowledge concerned with all goods and evils. This is a more

---

[25] As Tuckey points out (*Plato's Charmides* 87 n.1), "Knowledge of the Good" and "Knowledge of the knowledge of the Good" are in effect the same, since knowledge, if it really is knowledge, must be certain; otherwise it can only at best be true belief.

primitive suggestion[26] than that of the *Charmides*, for the speakers do not seem to have been able to raise themselves from the enumeration of a number of goods and evils to the discussion of them in terms of a general notion of what is good and what is bad; but for the moment this is not our concern. What is our concern is that in the *Laches* it is specifically stated that such a definition of courage as that given by Nicias tends to confuse courage, which is one of the virtues, with virtue itself. If a man is courageous, in the terms Nicias has suggested, he must have all the other virtues as well. Socrates claims in the *Laches* that this objection is fatal to Nicias' definition, though perhaps this is simply his εἰρωνεία. Be that as it may, the same objection would also apply to the definition of σωφροσύνη in the *Charmides*. If a man were σώφρων in the sense of possessing a knowledge of what is good and evil or in the sense which Tuckey believes to be implied, that of being able to do what is good with the knowledge that it is good, then such a man would no doubt possess all the other cardinal virtues in addition to σωφροσύνη.

This same idea, that a certain kind of knowledge is the basic ingredient in the whole of the good life (not merely with regard to courage, but to all the virtues) occurs in the *Euthydemus* (281E) where it is held that wisdom is good, ignorance is bad and, comparatively speaking, everything else is irrelevant. Thus it is not surprising that the discussion of the unity of virtue is brought up at considerable length in the *Protagoras*. In this dialogue, however, though the words ἐπιστήμη and σοφία occur continually in the discussion of the virtues, the object of knowledge seems to be neglected. In sections 329C–334A, Socrates compels Protagoras—at times apparently rather unfairly— to admit that σωφροσύνη and σοφία must be the same thing, and that justice and holiness are more or less the same. In 349D, restating his position, Protagoras admits that justice, holiness, courage, σοφία, and σωφροσύνη are all parts of virtue and that four of them are reasonably similar to one another, but that courage is very different from all the rest. By 360D, however, the argument has gone against him and he is unwilling to face the conclusion that the courageous man is he who knows what is dreadful and what is not. Socrates and Protagoras have previously agreed that the pleasant is good (358C) and that the best life depends on making a right choice of pleasure and pain (357A). Hence when the brave man faces what is not really to be feared but only appears so to the cowardly, he knows that he is choosing a course

[26]Cf. *Alcibiades* I, 110C, τὰ δίκαια καὶ τὰ ἄδικα.

which will give the most real pleasure. Such a course will be good and the brave man will recognize the fact. Thus the notion of the knowledge of the good is brought into the discussion of the unity of the virtues in the *Protagoras*, not explicitly, but still clearly.

The parallel between the discussions of courage in the *Laches* and the *Protagoras* is obvious, and hence we may put the latter side by side with the earlier dialogues and draw our conclusions as follows. It is the opinion of Socrates that Virtue is in some way an adequate general term for courage, σωφροσύνη, and the rest. This Virtue is a kind of knowledge that has to do with the good and bad. No detailed suggestions are made as to the nature of this good and bad, though, as we have seen, to do good brings pleasure to the extent that if one could measure real pleasures, it would be clear that the greater pleasure bore witness to the greater goodness. Moreover, what is good is shown in a long, and at first sight rather pointless speech of Protagoras (334A-C) to be always useful in some context or other, if not for men, then at least for some other part of the animal or vegetable kingdom. With these vague hints we must be satisfied for the present—though they are not so vague as not to suggest that the good may be treated in an objective way. To this matter we must finally turn our attention, in order to show how the claims made earlier about the priority of "knowing that" can be fully vindicated.

The simplest manner of proceeding is to enumerate certain passages from the dialogues. These passages show, with varying degrees of clarity, the pre-eminence of "knowing that." By themselves they are not all convincing; taken together, they point to an extremely high degree of probability.

(*a*) In *Alcibiades* I, 110C, Socrates asks Alcibiades whether even as a child he thought he knew which things were just and which unjust (ἐπίστασθαι τὰ δίκαια καὶ τὰ ἄδικα).

(*b*) In *Alcibiades* I, 111D, we read as follows:

SOCRATES: But what if we wished to know (εἰδέναι) not only what men or horses were like, but also which of them were runners and which were not, would the multitude be adequate to teach this?

ALCIBIADES: No, indeed not.

SOCRATES: Have you sufficient proof that they do not know this (ἐπίστασται) and that they are not proficient teachers in that they do not agree about it among themselves?

In these passages, despite Gould's objections, εἰδέναι, and ἐπίστασθαι appear to be interchangeable, as we have seen them to be in Xenophon's *Memorabilia*.

(c) In *Apology* 21D, comparing himself with the artisans, Socrates says that neither he nor they knew anything fine and good (οὐδὲν καλὸν κἀγαθὸν εἰδέναι). The implication of the passage is that if either party had known anything (εἰδέναι, not ἐπίστασθαι as Gould, p. 15, would have led us to expect from the connection with σοφία) he or they would have been σοφοί.

(d) *Laches* 194E, a passage already referred to, runs as follows:

SOCRATES: Come then, tell him what kind of wisdom (σοφία) courage, according to your account of it, may be. Presumably it is not knowing how to play the flute.

(Here it should be noticed that Socrates does not say "σοφία τῶν αὐλῶν" or "σοφία περὶ τῶν αὐλῶν," which would mean "knowledge of or about flutes," but "σοφία αὐλητική," a phrase which seems more ambiguous but which, as will become clear below, probably has the meaning I have assigned to it.)

NICIAS: Certainly not.
SOCRATES: Nor knowledge of how to play the harp (ἡ κιθαριστική).
NICIAS: No, indeed not.
SOCRATES: But what is this knowledge then, or of what? ('Αλλὰ τίς δὴ αὕτη ἢ τίνος ἐπιστήμη).

Here there are two alternative questions offered by Socrates: (1) τίς ἐπιστήμη, the answer to which might have been ἡ κιθαριστική or ἡ αὐλητική; (2) τίνος ἐπιστήμη, the answer to which would seem to be rather objective than in terms of "knowing how." It is this alternative which Nicias chooses to answer when he replies that courage is knowledge of what inspires dread or confidence in warfare and in other circumstances.

(e) In *Laches* 196D, Plato uses γνῶναι as the verbal representative of ἐπιστήμη, where, if a meaning of "knowing how" were required, ἐπίστασθαι might seem more appropriate, for ἐπίστασθαι can certainly at times mean to "know how," but γνῶναι primarily means to "recognize that."

(f) *Protagoras* 352BC and *Hippias Minor* 367A have been discussed earlier.

(g) *Hippias Minor* 375D. Here Socrates asks Hippias whether he would not agree that justice is either a sort of power (δύναμίς τις), or knowledge, or both. It is clear that δύναμις and ἐπιστήμη are alternatives, and if δύναμις implies something like "capability" or "ability," what else can ἐπιστήμη mean but "knowledge that"?

(h) Knowledge of good and evil in the *Charmides* has already been discussed.

(i) In *Euthyphro* 4E, Socrates, puzzled at Euthyphro's intention of prosecuting his father, addresses him as follows: "By Zeus, Euthyphro, do you think *you know about divine things and those that are holy and unholy* with such accuracy that . . . you are not afraid of committing an unholy act in prosecuting your father?" The italicized words are in Greek ἐπίστασθαι περὶ τῶν θείων ὅπῃ ἔχει, καὶ τῶν ὁσίων τε καὶ ἀνοσίων. "Knowing about" cannot mean "knowing how"; it must mean knowing facts. This is borne out by Euthyphro's reply that "I should be of no use, Socrates . . . if I did not know all such matters exactly (ἀκριβῶς εἰδείην τὰ τοιαῦτα πάντα)."

(j) In the "first act" of the *Gorgias*, Socrates tries to explain to Gorgias the difference between the rhetor and the τεχνικός. The rhetor has no knowledge, but employs great powers of persuasion as a substitute for it. In 459C, Socrates speaks as follows: "But as it is, let us consider first whether the rhetorician is in the same relation to what is just and unjust, base and noble, good and bad, as to what is healthful and to the remaining spheres of the other arts. He does not know (εἰδώς) what is good and what is bad but he has devised a persuasion on these topics so that he seems, among those who have no knowledge, to know more than the man who really knows. Or is it necessary to know (εἰδέναι) and must he who comes to you with the intention of learning rhetoric have a previous knowledge of these things (προεπι-στάμενον)?" Once again the alleged distinction between εἰδέναι and ἐπίστασθαι appears in contradiction to the facts of the dialogue; once again it seems to be a question of "knowing that" rather than "knowing how," of knowing what is good and bad, just and unjust, rather than of knowing how to act justly and unjustly.

A little later (460B) in the same discussion, we find the argument going as follows:

SOCRATES: The man who has learnt (μαθεῖν) τὰ δίκαια is just?
GORGIAS: Completely so.
SOCRATES: The just man, I presume, does just things.
GORGIAS: Yes.

Here again the course of Socrates' thought is from knowledge of what is just to the performance of just acts. As he goes on to remark, since the just man knows what is just and does what is just, he must *wish* to do what is just. This wish must be built into the nature of the justice that the just man possesses. A mere ability to do just deeds does not, as we have already pointed out, imply a wish to do them. Knowledge of what is just in some kind of objective sense has precisely this power, as the *Protagoras* has already taught us.

We may, I believe, conclude on the testimony of these passages and the evidence earlier discussed that "knowing that" is, in the mind of the Platonic Socrates, prior to "knowing how." We know too that by the time of the *Protagoras*, if not by that of the *Laches*, the virtues were thought to be closely related to one another and to be explicable as various aspects of the knowledge of what is good. Here we must revert to the relation between ἐπιστήμη (as Virtue) and τέχνη, and, stating the conclusion of the following argument in advance, point out that while ἐπιστήμη (as Virtue) is concerned with "what is good," or more fully, what is good in itself and the only good for the soul, the τέχναι, though concerned to promote the goods of their objects, as has been shown, deal not in the good, but in one of a number of "goods."

Socrates makes it plain in the *Apology* that he is a man who "knows himself." In the *Charmides*, Critias at one stage suggests knowledge of oneself as a definition of σωφροσύνη (165B). We may wonder what sort of knowledge knowledge of oneself is, and a partial answer to this question is given in the *First Alcibiades*, which, whether genuine or not, is, I think, illuminating. In 130D it becomes evident that one's self is one's soul. Hence to know oneself means to know one's soul. Now plainly if a man "knows his soul," he will know what is good and bad for that soul. Hence knowledge of one's soul implies knowledge of what is good and bad. Thus, in the *Charmides*, it is not surprising that the discussion of knowledge of oneself leads inevitably to the question of knowledge of good and bad.

To know oneself, then, implies knowing what is good and bad, and what is good and bad is good and bad specifically for the soul. Hence it is the mark of the best soul to know best what is good and bad, and in the widest sense σοφία is the ἀρετή of the soul (*Alc.*I 133B). Thus, while the τέχναι are each concerned with their own particular good, but not with the goodness of the soul, Virtue (which is ἐπιστήμη) is concerned with the good in general and, as the *Hippias Minor* tells us (376B), the good man is the man with the good soul. Finally, this good soul, this cause of the various acts of virtue, is good not because it performs these acts but because it knows what is good and what is not. While, as we saw earlier, there is a sense in which the τέχναι, properly so called, are morally superior to "knowing how," they in their turn must give place, in the moral sphere, to a correct "knowing that."

If ἐπιστήμη meant "knowing how," and "Virtue is Knowledge" meant that "the ability to do what is good" is ἀρετή, then Socrates' difficulty about "Who are the teachers, if virtue can be taught?"

would have been an unreal one. If virtue were a technique, then the claims of Protagoras or of Pericles, or even of the general public of Athens, to teach it would have been more feasible, for it would have been a mechanical skill which could be learned by imitation and similar methods, but since it is a "knowing that," and in particular a knowledge of good and evil, the lack of teachers can be seen to be due to the lack of people who know what good and evil are. Cleinias, in the *Euthydemus* (282C), is sure that *wisdom* is teachable, and Socrates is glad to hear it, but in the *Protagoras* the visiting sophist's claim to teach ἀρετή is shown to be unsatisfactory, and the *Meno* ends with the conclusion that since so far no one appears able to teach it (100A), we must assume that it "is neither natural nor taught, but by divine dispensation." This is an unsatisfactory position, and Socrates leaves the question in abeyance as to whether anyone will appear in the future who is capable of teaching it. The reason for all this would seem to be that if, as we have suggested, the Socrates of the early dialogues believes that Virtue is knowledge of the good, its teacher will need to have such knowledge himself. Socrates himself appears to be at the stage of knowing *that* there is a good and that it is beneficial to the soul, but not precisely *what* it is. As will later be clear, we hear no more about there being no recognizable teachers of virtue after a theory of *what* is the good has been worked out. One might object that the distinction between "knowing that" and "knowing what" is impossible for Plato—if it did not occur in the *Charmides* (170C).

It should by this time be evident that Plato makes use of notions both of "knowing how" and of "knowing that," but that when he speaks of the knowledge that is ἀρετή, "knowing that" is prior. Thus, regardless of the question of the validity of Ryle's distinction between these two kinds of knowing as a philosophical truth, we may conclude that Gould's application of it to Plato is an anachronism. Despite the evidence for the primacy of "knowing how" in the pre-Socratic period, it must not be assumed, without adequate proof, in the dialogues. It is a way of thinking which is either "primitive" or ultra-sophisticated. Its "primitive" nature is well brought out in the following remarks of Professor Onians:[27]

Where cognition and thought are so bound up with feeling and tendency to act, the relation of moral character, of virtue to knowledge, is closer than where cognition is more 'pure.' How emotional and prone to physical expression of their emotions Homer's heroes were we have seen. Greeks like Aristotle and we to-day have apparently attained to greater 'detachment,' power of thinking in cold blood without

---

[27]Onians, *Origins* 18.

bodily movement, as we have to a sharper discrimination and definition of the aspects and phases of the mind's activity. It is with the consciousness, the knowing self, the spectator aware of what happens within and without (emotions, sensations, etc.) that a man would tend more particularly to identify himself. As this spectator became more 'detached,' the purely intellectual, the cognitive bearing of such words as οἶδα would naturally prevail.

Our conclusions being clear about the use of "knowing that" by Plato, we may look at one last passage of Gould, this time (p. 18) an interpretation of the *Cratylus*. Gould translates *Cratylus* 390B 1ff. as follows: " 'Which man is going to know whether the right shape for a shuttle is embodied in this or that piece of wood? The carpenter who has made it, or the weaver, who will use it?' 'The man who is going to use it, I imagine, Socrates.' " He believes that this passage indicates that ἐπιστήμη is "knowing how," not "knowing that," or is so expressed in practice, and conversely that the true ἐπιστήμων is he who knows how to use whatever is in question. We may object, however, that to say that a weaver knows the right-shaped piece of wood for a shuttle because he knows *how* to use the shuttle is at best a half-truth. The weaver not only knows how to weave, but also *what* kind of tools he needs to do so. His knowing about the piece of wood is not merely a "knowing how," but *both* a "knowing how" *and* a "knowing that."

So much might be admitted, however, by someone who contended that, although both Plato and Truth admitted that there are two kinds of knowledge, "how" and "that," nevertheless the former is prior. Our discussion above of the *Laches*, *Protagoras*, and *Charmides* in particular, shows that, whether we like it or not, Plato is an "intellectualist." The justification of such a position is perhaps strictly beyond the scope of this essay, but we may look briefly at the question "How do we learn to know how?"

If I want to learn to play chess, I must learn, among other things, the knight's move and the fact that at the beginning of the game the white Queen stands on a white square and the black Queen on a black. Having learned these and similar facts I do not, admittedly, know how to play chess, yet I cannot know how to play chess without knowing them. Similarly, if I wish to learn to swim, I must learn that it is necessary to make certain movements with my arms and legs. Making these movements, again, is not knowing how to swim, but is an essential preliminary to it. Of course, it is possible that when I become "habituated" to swimming, I shall no longer be able to explain the things I once learned, since my movements will then be virtually mechanical, but this will not mean that the theory, the "knowing that," was never present.

On p. 31 of the *Concept of Mind*, Ryle points out that "A soldier does not become a shrewd general merely by endorsing the strategic principles of Clausewitz; he must also be competent to apply them. Knowing how to apply maxims cannot be reduced to, or derived from, the acceptance of these or any other maxims." That the outstanding general needs to know more than theory is obvious, but, unless he is an automaton, his knowing how cannot be viewed apart from his knowing that. Suppose that General X wishes to capture a town. His deliberations on the subject might be as follows: "I know that in order to relieve this town, the enemy will have to do this and that. I know how to prevent any such move. Therefore I can reduce the town by blockade." General X may never have read, or even heard of, Clausewitz, but his factual knowledge of the exigencies of war (e.g. that the enemy will do this or that in given circumstances) will, if he is competent, probably tally with the directions of the theorist in strategy. The claim that X knows how to win a battle but has no kind of knowledge that this or the other tactic is expedient is meaningless.

Once again, on p. 33, Ryle adduces an example, this time the performance of a clown. The spectators at the show are said to admire the clown's visible performance. This is true, and the clown certainly "knows how" to trip and tumble on purpose. But this tripping and tumbling is like knowing how to swim. It can only be learned by the clown if he has certain presuppositions *that*. When learning his art, he is told by his master *that* if he falls in a particular way he will hurt himself. If he is not told this specifically, he realizes from observation *that* there are ways of falling which will not break his arms or sprain his back. Having been told or having realized the fact, he then feels confident about learning *how* it is done. As Ryle says (p. 41), we learn *how* by practice, schooled indeed by criticism and example, but often quite unaided by any theoretical lesson. This is true, but even if no lesson is given on the theory, some prior knowing *that* is grasped by the learner.

We must leave this digression into contemporary philosophy, where, in the matter under consideration, Professor Ryle appears in the guise of Gorgias, and return to the theories of Plato, where Gould, who has been detected applying an inadequate theory to a thinker who did not profess it, has taken upon himself the rôle of Polus. It must first be mentioned that Ryle's debate is, formally at least, about what he calls "mental-conduct concepts" (p. 25), such as "clever," "sensible," "careful," etc. These words, or some of them, may have "moral" significance, but are not exclusively concerned with morality. The words with which Plato, and therefore Gould, are concerned are moral words: "just," "temperate," "brave," "good." Since Plato's views on the unity of the virtues leads to his seeing them all in terms of "knowledge" and "good," we may say that Gould applies to "good" what Ryle says of "clever." Unless one subscribes to an ethical relativism of the "Man is the measure" variety, it is hard to understand how "good" can be understood in terms of a "mental-conduct concept," particularly by Socrates and Plato who, as we have always understood, opposed ethical relativism. Could Socrates or Plato ever have agreed that "x is good" means "I know how to do x"? If so, assuming Socrates knew how to commit a murder, would he therefore assume that murder was good?

The conclusion of this argument must be that the knowledge which is virtue is a state of mind, that it is a knowledge of objects and that it will result in moral action when the circumstances demand. The Socratic "knowing that" implied a "knowing how." This unusual feature marks it off from the "knowing that" discussed by Ryle and Gould. For Socrates, if a man claims to know what is good and does not act upon his "knowledge," his "knowledge" is not knowledge at all.

Modern philosophy, and indeed most philosophy since Aristotle, first sets up a distinction between theory and practice and then, in some cases, tries to show that all theory is really practice, or vice versa. Aristotle talks about θεωρία being the highest form of πρᾶξις; Gould wants to adapt the pre-Socratic connection of σωφροσύνη with behaviour, not with mental outlook, to the philosophy of Plato; Professor Onians' nephew wants to answer "With my tongue" to the question "How do you know?"[28] All these possibly valid attitudes are, as we have seen, irrelevant to Plato, as is indeed the whole dichotomy of theory and practice. For Plato, a man cannot hold a correct moral theory without being morally upright. If his moral behaviour is doubtful, it is certain that he does not know what good and bad are. Hence Gould's statement (p. 13) that "Even for Socrates and Plato, to achieve ἀρετή is not to arrive at a valid ethical theory, but to attain valid moral behaviour" is misleading. However, while Plato thought that a correct moral theory made moral behaviour certain, he came to realize that moral behaviour does not necessarily imply the understanding of a correct moral theory, but merely the acceptance of guidance. But ὀρθὴ δόξα, in the time of the dialogues at present under review, remains a thing of the future.

[28]*Ibid.* 14.

With the priority of "knowing that" for Plato clear in our minds, we can answer the question "Is the proposition 'Virtue is Knowledge' analytic?" If knowledge meant "knowing how," then this would be the case. Since it primarily means knowledge of what is good, however, the answer is No. Virtue is a state of mind leading inevitably to action. Knowledge is knowledge of what is for Plato an external fact, namely the good. Thus "Virtue is Knowledge" is a synthetic, not an analytic proposition.

Virtue then is a knowledge of the good. It differs from the τέχναι in that it adds happiness to effectiveness. There is a famous passage in the *Charmides* (174D) where Plato makes it clear that the knowledge of good and evil is the only knowledge that will bring happiness to society. As Tuckey points out, we have here "a germ of Plato's later doctrine that humanity will only be happy when philosophers are kings and kings philosophers."[29]

[29]Tuckey, *Plato's Charmides* 79.

VIRTUE IN THE MIDDLE AND
LATE DIALOGUES

τὰ χρήστ' ἐπιστάμεσθα καὶ γιγνώσκομεν
οὐκ ἐκπονοῦμεν δ'....

Eur. *Hipp.* 380-1

IT is views of morality like Phaedra's that Socrates, in the early dialogues, is so anxious to oppose. He is looking for a knowledge that will determine actions and make men virtuous. Such knowledge of good and evil as Phaedra had, does not constitute, for him, real knowledge at all. For Virtue is Knowledge, and Phaedra is hardly virtuous. By the time of the *Meno* we can safely assume that Socrates is aware that knowledge of good and evil brings virtue. He is aware too, however, that whatever is knowledge must in some sense be teachable. Yet in the *Meno* there appear to be no teachers of virtue, nor pupils either (96C).

Socrates and Meno have been brought to an apparent impasse, but Socrates succeeds in avoiding the difficulty by suggesting (96E) that in the sphere of conduct knowledge is not the only guide to right action, for true opinion will produce the same effect. The distinction, here drawn for the first time, between knowledge and true opinion is important for all aspects of Plato's thought, but we must remember that it is introduced specifically to deal with a problem in ethics. It is in the realm of practical life that ὀρθὴ δόξα is introduced, and the implication is that in order to act virtuously we need only understand that certain things are good, without knowing the reason for their goodness. It is enough to believe that murder is wrong without knowing why.

The difference between one kind of knowledge and true opinion is said to be that the latter may run away out of the human soul and is of no great value unless it is secured by an αἰτίας λογισμός, a calculation of cause. This phrase has always appeared rather puzzling, and the ability to give an αἰτίας λογισμός has often been connected with that ability which is the mark of the dialectician and which is frequently described in the *Republic* as that of "giving an account" (λόγον δοῦναι). 'Αιτίας λογισμός is always associated with the ability to refer to general ideas as the background for particular statements. It is clearly linked by Plato with ἀνάμνησις (98A), with the soul's recollection of such general propositions as mathematical laws, which it has "seen" in a former life. In the sphere of ethics it is clear that knowledge includes a "calculation of the cause" of goods, while true opinion merely accepts that goods are good and acts accordingly. In other words, the "cause" with which we are concerned here is the good as distinguished from goods. The man who knows, knows that the good is the cause of the goodness inherent in certain activities.

We have seen how in earlier dialogues Socrates reduces the virtues now to knowledge of good and evil (as in the *Charmides*), now to knowledge of goods and evils (as in the *Laches*). He probably had not at this stage properly understood the difference between these two attitudes. At the time of the *Meno*, however, this difficulty may have been resolved. The man whose virtue is based on true opinion appears to recognize goods and evils, but the man who has knowledge recognizes the good. When the slave boy's true opinion about the geometrical problem has been elicited, Socrates says that by a continual repetition of such a process of enquiry true opinion can be converted into knowledge. Similarly, perhaps, he believed that by continual thought upon goods, one could eventually come to a knowledge of the good. The implication of this is that everyone could know the good, and thus become a philosopher in the fullest sense of the term.

Such confidence in the potentiality of the vast majority, if not the whole, of the human race is typical of the Socrates of the early dialogues and lasts at least until the time of the *Phaedo*. In that dialogue it is assumed that in a dialectical discussion agreement between the disputants will certainly lead to the discovery of truth, and that subjectivism will somehow be avoided. By the time of the *Republic* this confidence has vanished. Only a very few gifted individuals are there considered capable of philosophical discussion.

In the *Phaedo*, however, the question of the relationship between virtue and φρόνησις occurs in a much disputed passage (68–69). It is unnecessary to go into the details of the dispute;[1] what concerns us is that a sharp distinction is drawn between virtue with φρόνησις and a spurious virtue which may arise on utilitarian grounds. In accordance

[1]Cf. Hackforth's *Phaedo* 191–193.

with the elevated manner of the *Phaedo*, the latter is described as "fit for slaves"; it is a virtue which paradoxically often arises δι' ἀκολασίαν, since its practitioners abstain from certain pleasures merely to enjoy others.

The difficulty with this section is, as Hackforth points out (p. 193), that Plato appears to waver between a simple identification of virtue with φρόνησις and the regarding of φρόνησις as an indispensable aid to virtue. The former is of course the view of the early dialogues, the latter a refinement upon it. In this passage, especially at 69B2, the latter view is predominant.

Yet another kind of virtue is mentioned in the *Phaedo* (82AB). It has certain resemblances to the "spurious virtue" of 68–69, especially in that it arises without philosophy or reasoning (νοῦς). But Plato does not regard it as the product merely of a skilful choice of pleasures, the abandoning of the immoral because in the long run the moral is more beneficial, but the result of habit and training. This is clearly very like the virtue that is equated with true opinion in the *Meno*. It is a virtue that men *practise* (ἐπιτηδευκότες)—which means that its practitioners accomplish a number of goods without knowing what is the good. Such virtue is given short shrift in the *Phaedo*, where the souls of some of those who pursue it are said to be destined after death for transmigration into bees or wasps or ants, creatures which live their lives in similar unthinking respectability. Nevertheless, Archer-Hind[2] is somewhat too sweeping when he holds that for Plato all virtue which is not based on philosophy can only be practised by the multitude on utilitarian principles. Plato believes increasingly from the time of the *Meno* that such unphilosophic virtue can be practised by men who have been taught that there is a difference between good and bad, or perhaps accept this distinction as something given by their conscience, but who could not justify their ethical position. This attitude is a perfectly reasonable one to hold, and should be especially understood at the present time, when both among the educated and the uneducated words like "good," "better," etc. are continually bandied. Of those who use them, some have never thought about them in general terms, while others have thought, but can give no account of them even to satisfy themselves. As for Plato, as we shall see, the distinction between these varieties of virtue is maintained spasmodically throughout the dialogues from the *Phaedo* on. The three varieties are: (*a*) Philosophic virtue, which is either equivalent to or vitally associated with knowledge; (*b*) Virtue which is associated with ὀρθὴ δόξα, unthinking

[2]Archer-Hind, *Plato's Phaedo* Appendix I, 181–186, especially 186.

obedience to a standard; (c) A spurious virtue based on a calculation of pleasures. (It would appear that such calculations, devoid of true knowledge, must often be mistaken.) It should of course be remembered that both (a) and (b) will bring pleasure of the highest kind, but are not governed by it. Pleasure is not merely a concomitant of spurious virtue; spurious virtue, however, is merely a refined search for pleasure.

There is an important passage in the *Protagoras* which is most relevant to the present problem. In 357B, Socrates and Protagoras agree that since the salvation of our life depends on the ability to measure quantities of pleasure and pain, even such virtue *ought* to be related to some kind of knowledge. The fact that the practitioners of this kind of virtue often have no skill in judging pleasure and pain merely means that their "definition of virtue" is self-contradictory. Thus, properly speaking, (c) is not virtue but a spurious pretender. This is seen clearest of all, as Archer-Hind[3] has pointed out, in *Republic* 554C. Here, in the description of the oligarchical man, we are shown a person who seems to be just and is famed for this, but whose baser passions are constrained not by knowledge but by a fear that if they are indulged he will waste money and possessions which, as he values them highest of all, he is convinced are the sources of the greatest pleasure. Such a man, having no real title to virtue, need no longer claim our attention.

Let us now return to the man who is virtuous through the possession of ὀρθὴ δόξα, the man who has learned (or is by nature apt) to recognize that certain goods are good, but has no understanding of what good is. It is a commonplace that he comes increasingly to the forefront of Plato's thinking as Plato grows older. The tripartite division of the state and the corresponding division of the soul increase his importance. In *Republic* 429C 7 we find the old relationship between courage and a grasp of what things are to be feared. But here Plato is speaking not of the Guardians but of the Auxiliaries, and thus refers not to knowledge or wisdom but to an opinion created by law by means of education. Although it is beyond dispute, as the central books of the *Republic* make clear, that Plato at this period postulated a metaphysical Good as the ultimate source of all goodness, he makes no allusion to it in this passage. True opinion doubtless could not reach that far; it must limit itself to the plurality of δεινά, and presumably μὴ δεινά, in the world of particulars. Plato pretends in this passage of the *Republic* that courage is the specific virtue of the warrior-caste, but it is clear from elsewhere in the dialogue that the Guardians too

[3]*Ibid.* 181–182.

must be courageous. Their courage, however, could not be merely ὀρθὴ δόξα.

A commentary on the two kinds of courage is given by 401D 5ff., where we read as follows:

Is it then, Glaucon, for these reasons that an education in μουσική is most important, because rhythm and harmony sink most of all into the inner parts of the soul and, bringing gracefulness with them, take hold of it most strongly, and make a man graceful if he has been brought up rightly, but if not, the reverse? And also because he that has been duly brought up in this way will perceive defects either in art or nature most acutely, and rightly disdaining them will pursue objects that are beautiful, and rejoicing in them and receiving them into his soul will be nourished by them and become noble and good. He will rightly blame and hate all that is base even when he is a child, before he is able to grasp reasoning, and when reason comes, the man who has been brought up in this way will recognize it by his relationship to it and be most welcoming to it.

The potential Guardian will "know" what is to be feared by ὀρθὴ δόξα long before reason comes to explain the why. Before such a man knows the good, he will have become habituated to "goods." The underlying theme in the passage quoted is the production of the right habits and dispositions. As Plato grew older, he became more and more convinced that habit is the key to morals for the majority of mankind. As early as the *Meno*, he appears to believe that by a continual process of repeating an experiment or mathematical proof the mind of the prover will progress from the possession of ὀρθὴ δόξα to that of ἐπιστήμη. If pressed, he would have had to admit that this is not altogether true, but the basic point is that the continual repetition of ὀρθαὶ δόξαι leads the mind to the receptive state which the above passage of the *Republic* describes, if and when reason makes its appearance. This kind of ἕξις, these ὀρθαὶ δόξαι, are again referred to in 500D 8 as ἡ δημοτικὴ ἀρετή. This is the kind of virtue the philosopher-king can produce among his subjects. It is not spoken of here in the slighting manner of the *Phaedo*, for Plato is now more certain that this is all that the majority of men can achieve. Yet the earlier view can still be seen at times, even coupled, as in 619C 6, with a sneer at "habit." In this passage Er relates how in the choice of lives the man who chooses an absolute despotism with all its concomitant evils is one of those who previously lived in a well-order constitution and who attained a measure of virtue through habit, and without the sure basis that only philosophy can supply.

We may assume that this condemnation of habit arises whenever Plato looks back to his earlier view that virtue by knowledge was possible for all, and feels how inadequate and second-best is all that

can in fact be maintained. Most of the time, however, he is not remembering the over-optimistic past, but attempting to do the best he can
with human natures as he now sees them. The result is the ever-
growing importance assigned to the cultivation of right habits and
right opinion, under the guidance of those few who can attain to
something higher. In *Republic* 602, the man of right opinion is seen to
be he who has associated with the man who knows, and is instructed
about what is to be done. Here the rôle of authority, which is essential
to the production of right opinion by education, is explicitly
emphasized.

The obverse side of the increasing stress laid on the instilling of
right habits is Plato's anxiety lest good citizens be corrupted by the
theatre. As we have already noticed, good habits are produced by
repetition of good actions, by continually seeing what is good and by
thus becoming influenced by it. Conversely, the sight of heroes in
tears makes for the bad habit of cowardice and should be forbidden
the stage in the ideal state. If everything in the state is to be subordinated to the production of ὀρθὴ δόξα, Plato's views on poetry—
given the influence he ascribes to μίμησις—can hardly be disallowed.

However, the new vision of virtue as, for the majority, ὀρθὴ δόξα,
must not obscure another, related vision, that of virtue as "health"
or "harmony." Precursors of this view appear in the *Gorgias*, where
Socrates proclaims the importance of geometrical equality among gods
and men (508A), and indeed "health" is the underlying notion behind
the Delphic slogan μηδὲν ἄγαν and the discussion of σωφροσύνη in related
terms in parts of the *Charmides*. The idea that σωφροσύνη itself means
health of the mind is clearly in Plato's thoughts at the time of the
Cratylus, where, in 411E, he relates it by derivation to σωτηρία and
φρόνησις. Health had, at least since the time of Alcmaeon, been explicitly associated with ἰσονομία, "balance" or, in Platonic terms, "harmony." As Aëtius records:[4] "Alcmaeon holds that the bond of health
is ἰσονομία of the powers, wet and dry, cold and hot, bitter and sweet,
etc., while the sole rule of one of them is the cause of disease." Applying
this physical theory to the virtues, we arrive at the equation of virtue
with health in the *Republic* (444E). Plato's precise words here are
worthy of note, for they will recur. He writes: "Virtue then, it seems,
is some kind of health and beauty and good condition,[5] while vice is
a disease (νόσος) and a deformity (αἶσχος) and a weakness." This kind
of virtue clearly need not imply knowledge in the virtuous man; it

[4]Aëtius 5.30.1.
[5]Εὐεξία—"good condition"—is itself a medical term. Cf. *Gorgias* 450A.

VIRTUE IN THE MIDDLE AND LATE DIALOGUES 149

only requires to be implanted by knowledge. It need not be that virtue which is directly related to knowledge, but can often best be understood in the state of mind of the man who is virtuous through the possession of ὀρθὴ δόξα. The pragmatic definitions of justice as the doing of one's job (*Rep.* 443CD) and of σωφροσύνη as the agreement between the governing and governed parts both of the city and of the individual soul (431) are in accordance with this relationship of virtue with ἁρμονία.

Interesting commentaries are provided upon these doctrines in certain of the later dialogues. In the *Sophist* (227E–228E), all vice in the soul (κακία) is said to be either νόσος (the immediate source of evil-doing, of πονηρία) or αἶσχος, which is ignorance. Here again the medical terms occur and νόσος is related to στάσις, disorder in the soul. Clearly, for Plato, no philosopher could suffer from either νόσος or ἀμαθία, but we may suppose that, although ignorance is the fundamental problem, νόσος, disorder of the soul, is in a sense the more dangerous: for while the soul of the ordinary man is in such confusion, he must inevitably be guilty of ignorance also, since his reasoning soul is under bondage to his passions.

This is borne out by the *Timaeus*. Here (86BC) all evil in the soul is called ἄνοια, folly. Of this ἄνοια there are two varieties, madness and ignorance. Of ignorance nothing is said, perhaps because Plato believes that for the ordinary man knowledge in the highest sense is impossible, and hence it need not be discussed here. Madness, however, it is implied, can arise either purely in the soul or because of undue influence exerted by the body.[6] Such bodily interference is attributed to physiological causes such as the possession of too much semen. Plato is particularly concerned with this "madness," and says that he regards an excess of pleasures and pains as the greatest possible evil for the soul. The reason for this is that under such influences the ordinary man (The philosopher cannot possibly be under discussion here since he is always κρείττων ἑαυτοῦ) is unable "either to see or to hear anything correctly," and is then completely incapable of reasoning. Any chance he might have of avoiding ignorance is gone if he has not the opportunity even to think about a problem, being completely overcome by his passions. Here, as in the education of philosophers, the attainment of ἁρμονία must precede the recovery of knowledge or true opinion. The passions prevent the growth of habit, and without good habits no "higher" education is possible.

[6]Cornford is clearly right to remark: "It is not stated that *all* mental disorders are *solely* due to bodily states." *Plato's Cosmology* 346.

With reference to a passage of the *Laws* (863E–864A), Grube[7] maintains that "we thus find the Socratic formula (that goodness [ἀρετή] is knowledge) reasserted to the very last in Plato's works." It is true that virtue is associated with knowledge in this passage, and a similar association can be seen in the sections of the *Sophist* and *Timaeus* that we have just discussed. But the implications are different from those dear to Socrates. For Socrates—the Platonic Socrates— "virtue is knowledge" was true without much qualification. For Plato in the later dialogues, there is a direct relationship in the case of a few men between virtue and knowledge, but the virtue of the majority is the willingness to accept ὀρθὴ δόξα, the well-ordered disposition (ἕξις) of the soul, the harmony and balance of psychological factors which is the result not of personal, direct knowledge but of training in accordance with a code devised by those who know. It is well known that in the *Laws* the director of education is the most important official in the state, and that Plato there makes great efforts to raise the general educational level of his citizens. But this education is not to be like that of the philosopher-kings of the *Republic*—that would be impossible—but is to be approached in a practical rather than theoretical manner (819B). Of all this, and of the increasing importance Plato placed upon the production of harmony in the soul and good habits, any handbook of Platonic philosophy can provide an adequate account, and there is no need to say more of it here.

Before leaving the topic, however, it is worth looking at two passages where Plato is concerned to describe the fate of those who upset the established belief in a state. Of such a passage in the *Laws* (952C 5ff.) Gould writes as follows:[8] "Perhaps the greatest tragedy of the *Laws* is that it sets the final seal of doom on the Socratic approach: when Plato describes the Nocturnal Council condemning to death the man who, setting himself outside the tradition of the state, refuses to keep his views privately to himself, it is not only ironical but tragic that we seem to hear an echo of Socrates' judges." Plato's attitude here arises because the tradition of the state is based on the true knowledge of those who control it. Hence he knows that the man who "deviates" from it is certainly in error and insists on trying to lead others into his own error. A more gloomy picture is presented in the *Politicus*, where (299BC) not only is he who openly speculates "contrary to the written rules" to be brought to trial, but any kind of speculation undertaken in a private capacity is to be condemned. From

[7]Grube, *Plato's Thought* 229.
[8]*Gould* 109.

such passages it looks as though even knowledge is forbidden if it is not learned "through the proper channels."

We may now leave ἕξις and ὀρθὴ δόξα and return to the relation of ἀρετή with knowledge. All the above observations will be assumed in what follows, and only the ἀρετή of the best of men, the true philosophers, will be under discussion. First of all we must return to the remark of Hackforth about *Phaedo* 69.[9] Hackforth's point is that in this passage there is a wavering between the identification of φρόνησις with virtue and the notion that φρόνησις is a means or aid to virtue. In the earlier dialogues we saw how ἐπιστήμη that is virtue is a knowledge first of goods and then of "good." We regarded these as the preliminary stages in the progression of Plato's thought to the fully-fledged metaphysical doctrine of the Good as it occurs in the *Republic*. In this work, as 506A makes clear, Plato believes both that if a man does not know in what way just things and beautiful things are good, he will make a poor Guardian, and that no satisfactory knowledge of what is just and beautiful is possible for a man ignorant of the good. This leads to the doctrine that the Good is that which makes everything else knowable, and is in fact the very principle of existence (508E–509B). Our problem is: Is virtue to be understood quite simply as knowledge of the Good, or is some other factor, such as will, involved?

In the *Phaedo*, we recall, the difficulty discovered by Hackforth concerned the relation not of ἐπιστήμη but of φρόνησις to ἀρετή. Hackforth seemed to regard ἐπιστήμη and φρόνησις as more or less equivalent. Our first task is to discover their relationship. In *Meno* 98CD, φρόνησις appears to be used as an exact synonym for ἐπιστήμη. In the *Symposium* (202A), right opinion is said to be half way between ignorance and φρόνησις. A possessor of such true opinion is said not to know (ἐπίστασθαι). Again, φρόνησις appears to be knowledge rather than intelligence or the act of knowing, in other words a synonym for ἐπιστήμη. Again, in 209A, φρόνησις is said to be a product of soul. The best kind of φρόνησις is said to be that which concerns the management of cities and homes. It is wisdom, perhaps, of a practical kind; it is not the ability to understand. In *Protagoras* 352C, the meaning of φρόνησις is perhaps unclear: it may be synonymous with ἐπιστήμη; it may mean intelligence and thus be distinct from knowledge. The former is perhaps the more likely.

When we read the *Republic* the situation is even harder to unravel. At 505A Socrates says that the Form of the Good is the μέγιστον μάθημα.

[9] See footnote 1.

He speaks of the possibility of knowing (εἰδέναι) this Good. If we know it (εἰδέναι) we can then apprehend what is good and beautiful (φρονεῖν). He then makes the old observation that the majority of men regard pleasure as the good, while the more enlightened (κομψοτέροις) select φρόνησις. When asked what φρόνησις means, these savants reply "φρόνησις of the Good." Socrates thinks this ludicrous, and it is noteworthy that in this section he does not use φρόνησις when speaking of what he regards as the right kind of knowledge of the Good (506B 7). The word κομψοτέροις, too, suggests that Socrates regards such people with suspicion. Φρόνησις perhaps now seems to him too practical a wisdom, too much like the Aristotelian φρόνησις—a sense inherent in the remark in the *Protagoras* that the best kind of φρόνησις was concerned with the management of homes and cities. Presumably Socrates believes that the best kind of ἐπιστήμη is concerned with the Good, and that when the κομψότεροι speak of φρόνησις of the Good they are wrong. Φρόνησις for Socrates in the *Republic* does not seem to imply that specifically metaphysical kind of knowledge which he regards as the only true knowledge of the Good.

The suggestion of the κομψότεροι is that φρόνησις is the Good. Socrates reduces this to nonsense by asking, "Do you say that φρόνησις of the Good is the Good?" Perhaps the word φρόνησις was in use among intellectuals who claimed not, as did the Socrates of the earlier dialogues, that knowledge (ἐπιστήμη) of the good is virtue, but that knowledge (φρόνησις) is the Good. It is in intellectualist terms that the matter is again debated in the *Philebus*. Admittedly, Socrates begins (11BC) by putting the problem in terms of whether intellectual activities or pleasure are better, but the question is soon resolved into the simpler form (14B) of "whether one must say that pleasure or φρόνησις or some other thing is the Good for men"—in other words the dispute between the majority and the κομψότεροι in the *Republic*. As is well known, the *Philebus* concludes that neither φρόνησις nor pleasure is *the* Good for men, agreeing in this with the *Republic*, but that mental qualities are higher up the scale of goodness than pleasures. The intellectualist heresy thus disposed of, however, we are no nearer to the relation of φρόνησις or ἐπιστήμη with ἀρετή. It is time to look at Aristotle's comments on the matter.

In the sixth book of the *Nicomachean Ethics*, during the discussion on φρόνησις, Aristotle remarks on Socrates' view that "all virtues are φρονήσεις" (1144B 20), and then later (1144B 30) restates this in the form that "the virtues are ἐπιστήμαι." Clearly he holds that Socrates believed that "virtue is knowledge" and that ἐπιστήμη and φρόνησις were for him indistinguishable. Aristotle's own view, of course, is that moral ἀρετή is a kind of disposition (ἕξις προαιρετική) and that φρόνησις has a relationship with it but is not identical. There is thus a similarity between Aristotle's view of moral virtue as a whole and Plato's view of the virtue of the ordinary man. For Aristotle there is no Form of Goodness, and even if there were, it would be beyond human reach, and so irrelevant to conduct. Hence there cannot be a philosophic virtue in the Platonic sense of a knowledge of the Good.

When Aristotle speaks of Socratic φρόνησις in the above-mentioned passage of the *Nicomachean Ethics*, he is presumably using the word in his own sense—that of "practical wisdom." This implies that it is wisdom about particular goods and bads in the world of contingent things. 'Επιστήμη is synonymous with φρόνησις, and this accords with what we saw to be the case in the earlier dialogues. When in Book One of the *Nicomachean Ethics*, however, he speaks of knowledge of the Form of the Good, he uses words like γνωρίζειν (1097A 1), γνῶσις (1097A 6), εἰδώς (1097A 10). These words should be compared with those that occur with regard to such knowledge in the *Republic*: μάθημα (505A 1), ἴσμεν (505A 6), ἀγνοοῦντα (506A 6). Clearly it is to the doctrines of the Good like those of the *Republic* that Aristotle refers.

This being so, we can turn to *Rep.* 534C in the hope that it will solve the problem. Here, after describing the dialectical advance to a knowledge of the Good (εἰδέναι), Plato draws a distinction between real knowing (now ἐπιστήμη is used) and true opinion. There is no doubt that εἰδέναι and ἐπιστήμη are intended to refer to the same kind of knowledge. With these words may be associated γνῶσις and its cognates, as seen above. Thus γνῶσις or ἐπιστήμη are used for knowledge of the Good; φρόνησις is not. If Socrates used φρόνησις and ἐπιστήμη as synonyms, Plato has corrected him. The correction is shown, as we have seen, in the *Nicomachean Ethics*, where φρόνησις is used in a Socratic context but not in a Platonic, presumably because Aristotle felt that the sense he gave the word was suitable for Socrates but not for Plato.

It appears from the *Laws*, however, that Plato to the last felt himself able to use φρόνησις with regard to the virtues. In 710A, the Athenian stranger speaks as follows: "Yes, Cleinias, ordinary (δημώδης) temperance, not the temperance people doing philosophy speak of in their high-minded way when they assert that τὸ σωφρονεῖν is φρόνησις." It is hard to tell what is meant by this. It may mean that some people point out that σωφροσύνη is the prudent course and may therefore be equated with worldly wisdom; it may be the φρόνησις of the Good which is discussed in the sixth book of the *Republic* and for which Plato there prefers the term ἐπιστήμη. This view is perhaps the less obvious in view of our previous remarks, but it appears to be borne out by another passage in the *Laws* (631C). Here the Athenian is engaged in distinguishing "human" goods from "divine." Of "divine" goods, he holds, the greatest is φρόνησις, the next being a rational, temperate state of mind (μετὰ νοῦ σώφρων ψυχῆς ἕξις). The greatest good we can possess, then, is φρόνησις, and we must assume that this φρόνησις is in fact ἐπιστήμη τοῦ ἀγαθοῦ. In any case it is clear that, whatever be the appropriate Greek for "knowledge," in some sense the doctrine that virtue is knowledge is maintained right to the last of Plato's written works.

The question may be asked, however: Does Plato at the end of his life believe that for the philosopher the equation of virtue with know-ledge is the whole story? Is virtue knowledge and essentially nothing else, since true knowledge is an adequate well-spring of virtuous action, as it is held to be, contrary to popular opinion, in the *Protagoras*? Gould[10] suggests that in the *Politicus* Plato depicts the Forms of Courage and σωφροσύνη as incompatible. If this were true, then know-ledge of the Forms would be inadequate for virtue; indeed, knowledge of the Good would be incompatible with knowledge of the Forms of Courage and σωφροσύνη, if knowledge of these latter was only a cause of strife—which is not a good. Fortunately Gould is wrong here. Plato is not speaking of persons who are courageous or temperate in the highest sense. The man who had courage or temperance in the highest sense would not need to be bound by true opinion—the bond that the true statesman applies to hold his city together.

This digression being settled, we may return to the question: In what sense does Plato in his later work equate virtue with knowledge for the philosopher? The answer must be that philosophic virtue will only be attained when the philosopher crowns his earlier training with the knowledge of the Good. This earlier training is not all a training of the intellect, as is well known. In the *Republic*, the trainee philo-sopher undertakes courses in μουσική and γυμναστική. He acquires habits, learns techniques, learns to obey, and so on. His training is not purely an amassing of knowledge or even of wisdom; it consists first in pre-paring the individual by the use of persuasion and ὀρθὴ δόξα, and then in introducing him via the sciences to philosophy in its highest form. This "philosophy" culminates in a knowledge of the Good. Thus we may say that when a man attains to knowledge of the Good—the only

[10]*Gould* 215. Cf. Skemp, *Plato's Statesman* 223, n.1.

true knowledge—he is virtuous, but that before he can do this he must undergo many preliminary disciplines. In this sense, and only in this sense, is virtue the equivalent of knowledge in Plato.

However, we may still be puzzled. Why is it, we may ask, that Plato holds that if we know the Form of the Good, we are *bound* to act rightly? For the answer to this problem we must return to the doctrine of ὁμοίωσις θεῷ. At least from the *Republic* on, as we have observed, Plato sees the striving for virtue in the form of the attaining of likeness to God, and believes that to a very considerable degree such likeness is within the power of mankind. We have seen already that since the soul of the philosopher is able to grasp the Forms, it is by nature akin to the souls of the gods, and indeed the pre-existence of souls stressed in the *Phaedo* is additional evidence of this. It is the close association between the soul and God by nature that many Christian writers came to regard as the most hostile element of Platonism. To this theme we shall return. Our immediate concern is to show how the kinship of the soul with God is related to the impossibility of wrong-doing for those who truly "know." To discover this, we need to understand the relation, as Plato sees it, between God and the possibility of wrong-doing.

Fortunately on this topic the evidence is straightforward, and since much of it has been discussed earlier, a summary will be sufficient here. In Book Two of the *Republic*, Plato rejects the notion, commonly held by the unthinking, that God is the cause of everything, good or bad, that happens to mankind. On the contrary, since he is good, he is the cause only of what is good. As for what is bad, as it transpires in the myth of Er, God is guiltless, and man brings it down on his own head (617E). The goodness of God is alluded to again, by implication, in the *Phaedrus*, where at 247A we read that jealousy (φθόνος) is excluded from the divine realm. Finally, the *Timaeus* tells us (29E–30B) that since the Demiourgos is good, he desired everything else to be as like himself as possible, that θέμις forbade him who is excellent to do anything but what is finest. In brief, God and the Gods are, for Plato, naturally good, and such goodness entails the best possible conduct, if such a word may fitly be used of Gods. We are aware from the *Phaedrus*, as has been said above, that it is knowledge of the Forms which bestows on the Gods their divinity. Hence it is knowledge of the Forms which makes the Gods act as they act, namely as well as possible. Our conclusion must be that if a man can attain to knowledge of the Forms, he will attain, as far as possible for a mortal, to conduct like that of the Gods. Thus the philosopher who knows the Forms will be in a sense a god—since he is a purified soul—and will thus be sure to act virtuously. The guarantee that his acts will be virtuous may be expressed as follows:

(1) The likeness of the soul to God is shown by its pre-existence and natural immortality.

(2) Gods are good (and act well) because they know the Good.

(3) Souls, like Gods, can know the Good.

(4) Therefore the philosopher-king acts virtuously.

Clearly the important stage—and that which came in for the most criticism by later thinkers—is the suggestion that in essence the soul and God have equal or virtually equal potentialities. The natural immortality of the soul means that man is a kind of god. Hence his soul, when purified, cannot err. There is always something in the soul which by nature is acting for the best, and if this is allowed full control, sin is impossible. The man who has attained to knowledge of the Good *has*, in order to achieve such knowledge, put this divine, sinless element in control, and hence cannot err.

The kinship of man's soul with God is thus seen as the final source of morality. If this natural kinship is called in question, it is hard to see how Plato could guarantee that the virtue which is knowledge would result in action. Granted the metaphysical principle, however, we may conclude that Plato held up to the end of his life that for the philosopher virtue is knowledge, provided that this maxim be given all the qualifications that we have seen fit to apply to it.

Chapter Three

THE DISINTEGRATION OF THE PLATONIC DOCTRINE OF VIRTUE AND KNOWLEDGE

I

THE equation "virtue is knowledge" meant for Plato that he who knows the Good is bound to act in accordance with it. Such virtue is the highest life for man. It is a life in which there is no clash between theory and practice, a life in which the philosopher is at the same time a man of affairs directing his fellows in accordance with what is good. Yet already in Plato there are elements of dissension between theory and practice. In the *Republic*, when Socrates suggests that the philosopher must go back into the Cave (519D), it is objected that this is to condemn him to a life inferior to that of which he is capable. This objection is brushed aside. Socrates holds that to return to the Cave is just, and that the Guardians, being just men, will go. Yet even so they are said to return as to some unpleasant necessity (ὡς ἐπ' ἀναγκαῖον). The clash is there. One feels that "ideally" the Guardians should not have to return; they should spend their lives in contemplation.

Plato resisted the temptation to separate theory from practice in the lives of his perfect philosophers. Aristotle did not. For him, in the *Nicomachean Ethics*, the man of moral virtue and the man of θεωρία are rather further apart. Moral virtue is described in book two (1106B 36) as a ἕξις προαιρετική, ἐν μεσότητι οὖσα τῇ πρὸς ἡμᾶς, ὡρισμένῃ λόγῳ, καὶ ὡς ἂν ὁ φρόνιμος ὁρίσειεν. Moral virtue is a disposition; the prudent man (φρόνιμος) is the judge of the principle of action. This prudent man, however, is not the possessor of the highest wisdom. He is not a philosopher; he is the man who knows the ways of the world. The true philosopher, for Aristotle as for Plato, is he who attains to likeness to God as far as man can; who lives in accordance with what is divine in himself (1177B 30ff.). This life is purely that of the intellect (νοῦς). Man at his best is like the God who is defined in the *Metaphysics* as "thought thinking about thought." There is no time, and indeed no place, here

158 EROS AND PSYCHE

for the practical, day by day life of affairs. The philosopher is not a
statesman. Hence the question "Will knowledge of what is good enable
one to act rightly?" hardly arises for the Aristotelian philosopher,
since he has no interest in action, but only in thought. Whether or not
the *Protrepticus* of Iamblichus contains large sections of Aristotelian
material, a passage of it describes this aspect of the thought of the
Nicomachean Ethics very well: "We must either philosophize, or say
goodbye to life and leave this world, for everything else seems to be
a lot of babble and idle talk."[1]

At the end of Book Six of the *Nicomachean Ethics* we see Aristotle's
ideal relationship between the statesman (who possesses φρόνησις) and
the philosopher. It is suggested that just as the state looks after the
temples of the gods, but does not, obviously, command the gods themselves, so it is the duty of the φρόνιμος to look after the interests of the
philosopher. The rôles allotted by Plato are to be reversed. Instead of
the philosopher being the ruler and arranging affairs as well as possible,
it is now decided that the realm of θεωρία is too important to be deserted
for the merely mundane, and that it is the duty of experts in the merely
mundane to look after the best interests of their superiors.

In a sense the formula "The highest virtue is knowledge" is apposite
to Aristotle. The sense is that not knowledge, but rather contemplation
of the known is the highest activity of which man is capable. For
Plato, virtue means the knowing (and consequent doing) of what is
good; in Aristotle it means contemplation. Yet the ὁμοίωσις θεῷ motif
has remained. It all depends on the question "With what kind of God
does one wish to attain ὁμοίωσις?" For Plato it is ὁμοίωσις with a
God who is good, in whom there is no envy; for Aristotle, the God has
no moral attributes; he is purely intellectual. Hence he has no rôle to
play in the sphere of the motives of a man's ethical theory. God for
Aristotle is above mere virtue, for virtue involves doing what is just,
brave, and liberal, and to attribute such things to God is mere mockery
(1178B). Again, in 1145A 25ff., we read that the ἀρετή of God is more
exalted than ordinary ἀρετή, a statement which in its context can only
mean that the excellence of God is above mere virtue. This excellence
is pure intellect.

Even Aristotle hesitates over this doctrine of intellect. At 1134B
27ff., it is suggested as a possibility that among the Gods there is an
unwavering justice, and 1179A 25ff., admits, at least as a possibility,
that the Gods to some extent watch over human affairs and reward
those who are most like themselves. This may, in fact, be only a

[1] Iamb. *Prot.* 8 (Ross, *Fragmenta Sel.* 42).

concession to popular ways of speaking, but Aristotle not infrequently makes concessions about the nature of God which diverge from his formal theory. We can hardly neglect ὁ θεὸς καὶ ἡ φύσις οὐδὲν μάτην ποιεῖ. The least we can say is that he felt hesitant or uninterested enough in the matter to be inconsistent.

The substitution of God for the Good as the highest metaphysical entity, and the onslaught on the Good as a unity that accompanied this substitution in Aristotle's thought (cf. *N.E.* 1096A 12ff.) contributed further to the weakening of the relationship between virtue and knowledge as seen by Plato. For knowledge was understood by Plato as knowledge of the Good, and such knowledge was certainly relevant to ethics. But since Aristotle's God is not the Good (for there is no Good in this sense), he can hardly be relevant in the same way. In the seventh book of the *Nicomachean Ethics*, Aristotle does not adequately face the problem of why a man who is told what is right should ever feel obliged to act upon his knowledge. His suggestions for the practical world in which φρόνησις is the chief virtue must all depend either on the carrying out from force of habit of the so-called good acts one has been taught from childhood, or on a mere calculation of what will bring happiness. Why should the Aristotelian who knows of the theory of moral virtue as a mean be virtuous? Without the Platonic Good or the Platonic kinship of man with a *moral* Absolute become immanent in God, the necessity of good action is gone. Mere Aristotelians could quite well "know the better but do the worse," since for them human nature has not the natural associations with goodness that Plato tried to point out. For Aristotle to deny the Platonic Good would have been satisfactory provided he had substituted a moral rather than amoral God. This he failed to do, thus cutting away the fixed principles for an ethical theory which Plato had provided. Aristotle would not have defended a relativistic view of conduct, but he attempted to destroy the design of Plato to prevent it. As the *Laws* tells us, not man but God is the measure, and man is akin to God. While maintaining the kinship with God, Aristotle denies God's moral rôle in the universe. The only defence he can offer is that conduct is strictly not the concern of the man of θεωρία. This is inadequate, for as he himself admits, no man can live wholly "out" of the world, and for the philosopher in the world and the ordinary man at all times, morality needs to be based on a fixed principle.

As far as Aristotle is concerned, we need say no more here. For his highest man, the Platonic conception of virtue as a combination of contemplation and action is rather irrelevant, and without this link the ὁμοίωσις theory loses its original significance. We must accordingly pass on to the Stoa, a school which gave practice far more importance that it had had even in the days of Plato, while it still sometimes used notions of ὁμοίωσις as a theoretical support.

II

Unlike the Peripatetics, who in the days after Aristotle and Theophrastus devoted most of their energies to natural science or to commentaries on the founder of their school, the Stoics did not seem to put much emphasis on learning. Their main concern was with ethics, and in this they claimed to be going back from the over-learned and academic Plato and Aristotle to a man with whom conduct was all-important. Yet, although they were justified in some respects in their attitude to their predecessors, the outlook of Platonic thought affected them more profoundly than they often cared to admit. What Festugière describes as the "astral religion"[2] is influenced greatly by the *Timaeus*, and in general we may say that an alleged "return to Socrates" could hardly avoid emphasizing those points which Socrates and Plato had in common. One of these was the theory of the relation of virtue to knowledge.

For the Stoics, as we shall see, there was no dichotomy between theory and practice. In this they attempted to reverse a tendency begun by Aristotle. Proper theory implied practice; if it did not, it was mere juggling with words. As time passed, this attitude towards theory became ever stronger. It can be seen in Seneca,[3] and with Epictetus one sometimes feels that the master has degenerated from a philosopher into a moralist whose precepts are repeated and taught by rote.

The contradiction of Aristotelian accounts of virtue begins almost at the level of pedantry. Aristotle had defined virtue as a ἕξις; the Stoics objected to this term, for which they substituted διάθεσις on the grounds that a mere ἕξις admitted of various changes, whereas a διάθεσις was rigid.[4] This attitude is linked, naturally, with their usual doctrine that virtue once gained cannot be lost.

The second point at which the Stoics corrected Aristotle was over the question of the unity of the virtues. Plato had, following Socrates,

[2]Festugière, *Epicurus* 73–89.
[3]E.g. *Ep.* 71.6.
[4]Simplicius, *in Ar. Categ.* 8B26. Kalbfleisch ed., 237 (*SVF* 2.393).

reduced them all to aspects of knowledge of the Good. The Aristotelian treatment had not only abolished the notion of a general Good
but had tended to treat each one of the virtues in isolation, as a mean
between extremes. The Stoics wavered a little on this, but their general
view is given by Plutarch. Zeno, he says, held that the four main
virtues are inseparable (ἀχωρίστους) but distinct one from another.[5]
Aristo of Chios, a heretical Stoic, rejected even this slight distinction,
and holding that the virtues were simply knowledge, refused to divide
them. This view was rejected by Chrysippus, though it does not differ
radically from the generally received opinion of the school.[6] Chrysippus'
own opinion is not very far from that of Aristo. Stobaeus reports his
definitions of the primary virtues as follows:[7] "φρόνησις is knowledge
of what one ought to do, what one ought not to do, and what comes
under neither of these heads, or it is knowledge of the things that are
good and those that are bad and those that are neither good nor bad
for the nature of a political animal; temperance is knowledge of what
should be chosen, what should be avoided and what comes under
neither of these heads; justice is knowledge of what should be distributed to each man, while courage is knowledge of what is to be feared
and what is not to be feared and what is neither to be feared nor not
to be feared." Thus, despite disputes over the precise formulation of
the doctrine, the Stoics went a considerable way towards restoring the
relationship of virtue and knowledge.

For Plato, we saw that the guarantee that knowledge will produce
right action is that when a man possesses knowledge he is held to be
god-like. God can do no evil, for his nature is purely good. The human
soul when purified is like God, and hence knowledge—that is, real
knowledge—cannot but produce right action. We have now to look
at the Stoics to see whether they understood that the equation of
virtue with knowledge must, to be significant, be coupled with a
doctrine of the potentialities of man.

As Merki has pointed out, the specific notion of ὁμοίωσις θεῷ plays
no part in the doctrines of the early Stoa.[8] Yet from the very beginning
we find the text τὸ ὁμολογουμένως ζῆν, which led to similar ideas. According to Stobaeus,[9] this meant, in Zeno's opinion, καθ' ἕνα λόγον καὶ
σύμφωνον ζῆν, but Cleanthes interpreted it as meaning τὸ ὁμολογουμένως

5Plut., *Stoic. Repugn.* 7. 1034C.
6Cf. Galen, *De Plac. Hippocr. et Plat.* 7.2.591M (*SVF* 3.256).
7Stob. *Ecl.* 2.59. 4W (*SVF* 3.262).
8Merki, ὉΜΟΙΩΣΙΣ 7.
9Stob., *Ecl.* 2.75.2W. Cf. Merki, ὉΜΟΙΩΣΙΣ 8, Pohlenz, *Die Stoa* 117–118.

τῇ φύσει ζῆν, which meaning was further elaborated by Chrysippus. It will be immediately evident that "living in agreement with nature" is a doctrine that implies that "nature" is the real end of life, and that man is capable of attaining to this highest reality. Such a view bears strong similarities to the ὁμοίωσις doctrine and led inevitably to a synthesis with it.

For Plato, ὁμοίωσις θεῷ means obtaining knowledge of what makes the Gods divine, namely the Forms and in particular the Form of the Good. Stoicism would have no truck with Forms or indeed with any transcendent realm whatever. Their God is immanent in the cosmos, indeed in a sense is the cosmos itself. Hence for them ὁμοίωσις θεῷ would seem to have meant not knowledge of the Good but knowledge of Nature or of God. This ὁμοίωσις θεῷ comes to look remarkably like τὸ ὁμολογουμένως τῇ φύσει ζῆν.

The precise equation of the two expressions and outlooks was probably made by Posidonius[10] and is found in Cicero, Seneca, and succeeding writers in their accounts of Stoicism. The belief is that if we live according to nature (as understood by the Stoics) we are obtaining likeness to nature or God. Provided we know the facts of nature, we can obtain this ὁμοίωσις. It is within our powers. As Seneca puts it in the De Const. Sap. (8.2): "Sapiens autem vicinus proximusque dis constitit, excepta mortalitate similis deo." We may be confident of our ability to possess virtue. We are basically like God; all we have to do is to remember the fact. "Remembering the gods" is the path to virtue recommended by Marcus Aurelius (10.8), and he accompanies this precept with the observation that man should do man's work; in other words, that man should live ὁμολογουμένως τῇ φύσει, in accordance with his best nature, which is like the Nature of God itself.

Such a life will, for the Stoics, lead to a similarity between man and God which covers all that is important. "Inter bonos viros et deos amicitia est conciliante virtute. Amicitia dico? Immo etiam necessitudo et similitudo, quoniam quidem bonus tempore tantum a deo differt!" As in Plato, the difference between philosophers and gods has been decreased to a minimum. In loving God man is loving his best self and encouraging the growth of that self. "Time prius et ama deum, ut ameris ab eo." (Sen. fr. 5) Stoicism is the path to knowledge; knowledge makes the philosopher like God; God (Nature) can only act rightly. It is therefore not surprising that the motto of Seneca is: "Nec philosophia sine virtute est nec sine philosophia virtus."[11] It is

[10]Cf. Theiler, Vorbereitung 106–107.   [11]Sen., Ep. 89.8.

the rôle of philosophy to explain the kinship of man with God which
is so necessary as a firm foundation for conduct.

It would surely be out of the question to suggest that a good God
might cease to be good or that Providence might cease to provide.
One might suppose, then, that it would be impossible for the Stoic
sage, once he had obtained ὁμοίωσις θεῷ and was living in accordance
with nature, to decline from that happy state. When the sage is perfected, he cannot do wrong, any more than God can do wrong; he is
the possessor of all the virtues, for his soul, now that it is like God,
must act like God. Yet the Stoics, irrationally, appear to have been
in some doubt about this. Like Plato, who tells us in the *Republic*
(546ff.) how the ideal state may come to an end, some of the Stoics
believed that virtue can be lost. This problem, which recurred strangely
among the Neoplatonists (cf. *Enn.* 1.4.9) was disputed by Cleanthes
and Chrysippus.[12] The latter held that drunkenness or melancholy
could take away virtue, though why the sage should succumb to either
of these weaknesses must remain mysterious. Cleanthes' view that
virtue is unable to be lost was, however, that normally held in the
school, and indeed, considering the premises of the system, the only
one with any logical legs to stand on.

A further interesting inconsistency of the system may be noticed.
This is the dispute within the school about survival after death. It
might be supposed that the sage's soul must be immortal. For Plato,
ὁμοίωσις θεῷ was linked with the belief that man's soul had always
existed and could never die. It would appear logical for the Stoics at
least to have believed that the sage's soul survived as long as the
cosmos, or indeed as long as any πνεῦμα was left in being.

Cleanthes apparently held that all souls survived until the destruction of the world by fire, while Chrysippus limited this survival to the
souls of the wise.[13] Panaetius held that the soul perished at death,[14]
while Posidonius, under the influence of the Platonic theory of the
tripartition of the soul, believed that τὸ ἡγεμονικόν rose up to the ether.
Seneca speaks on several occasions of immortality,[15] and this is often
put down to his eclecticism, which allowed him to be much influenced
by Plato. Doubtless this is true, but the ὁμοίωσις theory, if it is to be
consistent, almost demands a belief in the immortality of the soul.
Without immortality, we might suppose the soul and God to be
different in *kind*; and if different in kind, then the whole theory of

[12]Cf. D.L. 7.127 (*SVF* 3.237).
[13]D.L. 7. 157.
[14]Cf. Cic., *Tusc. Disp.* 1.32.79.   [15]Cf. *Ep.* 65.16; 102.22. *Ad Marciam* 25.

conduct based on the power of knowledge to promote action will crumble.

It appears again that in the early Stoa there was a difference of opinion between Zeno and Chrysippus as to the nature of πάθη.[16] It was certainly the view of Chrysippus that πάθη, emotions, are misguided judgments. To correct them is to prevent irrational impulses from arising in our reason, for virtue is nothing but a διάθεσις τοῦ ἡγεμονικοῦ. Our emotions are in our own power; we can withhold assent to them if we wish. The "bit of theory" is in a sense prior. In the case of the sage, of course, emotions will be eliminated or the man would not be a sage at all. The reduction of πάθη to κρίσεις—so often held up to ridicule—is an over-simplified logical end of the doctrine that virtue is knowledge, and depends on the theory of man's nature which accompanies that doctrine. Emotions are the struggle that arises in a man who lacks self-control—and self-control is itself a form of knowledge.

Pure Stoicism had no truck with the aspirant to virtue, and presumably none with what might be equivalent to Platonic True Opinion. Men are of two kinds and two only: the wise and the foolish. The wise man (σοφός) and the good man (σπουδαῖος) are identical. Although the path to virtue was recognized even from the time of Zeno,[17] the learner was regarded as a fool until the moment of truth when he was transformed into a sage. This view is similar to Plato's in that it sharply marks off the sheep from the goats, but it differs in that it looks much less benevolently upon the goats. Compared with the philosopher-king, the other inhabitants of the Republic must in the Stoic's eyes be fools, yet they are not condemned as such by Plato. The Stoics would not have recognized the Platonic distinction between knowledge and true opinion. True opinion could only be held by the man who had knowledge, for the rest would be fools with their emotions sadly in control of their reason. The rejection of Platonic true opinion, except perhaps in the case of the προκόπτων, who is in any case a fool, reduces the Platonic tenet "virtue is knowledge" to a pious hope, for the Stoics themselves admitted that the sage is as rare as the phoenix. The Stoics have restored the joint realm of theory and practice denied by Aristotle, but the suggestion that virtue is an almost superhuman quality and has no degrees, since knowledge can only be complete, is a *reductio ad absurdum* of the original Socratic tenet.

[16]Cf. de Vogel, Greek Philosophy III. 169–170; Pohlenz, Die Stoa I.143; Galen, De Plac. 5.1.405ff. (SVF 3.461); D.L. 7.111; Plut., De Virt. Mor. 3. 441Bff. (SVF 3.459); Cic., Tusc. 4.7.14.
[17]Cf. Plut., De Prof. in Virtute 12.83Aff. (SVF 1.234).

III

Very little need be said here about Epicureanism, for the school subordinated virtue to pleasure. It is true that for them the best life is the life of virtue, for such a life brings pleasure in its train, but it is pleasure which is the τέλος and virtue is only a means to an end.[18] It is also true that Epicurus puts a high value on φρόνησις,[19] for this is the means of distinguishing lasting pleasures from the pleasures of sense, but in view of the direction of the whole system towards pleasure, little good is served in examining the relationship of virtue and knowledge. We are aware, of course, that the Epicureans only required such knowledge as would free them from anxieties about the world in which they lived.[20]

All that we need notice for the present purpose is that in a sense Epicurus shared with the philosophers of his time a conception of ὁμοίωσις θεῷ. This appears evident from two passages of Philodemus, one from the De Deorum Victu[21] (where we read too of the wise being the friends of the gods) and the other, discovered as a fragment of Epicurus by Jensen,[22] in the περὶ κακίων. Here we see Epicurus in conversation with the god Asclepius, who refers to the philosopher as a man under divine protection. Jensen himself supposed that this passage was paralleled by one from the letter to Menoeceus (D.L. 10. 124), but this seems to be incorrect.[23] Nevertheless, the two passages from Philodemus show an element of the doctrine of ὁμοίωσις even among the Epicureans. Thus this doctrine appears to have been partially shared by all the dogmatic schools of the day, and can be used to buttress theories of the relationship between virtue and knowledge when they occur. To criticize such theories without taking it into account is facile.

IV

Albinus as a Representative of Eclectic Platonism

It is worth looking at the doctrine of virtue taught by Albinus, since his theories on the subject, though of little real interest in themselves, are of importance as reflecting the general philosophic substratum of

---

[18]Cf. D.L. 10.140; Cic., Tusc. 5.26.73.; Plut., Adv. Col. 1117A.
[19]D.L. 10.132.
[20]Cf. D.L. 10.6 (Ad. Pyth.). Cf. Festugière, Epicurus 34–35.
[21]Vol Herc. 6. col. 1.   [22]Jensen, Ein neuer Brief.
[23]For a full discussion of this point, cf. Schmid, "Götter und Menschen," 97–155.

166 EROS AND PSYCHE

his age—and indeed of the whole period from Antiochus of Ascalon to Plotinus.

In the *Didaskalikos*, Chapter 29, he defines virtue as a διάθεσις ψυχῆς τελεία καὶ βελτίστη. An element of this is found in the "Platonic" *Definitions* (411Cff.), though it is not to be found in Plato. Witt[24] has suggested that Arius Didymus[25] was correct to attribute a similar definition to Aristotle, but διάθεσις is not an Aristotelian term in this context, and the passages quoted by Witt do not seem to prove the point. What is Aristotelian is the suggestion that virtue is a perfection of nature, which, deriving originally perhaps from Plato, certainly appears in the *Physics* and *Metaphysics*.[26] This notion reappears in a modified form in Stoicism, though the Stoics take great care to point out that there is little morality in the πρῶτα κατὰ φύσιν. Yet Albinus' version is probably derived from Antiochus, which explains the Stoic elements both in the word διάθεσις and in the notion of perfection.

Albinus continues his chapter with a discussion of the various kinds of perfection that are appropriate to the various aspects of the soul. The perfection of the rational part is φρόνησις, that of the spirited element is courage, and that of the appetitive temperance. This division of "perfections" is important, and though Witt[27] is able to find good Platonic ancestry for some parts of it, it involves a basic conflict with the view that virtue is knowledge.

We have already discussed how far Plato's theory of the tripartite soul involves a strong emphasis[28] on the divisions. The *Timaeus*, which locates the rational soul apart from the appetitive and spirited, appears to emphasize the division, but the evidence is not necessarily conclusive. For our purposes we may limit the discussion to the philosopher-king. This man, in so far as he has a grasp of the Forms, is akin to the Gods. He has attained ὁμοίωσις θεῷ. Yet even the Gods, as we remember from the *Phaedrus* (246A), have souls which can be likened to a charioteer and two horses. In their case, both the horses are good and work in accordance with the charioteer's directions. With wise men the position is similar. Their characters have different aspects, but their knowledge of the Good prevents them from being composite and hence liable to destruction. It appears almost certain that Plato, despite his theory of the tripartite soul, held that the souls of philosophers are primarily simple. Since they are primarily simple, their virtue, too, is one, and this is catered for by the metaphysical doctrine

[24]Witt, *Albinus* 89.   [25]Cf. Stob. *Ecl.* 2.50–51.
[26]*Phys.* 7.3.246A 13–17; *Met.* 4.1021B 20. Cf. Plato, *Laches* 190B; *Rep.* 353B.
[27]Witt, *Albinus* 89.   [28]Cf. Part One, pp. 105–108.

of the Good. Yet all the talk, in Book Four of the *Republic* and else-where, about subsidiary virtues, about a "mean," or about harmony and ὀρθὴ δόξα apparently distracted the Platonists. In Albinus we see the definition of virtue, apparently even the virtue of the philosopher, broken up into segments, among which only φρόνησις seems to have much to do with knowledge of the Good, and even here Albinus speaks rather of knowledge of goods and evils.

Let us look briefly at some of the Albinian definitions.[29] Φρόνησις is described as ἐπιστήμη ἀγαθῶν καὶ κακῶν καὶ οὐδετέρων. The καὶ οὐδετέρων is not Platonic, nor does it occur in the *Definitions*. Witt compares it with the view of Antiochus, and it occurs in a passage of Stobaeus dating back to Chrysippus, which we have already noticed.[30] Φρόνησις is thus concerned with knowledge of "goods" and "evils." We seem to have reverted from the Form of the Good to particular goods. Witt points out that the treatment of σωφροσύνη is akin to that of Antiochus—thus inevitably eclectic—while that of ἀνδρία, taken from the *Republic*, became similarly quite widely received. Neither σωφροσύνη nor ἀνδρία is defined in terms of knowledge of the Good. The account of Justice is Platonic, but depends on Book Four of the *Republic* rather than on the metaphysical section. Admittedly ἀνδρία is a form of knowledge; it is the preserving of a δόγμα ἔννομον and of an ὀρθὸς λόγος. It cannot arise without φρόνησις, which is knowledge of goods and evils. Yet the idea of preserving a "dogma" implies the loss of the theory that true knowledge is an infallible guide to right action. For Plato, true know-ledge would be eternal; there would be no need to emphasize the preserving of it, for once possessed it could hardly be lost. What could be lost, however, is courage based on a δόξα, for it is a perpetual theme that δόξαι are unstable.

Knowledge, as Plato sees it, is the state of God, and God can hardly lose his divinity! Yet despite Albinus' fragmentation of the virtues and his emphasis on the non-metaphysical varieties which Plato held to be only second-best, we must not forget that he still retains the doctrine of ὁμοίωσις θεῷ as the end of life. At the end of Chapter 27, he expounds the orthodox Platonic doctrine of "human" and "divine" goods and explains the good fortune of the man who possesses the latter, while at the beginning of the next chapter he recalls the consequence drawn by Plato, that man's aim must be ὁμοίωσις θεῷ. This doctrine, which we have seen appearing to a greater or less extent among Aristotelians, Stoics, and Epicureans, was not neglected by the Platonists. It appears

[29]*Didask.* 29.
[30]Stob. *Ecl.* 2.59.4W (*SVF* 3.262). Cf. Dyroff, *Ethik* 82.

in the anonymous commentator on the *Theaetetus* as well as in Albinus. In a sense its occurrence marks little more than a reflection of the general feeling of the age. What is more, a genuinely Platonic doctrine of ὁμοίωσις would appear to conflict with the fragmentation of the virtues which has been discussed above. It is true that Albinus adds the Platonic proviso that ὁμοίωσις can only be achieved κατὰ τὸ δυνατόν. Yet this limitation probably had little meaning for him, except in terms of man's being unable immediately to surmount the obstacle of physical death.

It has been pointed out again and again that for the true Platonist the virtue that is knowledge involves a complex of theory and practice. Albinus, as is well known, is an eclectic. His Platonism is much influenced by Aristotle and, through the medium of Antiochus in particular, by Stoicism. It is to an Aristotelian element that we must revert before leaving him: the emphatic contrasting, to which Witt[31] rightly draws attention, of θεωρία with πρᾶξις, and the belief in the superiority of the former to the latter. In this belief we can see part of the reason why the individual virtues are in general not closely associated with the Idea of the Good. Only the intellectual virtues are truly worthy of the philosopher. Man as a being like to God has been reduced to Mind, and one might almost say that only mental activities are truly virtuous. Albinus does not see why or how this is unplatonic. Ὁμοίωσις θεῷ for him means likeness to the Aristotelian God, not to those Gods of Plato who are active and full of a goodness which is by its very nature creative. A philosopher who put an Aristotelian νοῦς at the head of his system could not, despite all his protestations, remain true to the Platonic equation of Virtue with Knowledge.

[31]Witt, *Albinus* 8.

Chapter Four

PLOTINUS AND VIRTUE

S T. Augustine said that in Plotinus Plato lived again.[1] We must now consider how far this is true in regard to theories about the nature and importance of virtue and its relation to knowledge.

It should be observed from the outset that the word ἐπιστήμη is not common in the Plotinian *corpus*. Bréhier's index to the *Enneads* gives only three examples of its use. While this fact alone is inadequate to prove anything, it is yet a certain indication that, compared with Plato, Plotinus finds ἐπιστήμη of less interest. His normal word for knowledge is γνῶσις, which better emphasizes what is intuitive than what is rational in the process. However, this difference may be only a matter of words. Plato, as much as Plotinus, valued intuitive knowledge, the "seeing" with the eye of the soul, which is a constant theme in his works.[2] If either of them was negligent of some aspect of knowing, it was rather Plotinus, who concentrated too much on the intuitive. But this subject must be deferred for the present.

We recall the Platonic distinction between civic and philosophic virtue, and note that it is emphasized frequently by Plotinus.[3] In 1.2.1 it is pointed out that the Civic Virtues cannot exist in the world of Νοῦς since they concern the relation of the lower parts of the soul to the higher, and the question is raised whether they can therefore be of any real help in attaining to ὁμοίωσις θεῷ. The answer given in the next section is that even these lesser virtues bear with them a certain trace of the higher Good. They are therefore useful and can be satisfying to such an extent as even to mislead men into supposing that it is possible, while still within the hypostasis of Soul, to see God in his entirety. This is a delusion, but the civic virtues are useful nevertheless, although, as 1.2.3. points out, their essence cannot be properly

[1]St. Augustine, *Contra Academicos* 3.18.
[2]Cf. *Soph.* 254A, etc.
[3]It should not be forgotten that Plotinus equates the Platonic πολιτικὴ ἀρετή with Aristotle's ἠθικὴ ἀρετή, and Plato's καθαρτικὴ (higher) with Aristotle's θεωρητική. Cf. W. Theiler, Review of Schissel's *Marinos von Neapolis und die neuplatonischen Tugendgrade, Gnomon* 5(1929)312.

understood save by the man whose virtue is on an altogether different level. In this chapter, civic virtue is distinguished from virtue seen as the attaining of likeness to God and is said to be insufficient to achieve that end. Indeed in 5.9.1 it is shown to be a possible hindrance to the attainment of ὁμοίωσις, since it offers a lesser good which can too easily be accepted for a greater. As Plotinus says: "Others have raised themselves a little from things below, under the urge of the better part of their soul, which moves them from the pleasant to the more noble, but have not had the power to see what is above, and thus not having anywhere to stand firmly have been carried down—and taken the name of virtue with them—to actions and choices among what is below, from which at first they tried to raise themselves." Civic virtues are lesser perfections, and like others of their kind are valuable so long as they do not distract the mind from those which are superior.

It is inevitable that civic virtue should concern itself with action. Its very name implies that it is the concern of men in society. To understand its importance or unimportance in the Plotinian system more clearly, it is necessary to consider the rôle of action in the Plotinian philosophy as a whole. This is expressed in the clearest terms in *Enn.* 3.8.4, where we read: "In the same way, human beings, when they are weak in respect of contemplation, make for themselves in action a shadow of contemplation and reasoning. Because their soul is weak and inadequate for contemplation, because they are unable to grasp the vision properly and are therefore left unsatisfied, though [still] desirous of seeing it, they are carried off into action in order that they may see what they could not see by intellection." A little further on, we find that πρᾶξις or ποίησις is either an enfeebling (ἀσθένεια) of contemplation or its "accompaniment" (παρακολούθημα).[4] The chapter is rounded off with the remark that the relation of contemplation to action can be seen from the fact that those children who are incapable of μαθήσεις καὶ θεωρίας take up crafts and manual work. The whole position is summed up by the opening of 3.8.6: ἡ ἄρα πρᾶξις ἕνεκα θεωρίας καὶ θεωρήματος. Those whose life is given up to action are compelled to achieve by a more indirect route the end which for the philosopher can be directly attained by contemplation.

It will be clear that Plotinus has little time for the return to the Cave. Contemplation leading to ὁμοίωσις θεῷ is the only important end for the philosopher. Earlier it appeared that this stress on θεωρία was an Aristotelian element in Albinus. Plotinus has taken it up and fathered it on Plato. He considers all action a feeble attempt to achieve

[4]Cf. Trouillard, *La Procession plotinienne* 29.

the end of contemplation. Hence virtue, understood, as Plato understood it, to include the philosopher's attempt to bring about the good
life in the rest of the human race, is impossible. Virtue is contemplation, and contemplation is the source of creativity in Plotinus' thought.
Hence virtue will have its effect on the world, but as a by-product and
on a cosmic scale. As Father Cilento has expressed it,[5] Plotinus equates
θεωρία with ποίησις, and the equation enables him to diminish the
importance of both ποίησις and πρᾶξις in their more normal sense.
Θεωρία is the kind of ποίησις which enables man to share in the creativity
of God. Compared with this, the management of merely human
society seems trivial.

Among the Greeks, perhaps the greatest exemplar of noble action in
the world—action leading to apotheosis—was Heracles. Even Plotinus
cannot deny (*Enn.* 1.1.12) this superhuman service, but he makes a
point of saying that Heracles' heroism was shown in practical affairs,
not in contemplation, and that the result is that he is not entirely in
heaven, for although he himself is among the gods, his shade remains
in the Underworld. Because of his καλοκἀγαθία Heracles was worthy to
be a god, but he took only the second-best way of attaining this end.
This is parallel to what we have seen in 1.2.1, where it is only in such
a grudging sense that civic virtue is admitted to lead to ὁμοίωσις.

In view of all this, what is one to make of Plotinus' scheme to found
a city to be named Platonopolis and governed in accordance with
Plato's Laws? Many suggestions have been made about this. Bréhier[6]
speaks of a city-state "devenue couvent," Harder[7] of "eine Art
heidnischer Klosterwirtschaft," and Katz[8] of a "philosophical school."
All these suggestions contain elements of truth, but the objection is:
Why did Plotinus think it necessary, if he was interested in monasteries
or philosophical schools, to found not a school but a city? The first
part of this essay offers a strong reason for Plotinus' abandoning his
normal preference for θεωρία over political activities, namely his desire
to carry out the intentions of his revered master Plato. Given the
opportunity, Plato would certainly not have limited himself to found-
ing a school or monastery. The second would have been out of the
question; the first was carried out in the form of the Academy, but
even this establishment did not prevent its founder from making
attempts to construct a philosophic state at Syracuse. Nor should we

[5]Cilento, "La Contemplazione," 206.
[6]Bréhier, *Ennéades* 1.13.
[7]Harder, "Zur Biographie Plotins," 286. Cf. *Entretiens Hardt* (1960) 321.
[8]Katz, *Plotinus' Search* 72.

forget that the highly practical *Laws* was the last work of Plato's old age, written many years after the foundation of the Academy.

In Chapter 12 of Porphyry's *Life of Plotinus*, which is the only evidence available for the scheme to found Platonopolis, the whole project is described with tantalizing brevity. Porphyry believes that it was the spiteful objections of some of the court circle which caused Gallienus to have the scheme shelved. Be that as it may, the emperor finally rejected the proposal. We may ask what were the underlying reasons for this decision, and the answer will show us more about the project itself. Had Platonopolis been intended merely as a monastery, it is hard to see what objections could have been raised, and certainly there would have been none to a philosophical school. But had Plotinus hoped to found a city, the city would have had to be peopled and a reasonable amount of land given over to it. Land at this time was abundant, and Plotinus' city would have helped repopulate a desolate area. But who would have been the citizens? The only people available for land-settlements were veterans, troops largely drawn from the Balkans, whose mutinous demands were a continual menace to the Empire. These were men whose wishes were catered for as far as possible, and it is hard to imagine them choosing to live in a city governed by a group of philosophers in accordance with Plato's Laws, for these Laws would certainly have put Plotinus and his friends in office. To this it may be objected that a school or monastery would not need many additional citizens—but as we have said, a school or monastery would hardly have been rejected by the Emperor. In any case, Porphyry's words, νόμοις δὲ χρῆσθαι τοὺς κατοικεῖν μέλλοντας τοῖς Πλάτωνος καὶ τὴν προσηγορίαν αὐτῇ Πλατωνόπολιν θέσθαι, ἐκεῖ τε αὐτὸς μετὰ τῶν ἑταίρων ἀναχωρήσειν ὑπισχνεῖτο, hardly imply that Plotinus and his school would have been the majority of the inhabitants.

It being accepted, then, that Platonopolis was to be a city-state, the question arises as to what was to be the rôle of the philosophers. Had Plotinus given up all chance of permanent θεωρία in favour of the administration of a city? Was he preparing to go back into the Cave? This seems unlikely. It is more credible that just as Plotinus' general thought contains a mixture of Platonic and Aristotelian elements, so does his concept of a city. In the *Nicomachean Ethics*, we remember, the relation in the best state between the φρόνιμοι and the σοφοί is that the former run the state for the benefit of the latter, though these latter are their acknowledged superiors. It seems that in the case of Platonopolis the state was to exist for the sake of the school, admittedly an unplatonic notion, though the only one possible for a man so committed to θεωρία as Plotinus. There is no doubt that this concept of the state clashes with the ideal of a city ruled in accordance with Plato's Laws, yet it seems the only solution. Perhaps Gallienus saw the clash between Platonic and Aristotelian political theory more realistically than Plotinus. If Plotinus would not return to the Cave for the benefit of the Pannonian veterans, would they have acknowledged that the interests of the school were superior to their own?

We may conclude this survey of contemplation and action in the thought of Plotinus with the clear statement that contemplation alone is worthy of the philosopher, and that contemplation is itself a kind of action—the higher and only valid kind. If we then wish to ask about the attitude of Plotinus to Plato's belief that knowledge in the full sense of the word implies action, since it makes the soul like God, these are the terms in which we must discuss the matter. Plotinus shows in at least one passage (*Enn.* 1.2.4) that he accepts the motivating force of knowledge. If a man does not act in accordance with the knowledge he has, this knowledge is alien to him (ἀλλότριος). He has not fully taken it into his soul. This is one of the few passages where the word ἐπιστήμη occurs in the *Enneads*. Plotinus is almost certainly not thinking of any of the more elevated (in the Platonic sense) kinds of knowledge, not of knowledge of the Forms or of the Good, but knowledge of particular crafts. In such cases action and theory go hand in hand, or the theory is ἀλλότριος. Similarly with knowledge of universals, which Plotinus would more generally refer to as γνῶσις, such knowledge would only go hand in hand with the "higher action," which is, as we have recalled, a sharing in the creativity of God. Yet just as for Plato the truly moral action must be linked with true knowledge, so for Plotinus the "higher action" is inextricably linked with contemplation. The connection between contemplation and creation is familiar to every reader of Plotinus and has been discussed so frequently by the commentators that there is no need to examine it again here.

Wisdom and dialectic are shown in *Ennead* 1.3.6 to be the link between the "natural" virtues—by this is presumably meant the civic virtues we have discussed above—and the perfect virtues of the philosopher. The natural virtues are here said to be imperfect, and one of the reasons for this imperfection is certainly that they are not closely associated with wisdom. When wisdom comes, the process of transforming them into their higher counterparts has begun. Hence we have some form of that relationship between virtue and knowledge (seen as dialectic) which we have discussed in Plato. The next stage is for us to notice what the "higher virtues" are.

The first claimant to the title "higher virtue" to appear in Plotinus' treatise on the virtues (*Enn*. 1.2) is purification. At the beginning of 1.2.4 Plotinus asks whether purification is the same as virtue or whether virtue merely follows upon purification. He decides in favour of the latter, though insisting that the former is the essential cause of virtue's being brought into existence. Finally he says that the good for the soul, and therefore the virtue of the soul, is to be found in its association with what is akin (τὸ συγγενές)—an obvious echo of the *Phaedo* (79DE). It is then in accordance with this attaining of likeness that all the higher virtues exist. In 1.2.6, wisdom and understanding (φρόνησις) consist in the contemplation of the contents of the hypostasis of Mind; justice is τὸ ἐνεργεῖν πρὸς νοῦν; σωφροσύνη is an inward bending towards νοῦς; courage is being impassive in the likeness of that (i.e., νοῦς) towards which the soul looks. It is evident at once that all the higher virtues are thus defined as mental states which have no necessary connection with action in the normally understood sense of the word.

This conclusion is repeated in *Ennead* 1.4.2, where virtue is defined as the perfection of reasoning, and in 6.3.16, where again the higher virtues are marked off from the practical virtues by their leading of the soul up to higher things and out of the sphere of action. We shall now take it as proven.

We have observed the higher virtues and the lower. We have noticed how dialectic and wisdom are said to raise the soul from the latter to the former. We might assume, therefore, that the distinction between knowledge and true opinion, so important for Plato, would recur in Plotinus, and that true opinion would be confined to the practical life, as in Plato it is confined to the world of particulars. This is in fact the case. Perhaps it is expressed most clearly in *Ennead* 5.9.7. In the reasoning soul, says Plotinus, there are two kinds of ἐπιστήμη, although one of them, namely that which deals with particulars, hardly deserves the title ἐπιστήμη and should rather be called "opinion."

A second interesting passage occurs in 3.6.2. Here Plotinus first adopts a suggestion of the *Phaedo* (93E) that virtue—he means practical virtue—is a harmony. Admitting this, he goes on to point out that the harmony of the whole soul must depend on the harmony of its faculties. He continues that in the case of the reasoning faculty this harmony can very easily be upset by the intrusion of false opinions. It is these false opinions which are the chief cause of vice. Behind this latter remark is all the Platonic fear of the impossibility of testing whether an opinion *qua* opinion is true or false. Opinions are ἄλογοι.

Plotinus, then, has refined the Platonic position one stage further. For Plato (at the time of the *Republic*), knowledge is of the Forms. It is the only infallible guide to action, and action is necessary. Such knowledge is in a sense itself a virtue. Plotinus tacitly corrects this view. He holds that knowledge properly speaking (perhaps he would normally use the word γνῶσις here) is of the world of Νοῦς, and is associated with the higher virtues of contemplation and the higher action of creation. The practical virtues will then be the products of the right education and of ὀρθὴ δόξα. For Plato, the same good act done by a philosopher and a non-philosopher can be called in the former case an act of higher virtue, and in the latter an act of civic virtue. For Plotinus, the higher virtues do not lead men back into the Cave, but out of the Cave for ever into a higher sphere.

We have already spoken of the "higher action" and "higher virtue" of the Plotinian philosopher. It has been seen in what sense "virtue is knowledge" is intelligible in Plotinian terms. It is translated into "contemplation of the Divine mind is the higher action or virtue." When treating of Plato, we noticed that it is because the soul of the philosopher-king becomes like that of God, who can do no wrong, that there is a guarantee that the philosopher-king will not, like Phaedra, know the better course but follow the worse. Similarly, in Plotinus we have met the notion of the kinship of the soul to god, and we must expand our earlier remarks by a discussion of the Plotinian idea that even during a man's unreformed life on earth, even if he is not a philosopher, some part—indeed the essential part—of his soul remains "above" in the realm of Νοῦς.

This notion of the unsullied spark within us is already in Plato. In the *Republic* (611CD) we read of the soul's likeness to the sea-god Glaucus, who by living in the ocean has been mangled and deformed by the action of the water and by the seaweed and other such débris which clings to his body. Like the soul entangled in the body, Glaucus' original nature—that of a God—is not easy to see, yet it is continually present all the same. Similarly for Plotinus, despite the general preoccupation of even the best of men with things of the body, even in the worst of men the divine part remains intact. This doctrine is as necessary for Plotinus as for Plato, with respect to the doctrine of the higher virtue. It is because of the innate divinity of man that he can attain to the higher virtue without external assistance. This theory was attacked by the Christian apologists, but is, as we shall see, essential to any validly Platonic ethic. Its abandonment is fatal unless drastic changes are made in the whole Platonic outlook. For Plato, it is the guarantee that the man who knows the Good will act for the best; for Plotinus, it is the prerequisite of any kind of "higher action." Furthermore, as we have seen in our brief glance at various non-Platonic systems, it was a doctrine shared in some form by all the leading schools of antiquity, a vital part of the *Weltanschauung* which could not be abandoned without a permanent and irremediable weakening of the structure as a whole. Let us therefore look at the doctrine as it is taught by Plotinus.

There are two passages in which the theory of the undescended part of the soul is taught most precisely: 4.8.8 and 5.1.10. In the former, we find Plotinus admitting that other philosophers do not by any means agree with him on this point—though we have seen that to deny it altogether must have meant either illogicality, which was the more usual result, or a transformation of the system. Be that as it may, it is here the opinion of Plotinus that our whole soul has not descended (οὐ πᾶσα ἔδυ) but that some part of it remains in the intelligible world. Individual souls, he continues, are in general taken up with the distractions produced by sensation, and this blinds them to that upper part of themselves which is constantly rapt in contemplation. This part is unattracted by transitory pleasures and maintains a smooth, contented, and unchanging tenor of life in the world of pure intellect. In 5.1.10 the same idea is repeated as follows: "Therefore our own soul too is a divine thing, and belongs to another order [than sense], as is everything that is of the nature of soul. But [above] there is perfected soul which contains intellect, both the intellect which reasons and that which gives the power to reason. This reasoning part of the soul (τὸ λογιζόμενον) needs no bodily organ for its reasoning, but it maintains its activity in purity in order that its reasoning may be pure. We should not be in error if we placed it within the first intelligible world as separate (χωριστόν) and unmixed."

Dean Inge remarks of this passage that "Plotinus tries to father his doctrine on Plato."[9] I cannot understand this comment. There can be no doubt after the preceding discussion that the doctrine is essentially Platonic. In the sentence before that just translated from *Enn.* 5.1.10, Plotinus quotes Plato on the subject of "the inner man,"[10] and the "divine spark" theory of the soul has already appeared a necessary concomitant of the doctrine of ὁμοίωσις θεῷ. Not only could Plotinus have found his doctrine in some form in Plato; he could have reinforced it from Aristotle. It is not impossible that the separable element of the soul is in part a descendant of the νοῦς χωριστός of the third book of the

[9]Inge, *Plotinus* 1,262.
[10]*Rep.* 589AB.

De Anima (Ch. 5). At any rate, the "inner man" occurs prominently
in the tenth book of the *Nicomachean Ethics* (1178A)—and, it should
be noticed, in a passage which is full of Platonic echoes and refers
explicitly to the attaining of likeness to God.[11]

It would seem that no intelligible doctrine of the natural immortality
of the soul could be free of this "divine spark" theory, and without the
doctrine of natural immortality a Platonic attainment of ὁμοίωσις θεῷ
is impossible. And if this is impossible, as we have seen, all basis for
the assumption that the man who knows the Good will act rightly
disappears. On these grounds, Plotinus was right—as against the
"general view" he dismisses in 5.1.10—to insist that the soul does not
wholly descend. He might further have added that to assert the descent
of the soul was to deny the possibility of ascent—a possibility he knew
from experience to be real.

It has recently been suggested by Himmerich[12] that even the highest
part of the soul could be affected by ignorance. In *Enn.* 3.6.2, the
passage he quotes in support of this idea, we read that τὸ λογιστικόν is
what is marred by ignorance. In view of what has already been said,
we should be hesitant about accepting this as referring to that part of
the soul which does not descend. Armstrong[13] has pointed out that
τὸ λογιστικόν is here probably identical with the "discursive-rational
part which in 2.9.2 Plotinus calls τὸ μέσον," the part which is concerned
not with intuition but with the dialectical prelude to intuition, the
part which in 2.9. is distinguished from that which always remains
above. In *Enn.* 1.1.7, Plotinus distinguishes διάνοιαι from δόξαι and
νοήσεις. Διάνοιαι are probably the functionings of that middle part of
the soul that is tied to the earth, while νοήσεις are the sphere of what
cannot descend. Himmerich's attitude implies that νόησις is the functioning of the λογιστικόν of 3.6.2 *qua* λογιστικόν. But it is rather the
culmination of the dialectical process. This being so, Himmerich's
attempt to moderate the Plotinian doctrine of the undescended part
of the soul must be judged a failure.

For those who declare that the whole soul descends, the only hope
rests in some kind of doctrine of salvation produced or given by
external powers. We have already said something of Plotinus' attitude
to such doctrines and will return to the topic later. We may profit
first, however, from a consideration of the attitude taken up by certain
of those who believed in salvation towards the Platonic-Plotinian

[11]Cf. *N.E.* 1166A 15ff., 1169A 2-3.
[12]Himmerich, *Lehre des Plotins* 126.
[13]Armstrong, Review of Himmerich, *Lehre des Plotins, Gnomon* 36 (1960) 319–320.

theory of the "divine spark" which does not descend. To this doctrine these persons were vigorously opposed, though perhaps they did not realize that in attacking it they were pulling down not only the Platonic theology and theory of man, but the theory of conduct as well. It may be objected that the Christian apologists, a few of whose remarks we shall consider, were aiming specifically at the doctrine of the natural immortality of the soul and not specifically at the question of the descent of the soul, but we should remember that if the soul is regarded as wholly descended, as it was by Iamblichus and Proclus, its cosmic status cannot but be affected. A natural immortal can hardly logically "wholly descend." The acceptance of a complete descent is the thin end of the wedge which will introduce the abandonment of belief in the natural immortality of the soul. Hence it is relevant at this point to discuss attacks on this immortality.

Perhaps the fiercest critic of the Platonic viewpoint was Justin. In the opening chapters (4-6) of his discussion with Trypho, he relates how his meeting with a venerable old man caused him to see the fallacies in the Platonism to which he had previously been committed. The chief of these fallacies, in the view of the Christian, is that the natural immortality of the soul leads to the abandonment of monotheism, since souls too are thus deified. The soul is not life itself, but rather it *has* life. If it were life, it would have the power of producing life in other things, just as movement has the power of creating movement in other things rather than in itself (Ch. 6). No, in contradiction of the views of the Platonists, the soul is created, as the world is created, and is similarly liable to death. The soul only partakes of life when God wishes it to live. It is wholly inferior to God and wholly dependent on him. If it were immortal and uncreated, it could not sin (οὔτ' ἂν ἐξημάρτανον) nor (a *reductio ad absurdum*) could it migrate of its own choice into an animal body. Hence it follows that the so-called kinship of the soul with God is, understood Platonically, an illusion (Ch. 4). Justin's interlocutor queries both the kinship of the soul with God and the success likely to attend a search for God under the guidance of Platonic Eros, without the help of the Holy Spirit.

In his *Oration to the Greeks* (1.13), Justin's pupil Tatianus takes up the same theme, though a somewhat more Platonic line appears in his speculations. Tatian begins with the emphatic exclamation: Οὐκ ἔστιν ἀθάνατος, ἄνδρες ῞Ελληνες, ἡ ψυχὴ καθ' ἑαυτήν, θνητὴ δέ. Immortality is not a natural possession of the soul, but this is fated to perish with the body "unless it knows the truth." Yet Tatian continues with some rather more Platonic remarks about the Holy Spirit's being present in the good. The Spirit originally appears to be God, but it becomes clear that Tatian is thinking rather of the "divine spark" which is originally present in the soul but often finds its habitat uncongenial. Not only that, but this Divine Spirit is not present in the whole of mankind, but only in a certain number of those who live aright. It seems that we may say of this passage as a whole that Tatian tries to deny the natural immortality of the soul, but sees no hope that men, without a divine spark, will attain the vision of God. Thus Platonism (perhaps *via* the Gnostics) has returned at the back door.

The next source to be considered is Tertullian. Tertullian, as is well known, believed that there must be a great gulf fixed between philosophy and Christianity. Athens and Jerusalem are incompatible. A less famous, but equally typical outburst is the following from the *Apologeticus* (Ch. 46): Quid adeo simile philosophus et Christianus, Graeciae discipulus et caeli, famae negotiator et salutis, verborum et factorum operator, rerum aedificator et destructor, interpolator erroris et integrator veritatis, furator eius et custos?" This onslaught, though not unparalleled among the Christian apologists,[14] marks a more determined opponent of philosophy in Tertullian than in many of his fellows. Tertullian was particularly uncompromising towards Platonism. Chapter 23 of his *De Anima* contains the words: "Doleo bona fide Platonem omnium hereticorum condimentarium factum." His objections to Plato, both here and elsewhere, centre on Plato's views on the nature of the soul, in particular on his belief in the kinship of a "divine spark" within the soul to God. In Chapter 24, Tertullian declares that the soul could not forget the Forms (and hence needs the help of ἀνάμνησις to attain to knowledge) if it were constituted in the manner described by Plato, for "illi concessit divinitatem, ut deo adaequetur." Christians, says Tertullian, place the soul far below the level of God.

In his edition of the *De Anima*, Waszink[15] pionts out that Tertullian's view on this point is unlikely to have been influenced by the Greek apologists (Justin, Tatian, etc.), and this makes his testimony especially valuable, since we thus see a universal Christian opposition to the view of the "philosophers." It is well known that Tertullian regarded the soul as material, on lines that are Stoic rather than Platonic. In Chapter 27 he tells us that the soul and the body are born at the same time—the implication being that, barring the action of Divine Grace, they will die at the same time. The extreme position of

---

[14]Cf. Justin, *Dial.* 1.3.16.
[15]*De Anima*, ed. Waszink (Amsterdam 1947) 309.

the materiality of the soul is in conscious opposition to Gnostics and heretics like Tatian who, as we have seen, maintained the existence of a divine spark in the soul even while accepting the normal Christian denial of natural immortality. In Chapter 11, the whole notion of a *spiritale semen* is rejected as heretical. The context here is a reference to those Gnostics who spoke of the *aeon* Sophia, but the remark has a wider application and is valid for Tertullian against all Platonic or Platonically-influenced theories of the soul.

The above passages will suffice to show that the Christian opposition to the essential Platonic doctrine of a divine part of the soul which does not descend was strong, but that the seductions of quasi-Platonic positions were great. Tatian's acceptance of the "divine spark" theory arose because he failed to see how, without such an element in its constitution, the soul could ever be saved. In Platonic terms, this is expressed by saying that it appeared doubtful how, if the soul had no natural divinity, it could ever attain ὁμοίωσις θεῷ—the necessary guarantee of the good life.

What then, we may ask, are the prerequisites for the good life? For Plotinus, it is effort and love of one's spiritual home which alone will lead to the attainment of happiness. This is the legitimate result of his doctrine of the inherent divinity of the "higher soul." As against the Christians, who insisted that without Divine Grace the salvation of man is not possible, Plotinus put the onus on man alone. Man needs no additional "grace," since the soul is capable of "saving" itself if it undergoes the proper purifications. To demand a saviour is to demand that Gods or beings higher than man take up a life which is human rather than divine, corporeal rather than spiritual.

Before dismissing this point, we should observe again that the Plotinian position is not only unchristian[16] but also unplatonic. Plato requires his philosopher-kings to go back into the Cave, to become in a sense the saviours of mankind, to live a life apparently worse than that of which they are capable. We recall how in the *Republic* (519D 8), Glaucon, objecting to Socrates' insistence that the philosopher return to the Cave, says: "Then shall we do them an injustice and make them live a worse life when they have the possibility of a better?" These words could almost have been uttered by Plotinus. Plato's answer to them, however, is: "You have forgotten that the law is not concerned to bring it about that any one class live well, but that well-being be engendered in the whole city." In Plato's view, Glaucon is under a delusion, for he thinks that the life of pure contemplation is the best

[16]Cf. Trouillard, *La Purification plotinienne* 200-203.

possible life, whereas the true contemplative knows that the purpose of such a life is to help one's fellows, for by doing so one shares in the active goodness of God and in his work of bringing order out of chaos. Plotinus, in his turn, thinks that Plato himself has missed the point. Certainly, he agrees, the philosopher should be sharing in the work of God, for he possesses likeness to him, but the creativity of the philosopher is best shown not in arranging the petty everyday concerns of the state, but in the higher action of contemplation, that action which is eternally the source and spring of being in the universe.

Finally, before leaving this matter of salvation, there is an important point to be recalled. This is that the impulse to raise oneself back to one's spiritual home is, admittedly, a part of human nature, but it is also, along with the rest of that nature, itself the result of the exuberant expansiveness of the One. The power to return to higher realms is itself the "gift" of the procession from the One. Armstrong[17] has rightly selected a sentence from *Enn.* 6.7.31 to express this aspect of the Plotinian position. Plotinus writes here that "the soul loves the Good because it has been moved by it to love from the beginning." Thus the inherent power to save oneself is given to man in the nature of things, and once given it can always be used if man is prepared to make the effort. Man's existence is always supported by the power of emanation from the One, and the support is adequate for salvation. The One is always turned towards mankind; mankind has only to turn to the One.

We have digressed a little to discuss salvation. It is time now to return to the question of virtues. We have already seen that the higher virtues are to be regarded as purifications leading to ὁμοίωσις θεῷ. The θεός here is originally understood (as in *Enn.* 1.2.1) as "the soul of the cosmos and the ruling principle within it, which possesses a wonderful wisdom" (φρόνησις). This ruling principle is certainly Νοῦς. Therefore we might suppose that since we must attain ὁμοίωσις θεῷ and perfect ourselves in virtue, the World of Intelligence also must be virtuous. This Plotinus explicitly denies (1.2.1) by a series of arguments, some of which are rather strange. First he asks whether, if a fire warms something, that fire must itself be warmed by another fire. To this analogy, however, he recognizes objections, especially that which would state that the fire does not need to be warmed by another fire since its own nature is already such as to be warm, and must be so.

---

[17]Cf. Armstrong, "Salvation," 128. As Armstrong points out, it was Trouillard, in his two books cited above, who most clearly drew attention to the fact that the power of the soul to raise itself is something *given*. See above, p. 89.

A more useful analogy follows. Plotinus is trying to show that virtue must be regarded as separate and distinct from the source of virtue, and draws an analogy with house-building. The material house, he says, is not the same as the house conceived in the mind of the designer, though it is a "likeness" to it. The material house "partakes of τάξις and κόσμος," while the house in the mind does not. So it is, he continues, that we derive κόσμος and τάξις from higher regions, and for us these things are virtues, but the higher hypostases have no need of them, nor of virtue (ἀρετή) at all. Yet it is by means of the presence of virtue in us that we ourselves attain ὁμοίωσις. Thus we need to possess virtue, while the whole notion of virtue is irrelevant to the higher hypostases.

If it is asked why virtue is irrelevant to them, the answer is simple. Plainly the civic virtues cannot be current in the hypostasis of Νοῦς. But what of the higher virtues and the higher action that we spoke of before? Surely Νοῦς, being a hypostasis nearer the Supreme than the Soul, should display these higher virtues to an eminent degree. Plotinus' denial of this supposition, which at first sight would seem necessary for his system, arises from his connection of virtue with the life of the aspirant to divinity, the προκόπτων. Following an idea already noticed in Aristotle's *Nicomachean Ethics*, he finds the idea of attributing "virtue" to a superhuman world impossible. There is no question of the Second Hypostasis having virtue and being virtuous, rather, as appears from *Enn.* 6.8.6, δεῖ δὲ τὴν ἀρετὴν ταύτην νοῦν τινα λέγειν εἶναι; the Second Hypostasis, Νοῦς, *is* some kind of virtue. And at last we are back to a quasi-Platonic equation of virtue with some kind of intellectual condition, but in what different circumstances! Plotinus is now saying that virtue is mind intuiting the Forms within a realm in which all action, all merely moral or civic judgment, is irrelevant. Virtue is no longer a knowledge of the truth coupled inevitably with the urge to bring that truth into an authoritative position in the world; rather it is a metaphysical and supra-sensible description of the functioning and nature of Being. That this transformation is connected with and indeed necessitated by the transformation of the theory of Forms and their relation to Mind is obvious and need not be expounded here. It is sufficient for the present purpose to recognize it and observe its effects. Virtue is now purely metaphysical and a manner of describing the Second Hypostasis.

Hence we must proceed to the consideration of virtue surpassed. In Platonic terms it is impossible to transcend virtue, for in a sense the Gods may be said to be exemplars of virtues, and man, when he attains ὁμοίωσις, is an exemplar too. For Plato, God and the Good are not identical; the world is not seen as a fundamentally unified whole. Hence even Gods have something in a sense "higher" than themselves, and ὁμοίωσις θεῷ does not raise man to the pinnacle of existence. For Plotinus, on the other hand, ὁμοίωσις θεῷ, which starts, as has been seen, with the attempt by man to raise himself to the level of νοῦς seen as the highest level of soul, leads him on till he achieves, through the essential unity of the Plotinian system, union with the One or Good. It has already been noticed that even the Second Hypostasis, the Divine Mind, is not virtuous, but rather is virtue. Virtue, then, is another name for, or way of looking at, true Being—and the One is raised above all Being, since it is Being's source. Hence it might be expected that in the union with the One, virtue itself should be surpassed. Virtue is the Second Hypostasis; it is mind, the intuitive grasp of object by subject, which makes the knower and the known a unity. But the One is above all knowledge. Therefore it must be above all virtue, and when a man attains the mystical experience he will be above all virtue too.

This is precisely the teaching we find in *Enn.* 6.9.11, where Plotinus comes nearest to describing the nature of mystical experience. In line 16 he writes as follows: "He does not belong to the beautiful, but he has already risen even beyond beauty; he has gone beyond the choir of the virtues (ὁ τῶν ἀρετῶν χόρος), like a man who, having penetrated the inner sanctuary, has left the temple images behind him." Thus the highest state leaves virtue behind, for if the Divine Mind is virtue, the One is something higher.

I have suggested elsewhere that this "something higher" is best regarded as a kind of Ἔρως, only an Ἔρως which is not appetitive but creative, creative of being.[18] There is no need to repeat here the arguments used to establish this position; here it may be taken as established. Our conclusion, therefore, is that if the "flight of the alone to the alone" is to be carried to its farthest limits, the soul transcends virtue and becomes a creative Ἔρως. This is the culmination of that "higher action" of which we have spoken above.

To arouse one's virtuous instincts is, as the last few sentences of *Enn.* 6.9.11 remind us, the way to begin the long journey of the soul back to unity with the One. It is virtue that will raise us to the hypostasis of Νοῦς, which *is* virtue. Then we shall attain the φρόνησις of the Second Hypostasis, which will eventually lead us back to the One. This return is always possible, human nature being what it is—or,

[18]See above, pp. 76–86.

more precisely, being created what it is. As 6.9.8 tells us, we cannot be out of the sight of the One, for such a state would be dissolution. While we are always before him, however, and within his view, we often, through our own folly, turn away from him and fix our eyes upon matter or pleasure or some other distraction. When we realize our error and proceed to mend our ways, the path to salvation, as we have seen, is clear before us. At the end of the path is rest.

For Plotinus, both virtue and knowledge are surpassed in the mystic union. This fact should draw attention to a problem in the whole notion of ὁμοίωσις θεῷ as taught by the Platonists. The problem is that there is a fundamental clash between their doctrine of ὁμοίωσις θεῷ and virtue in the ordinary sense. 'Ομοίωσις θεῷ, as an aim, is originally formulated by Plato as an exemplification of the principle ὅμοιος ὁμοίῳ; virtue is seen as the knowledge of the Good and the concomitant desire to act in accordance with it. It has already been observed how these doctrines are inextricably linked, since the guarantee of right action is the true nature of the soul. Practical virtue can continue to be an ultimate aim, however, for Plato, since it means the organizing of the chaos of matter and society, the action, that is to say, of the Gods and the philosopher-kings. When the aim of ὁμοίωσις θεῷ reaches the level of hoping for the mystic union, however, virtue, as has been seen, is bypassed. Ultimately it comes to be regarded as somehow inferior: not in any sense the end of life, but a mere stage. As the emphasis on ὁμοίωσις increases, so the importance of virtue, and especially of moral virtue, tends to decline. The logical end of this process was the antinomianism of certain Gnostic sects, such as the Carpocratians, who, confident in their likeness to God, found moral action irrelevant to their lives. Such persons were extremists whose basic views on morality were wholly alien to the majority of Neoplatonists, but their existence helps to show up in the clearest light a process which was making itself felt in more reputable thinkers, such as Plotinus.

A few examples will help to show this Gnostic viewpoint clearly. In the first book of his work against heretics, Irenaeus tells (1.6.2) of various attitudes of the Valentinians. These Gnostics divided mankind into two classes, "spiritual" and "animal" men, and agreed that the lower class was bound to observe the moral law. For the higher, "pneumatic" group, who are regarded as "in" the world but not "of" the world, it is right to be immoral. The "spiritual" men cannot in their essence take any harm, any more than gold, when dipped in excrement, loses its essential beauty. A merely moral life, according to the Valentinians, can never lead to the Pleroma, but is a second-best which should be taken up only by those incapable of anything better. Similarly when speaking of the followers of Carpocrates (1.25.3), Irenaeus tells us that they too believed that all kinds of action, good and bad, were permissible for themselves. The Carpocratians apparently held that it was only "opinion" current among men which determined moral laws, and that, being higher than the average of mortals, they themselves could disallow these absurd conventions. Finally, in 1.26.3, we hear of the followers of Nicholas, who apparently taught that it is a matter of indifference whether one commits adultery or not, or whether one bothers to restrain oneself from eating meat which has been sacrificed to idols. It is unnecessary to produce further examples; the trend towards antinomianism is obvious. The importance of virtue in the moral sense is denied.

I am, of course, far from wishing to attempt to blackguard the reputation of Plotinus by saddling him with any moral aberrations. To such excesses we have seen him unreservedly opposed.[19] Yet let us look again briefly at his brush with Diophanes as Porphyry describes it. Diophanes suggested that Alcibiades' attitude to Socrates is defensible on the grounds that for the sake of obtaining virtue the pupil should submit to the sexual desires of the teacher. It is worth noticing here that the submission is to be for the sake of virtue—in other words, virtue has no connection with a moral life. It is rather something "higher," something, we may say, for the élite, although we know from the sources that the morals of many of the self-styled teachers of the day were often disreputable. There is quite possibly a Gnostic influence at work here upon the attitude of Diophanes. His attitude tallies very well with that of those Gnostics mentioned by Irenaeus, who held that morals and the moral life are irrelevant to those who are perfect. Perfect virtue, for Diophanes as for the Gnostics, is handed down from master to pupil; it is understood only if the pupil, like Alcibiades, belongs to the "spiritual" group of mankind.

Plotinus has no time for Diophanes, and directs Porphyry to write and deliver a refutation of his views. He learned to have no time for Gnosticism either. A link between the views of Diophanes and those of the Gnostics is that they both associated "virtue" with knowledge, albeit a very different form of knowledge from that taught and beloved by Plato. Yet with the Gnostics, as we have suggested, we see the tug of war between doctrines of ὁμοίωσις θεῷ and virtue, in either the ordinary or the Platonic sense, which in an attenuated form is also visible

[19]See above, pp. 100–102.

186   EROS AND PSYCHE

in Plotinus. Ὁμοίωσις θεῷ naturally has a different value according to one's different conceptions of God. Both for Plotinus and for the Gnostics the supreme God is above virtue. For Plotinus the One is above the Virtue that is the Second Hypostasis, since it is above Being; and since it is above the higher Virtue, it is *a fortiori* above the inferior, civic variety. For the Gnostics the ordinary virtue of morals is not only outgrown but rejected as worthless and fit only for men scarcely worthy of the name. No higher virtue is demanded; the place of virtue is taken over by γνῶσις. In both Plotinus and the Gnostics there are shadows of Plato, but no more than shadows.

In this connection there is a further point to be noticed. When Plato speaks of ὁμοίωσις θεῷ, he normally adds κατὰ τὸ δυνατόν,[20] as though very conscious of a greater difference between Gods and men than one might suppose from his normal attitudes about the soul and the philosopher-kings. This reserve is also adopted by Aristotle, who, in a famous platonizing passage of the tenth book of the *Nicomachean Ethics*, writes that "We ought not to obey those who suggest that a man should think the thoughts of man and a mortal the thoughts of mortality, but we ought *as far as is possible* to become immortal and do everything in man's power towards living in accordance with what is highest in him." The original formulation of this doctrine, then, was accompanied by a good deal of restraint—and even Albinus pays lip-service to this restraint when he refers to the *Theaetetus* passage (176) in Chapter 27 of the *Didaskalikos*. When we come to Plotinus, however, restraint is far less evident. The nearest he comes to the Platonic formula is in a section of *Enn.* 2.9.9, where, refuting the claims of certain of the Gnostics to be nobler than the Gods and by their very nature more elevated than the Intellectual Principle, he says that such notions deprive man's soul of the chance of becoming god as far as is possible (καθ' ὅσον ἐστὶ δυνατὸν ψυχῇ ἀνθρώπου θεῷ γενέσθαι). There is no direct reference here to the *Theaetetus*, but the similarity of doctrine is clear. Yet in a number of passages where Plato is expressly quoted, the κατὰ τὸ δυνατόν is left out.[21]

From Albinus' apparently conservative position, which is echoed by Justin's comments on the τέλος of Platonism as the "sight"[22] and presumably the contemplation of God, Plotinus has made a considerable advance. His aim is to become god. He speaks in *Enn.* 1.2.5 of ταυτότης τίνι θεῷ and, in 1.2.6, there is the famous sentence ἡ σπουδὴ οὐκ ἔξω

[20]Cf. *Rep.* 613B, *Theaet.* 176AB, *Tim.* 90A; also *Rep.* 500D.
[21]E.g. *Enn.* 1.2.1.4; 1.2.3.5–6; 1.6.6.19–20.
[22]Justin, *Dial. cum Tryphone* 2.45.

ἁμαρτίας εἶναι, ἀλλὰ θεὸν εἶναι. Plato's hesitancy in this matter, marked by the κατὰ τὸ δυνατόν, is partly a reflection of the fact that the Good and God are separate, that the universe is not wholly derived from a single principle as it is for Plotinus. Hence, perhaps, arose his realization that even at the highest level there still remains a certain weakness in man. Although in the *Phaedo* the soul is repeatedly said to be συγγενής with the Forms, it is never said to *be* a Form, and indeed it could not be. Hence, since man cannot, even at his best, rise to the highest limits of Being, the incentive not to cast away his more limited capabilities in the sphere of virtue is perhaps increased.

Plotinus' clear enunciation of the possibilities of man's attaining to the mystic vision, an experience which unifies him with the One, the summit of all that is, radically changes the position. Dodds and Festugière have thought that knowledge of God by ecstasy—in a manner like that spoken of by Plotinus—had already been mentioned by Albinus in Chapter 10 of the *Didaskalikos*. Dodds remarks that "the other three ways (of knowing God) all form part of the Platonic tradition before Plotinus, as appears from Albinus . . . where they are clearly stated and distinguished."[23] This seems to be inaccurate. In the relevant passage of Albinus, it is true, θεωρία is regarded as the third way of knowing God, and the progress of the philosopher is described in the terms of ascent of Plato's *Symposium*. But the Albinian doctrine is no more a doctrine of ecstasy than is the Platonic. The question before us, therefore, is not whether doctrines of ecstasy are in Albinus, but whether they are to be found in Plato's *Symposium*.

The relevant section in the *Symposium* is 211. Plato tells us how the philosophic lover proceeds from the love of a beautiful body to the love of beautiful bodies in general; how he next proceeds to the beauty of observances and knowledge; how he finally reaches Beauty itself. He is then spoken of as contemplating Beauty (θεωμένῳ αὐτὸ τὸ καλόν). It is said that when he *sees* it, lesser beauties will pale into insignificance. He is said to *behold* divine Beauty itself in its unique form (αὐτὸ τὸ θεῖον καλὸν δύναιτο μονοειδὲς κατιδεῖν). In this happy state he grasps reality and "begets" true virtue. It should then be evident that this passage gives no support to a doctrine of ecstasy or of the ecstatic knowledge of God *in the Plotinian sense*. The *Symposium* passage describes the advance to an intuitive knowing or seeing of the Good or the Beautiful. All the other Platonic passages which speak of the "flash" of insight, the "vision" of the eye of the soul, do likewise. This is not the Plotinian ecstasy; there is nothing in the *Symposium*

[23]Dodds (ed.), *Proclus* 312. Cf. Festugière, *Contemplation* 228.

passage to suggest "becoming Beauty"; all the talk is of seeing the beautiful or of knowing it. And Albinus in the *Didaskalikos* follows Plato.

Having disposed of Albinus as a precursor of the Plotinian doctrine of union with God, we must now consider Philo. In the innumerable attempts to find "sources" for certain key aspects of the Plotinian mode of thinking, Philo has often been mentioned, though perhaps in rather a cavalier fashion. His influence on Plotinus is sometimes supposed to have come through the writings of Numenius, which were read, Porphyry tells us, at Plotinus' school.[24] Assuming this influence to be real, our problem is to decide whether doctrines of the unity of man with God appear in Philo in such a form as to have any meaning for Plotinus.

Prima facie evidence is against it. Philo is sufficiently Jewish to recognize the distinctness of Creator from creation. Quoting Genesis, he says that man is created in the image and likeness of God.[25] His spirit, though immortal by nature, is only made so by Creation. For Plotinus, however, the soul is eternal because the process of emanation on which it depends is eternal. In contrast to the Platonists, Philo's view is that the soul is created in time. This being so, any doctrine of man's becoming God in the Plotinian sense would appear very strange.

Professor Dodds has long since pointed out that ecstasy according to Philo is very different from ecstasy according to Plotinus.[26] Philo speaks regularly of four kinds of ecstasy, of which only the fourth is relevant to the present discussion. The fullest treatment of the matter occurs in *Quis rerum divinarum heres?*, and arises in connection with the following passage from Genesis: "At sunset, ἔκστασις fell on Abraham, and lo, a great, dark terror falls upon him."[27] This ecstasy, which is the best form of ecstasy, is described (51.249) as ἔνθεος κατοκωχή τε καὶ μανία—clearly a reminiscence of Plato's *Phaedrus*.[28] A little later (53.263–265) a fuller description is given, which is worth trans-

[24] *Vita Plotini* 15.
[25] Philo, *De Opif. Mundi* 23.69. Philo holds, of course, that the creation of man described in Genesis 1.26 as in the image and likeness of God is the creation of an Ideal Man, whose being is purely intellectual (*De Opif. Mundi* 46.134). The creation of a particular man does not come about, for Philo, until Genesis 2.7. Here it is man as a composite of soul and body that is described. Cf. *Legum Allegoria* 1.12.31, and Ladner, "Philosophical Anthropology," 81.
[26] Dodds, "The *Parmenides*," 142.
[27] *Quis rerum div. heres?* 51.249 (Genesis 15.12).
[28] On the *Phaedrus* as source, see Jones, "Posidonius," 102.

lating in full so that its difference from Plotinian ecstasy may be
clearly visible. Philo writes as follows:

The word "sun" he uses symbolically as a name for our mind. For when λογισμός
is in us, this is the sun in the world, since both sun and mind bring light, the one
sending forth upon the universe a light perceived by the senses, the other sending
mental rays upon ourselves by means of our apprehensions. Therefore while our mind
shines about us and surrounds us, pouring as it were a noonday light into our whole
soul, we are self-contained and not possessed. But whenever it sets, naturally ἔκστασις
and divine possession and madness fall upon us. For whenever the light of God shines
on us, the human light sets, and when the divine sets, the human dawns and rises.
This is what normally happens to the prophets. The mind is turned from its home on
the arrival of the divine Spirit, but on its departure returns to its own home; for it is
not right that what is mortal should live with what is immortal. Therefore the setting
of the reason and the darkness associated with this setting produce ἔκστασις and
inspired frenzy.

At first sight, there might appear to be some similarity between
this passage and the description of ecstasy in *Enn.* 6.9.11, where
we find the words ἀλλ' οὐδὲ λόγος οὐδέ τις νόησις, οὐδ' ὅλως αὐτός, εἰ
δεῖ καὶ τοῦτο λέγειν· ἀλλ' ὥσπερ ἁρπασθεὶς καὶ ἐνθουσιάσας . . . .
In both Plotinus and Philo λόγος (λογισμός) and νοῦς (νόησις)
are transcended. Yet this similarity is only superficial. There
are two great differences, the one a sequel of the other. The first and
more important is that Philo is speaking of the driving out of the
human by the divine, while Plotinus thinks of the union of the soul
with the One, a union in which man is not superseded by God, but
restored to his proper assimilation with God.[29] From this first difference follows the second. In Philo there is talk of darkness, in
Plotinus there is not. The darkness is the emptying of the soul and
its replacement by the Divine Spirit, a notion unacceptable to Plotinus,
who would rather believe in the stripping off of those encumbrances
which darkened the soul and seduced it from its true home.[30] These
two insuperable difficulties should dispose once for all of the suggestion
that Plotinus' doctrine of ecstasy is indebted to Philo.[31]

[29]Armstrong (*Architecture* 71–73) tries to show a greater similarity between the
Plotinian ecstasy and the Philonic. His proof depends on a playing down of those
parts of the *Enneads* which teach the omnipresence of the One, and on a misinterpretation of *Enn.* 5.5.8, where the *presence* of the One is affirmed and its *coming* denied.
[30]Cf. *Enn.* 6.9.9.
[31]For further discussion of "ecstasy" and its relation to prophecy in Philo, see
Wolfson, *Philo* 24–43. For a denial that Philonic ecstasy is mystical, see Bréhier,
Idées 204.

Having rid ourselves of the encumbrances of Philo and Albinus, we may feel free to return to Plotinus' understanding of the mystic union. The first striking fact is his empirical approach. Plotinus knows what man can achieve in this field because he has achieved it himself. As Porphyry says of him:[32] "The Aim ever near appeared to Plotinus. For his aim and end was to attain unity and draw near the Supreme God. And he achieved this Aim four times, while I was with him, not just potentially but in ineffable Act." Plotinus himself, on one of those rare occasions when he directly describes his personal experiences, begins *Enn.* 1.6.7 as follows: "Therefore we must ascend again towards the Good, which every soul desires. If anyone has seen it he knows what I mean when I say that it is beautiful." This expression occurs again in 6.9.9, which reads: "If anyone has seen it, he knows what I mean." In similar vein are the opening lines of *Enn.* 4.8.1: "Many times has it happened: lifted out of the body into myself; becoming external to all other things and self-encentred; beholding a marvellous beauty; then, more than ever, assured of community with the loftiest order; enacting the noblest life; acquiring identity with the divine; stationing within it by having attained that activity; poising above whatever within the Intellectual is less than the Supreme. . . ." (Trans. MacKenna-Page.)

These passages bear out the statement of Porphyry. Plotinus describes what he has experienced, and from this we can understand better precisely how and why he differs from Plato. Plato's aim is contemplation of the Forms, the attainment of likeness to God κατὰ τὸ δυνατόν; the aim of Plotinus is union, and since he knows from his own experience that union is possible, the κατὰ τὸ δυνατόν, as has been seen, tends to be dropped. It is well known that, with the exception of Porphyry, no other Neoplatonist claimed mystical experience of the Plotinian type. And Porphyry almost certainly enjoyed it through close association with Plotinus and through directing his contemplation along his master's lines. The fact of this experience's not being repeated may in some way be related to Porphyry's watering down of some of the purer elements of Plotinianism in favour of a more eclectic piety buttressed by borrowings from the mystery religions. Be that as it may, none of his pagan successors succeeded even to his limited extent and, as Dodds[33] has said of Proclus, union becomes for them a dogma rather than a personal experience. Lip-service is paid it, but it is associated with the great men of the past.

[32] *Vita* 23. (Trans. MacKenna-Page.)
[33] Proclus, *Elements* xix.

Plotinus, then, was convinced both by theory and by practice that ὁμοίωσις θεῷ led to the mystical union. Plato, on the other hand, supposed that it led to contemplation of the Forms and to an intuitive grasp of the Form of the Good. The difference is obvious. While the theoretical difference is partly to be accounted for by Plotinus' inclusion within his system of the Aristotelian noetic—the view that thought and its object are identical—it should further be remembered that even without this particular theory to separate him from Plato, he could never have subscribed to Plato's dualism of Forms and Gods, and would have had to find some means of relating them in a monistic whole. There is all the difference in the world between contemplation and union in the Plotinian sense. The latter may be a development of the former, but it is not the same thing. We have already seen how Plato's *Symposium* does *not* describe the Plotinian ecstasy.

Let us now list our conclusions briefly. When Plotinus speaks of virtue in its noblest sense, he is adopting the Platonic notion of "philosophic virtue," as apart from the virtue of a citizen. But philosophic virtue implies ὁμοίωσις θεῷ, and this has a different connotation in the two philosophers. For Plotinus the highest virtue is far above concerns of statesmanship, whereas for Plato it is the guarantee of statesmanship of the highest kind. For Plato virtue means being like the Platonic God; for Plotinus it means that state which leads to union with the One. We have seen in what sense, for Plato, virtue is knowledge: it is knowledge of the kind that guarantees action. For Plotinus, virtue—if we may use the word at all of the crown of philosophy—is creativity, since the One is eminently creative. Earlier in this study an attempt was made to show that in a sense the One is Ἔρως—and Ἔρως not directed upwards. Applying such an account of the One to the present problem, we may conclude that whereas for Plato virtue is knowledge, for Plotinus it is love, that love which is the source of all.

PART THREE

ORIGEN

IT is regrettably true that, in the words of Daniélou: "Controversy continues as to whether Origen is a biblical theologian or a neo-Platonic philosopher,"[1] and it is doubtful whether the controversy will ever be resolved. This is not because we have insufficient knowledge of Origen's works, but because it is a perpetual weakness of the scholarly mind to wish to give labels and definitions and to lay down hard and fast rules. Furthermore, certain writers who themselves deplore speculative philosophy wish to diminish its importance in Origen compared with that of the Scriptures, while "pure" scholars of Neoplatonism go to the other extreme. It would therefore be a much safer guide to go back to the famous words of Porphyry, as quoted by Eusebius: κατὰ μὲν τὸν βίον χριστιανῶς ζῶν καὶ παρανόμως, κατὰ δὲ τὰς περὶ τῶν πραγμάτων καὶ τοῦ θείου δόξας Ἑλληνίζων καὶ τὰ Ἑλλήνων τοῖς ὀθνείοις ὑποβαλλόμενος μύθοις.[2] In quoting these words, the Christian Eusebius is in agreement with the Neoplatonist Porphyry that there was at least some intermingling of Christian and non-Christian elements in Origen's thought. We must without doubt agree with Father de Lubac[3] that the basis of his thought is the Scriptures, but this is not to preclude certain elements of a Neoplatonic super-structure.[4] If we concentrate on a few of these Neoplatonic elements, it does not imply that we are regarding them as the more fundamental; it is only because we are particularly concerned with certain ways of thinking about Platonism and with how later thinkers who attempted to use the Platonic philosophy as a system brought out the latent contradictions in it and attempted to resolve them.

Returning to the words of Porphyry as quoted by Eusebius, we read that Origen was always studying Plato and a host of Middle-Platonists and platonizing Pythagoreans as well. His detailed answer to the anti-

---

[1]Daniélou, *Origen* 339.   [2]Eusebius, *H.E.* 6.19.   [3]De Lubac, *Histoire*.
[4]Cf. Crouzel, *Théologie* 33. "Les thèmes que nous étudions chez Origen ont donc, comme tout l'ensemble de sa pensée, une origine double, hellénique et scripturaire. Il ne les appuie que sur l'Ecriture, mais il les exploite à l'aide des matériaux que lui fournissait abondamment la philosophie grecque."

Christian polemic of Celsus shows that he knew a good deal of his adversary's ground. Dean Inge understates the matter when he says that Origen "knows the Stoics fairly well, Plato a little, Aristotle perhaps not at all,"[5] but even if we admit that he has a fair knowledge of the Platonic systems, it might still be the case that he has studied the philosophers only to deny the validity of their work. Even the great work against Celsus, however, filled though it is with argument and ridicule directed against the Platonists, does not point to the conclusion that Origen regards Plato as valueless and derives little from him. No doubt he finds great faults, being especially scornful of the toleration of polytheism.[6] At times he exaggeratedly claims to regard this as Plato's only error, though elsewhere he finds other weaknesses. He is particularly opposed to the aristocratic notion that the good life is only for the very few. Plato and his followers are, in Origen's opinion, like doctors who are only willing to give their attention to cultured patients[7] and have no interest in the vast majority of mankind. But Origen too, in his own way, has a more esoteric doctrine, as we shall see, and he does less than justice to certain aspects of Plato's thought in suggesting that the philosophers have in mind only the good of the few. Admittedly only the few shall rule in Plato's Republic, but their rule is not to be in their own interest but to promote the common good and to allow all classes to fulfil themselves to the best of their capacity.

The Platonic tradition in Origen's day was not regarded with quite the same distaste, at least among Alexandrian Christians, as it had been a few decades earlier, when, for example, it had been held by Tertullian that the Theory of Ideas was the origin of the Gnostic doctrine of *aeons*.[8] Since then, philosophy had to some extent been tamed by Clement, but in the eyes of the simpler believers it was still a dangerous occupation. Origen himself met with opposition, and this opposition was certainly justified, for his Platonism led him into certain doctrinal vagaries, as was afterwards discovered.[9]

[5] Inge, *Christian Mysticism* 101.   [6] *Contra Celsum* 5.43; 7.47 and 59.
[7] *Contra Celsum* 5.43.
[8] Irenaeus also asserts that the Platonic writings are the origin of this heresy. *Adv. Haer.* 2.14.3; 2.16.1–2.
[9] On the subject of how the Platonic tradition tended to verge into heresy, see Arnou, "Platonisme des Pères," cols. 2258–2390. Among the chief later objections brought against Origen were:
(1) That he believed in the pre-existence of souls.
(2) That he tended to subordinate the second and third Persons of the Trinity.
(3) That he held that all souls would eventually be saved.
Plato's *Phaedrus* can often be detected behind Origen's "errors."

Before Clement, Stoicism had often been looked upon with more
favour among Christians than Platonism, and Clement had made use
of the Stoic term ἀπάθεια in his account of God. The Bible, he maintained, is not to be taken seriously when it attributes πάθη to God,
who is ἀπαθής, ἄθυμος, ἀνεπιθύμητος. As De Faye[10] pointed out long ago,
however, when Clement attributes ἀπάθεια to God, he gives it a meaning unacceptable to the Stoics, who called a man ἀπαθής if he had freed
himself from irrational impulses, whereas for Clement ἀπάθεια means
"la suppression des passions péchéresses." To say that God is ἀπαθής
then is for Clement not to say that He is passionless, but that He is
sinless. In the *Paedagogus*[11] the soul of Jesus is said to be ἀπαθής, and
Casey[12] can properly say of the *Christian* sage that he "acquires
ἀπάθεια which is the sign of his union with Christ."

It is then clear that when Clement declares that God feels pity,[13]
he is not contradicting his own view of divine ἀπάθεια, though he is
dismissing that of the Stoics, for whom "even divine benevolence was
a passive virtue."[14] When we come to Origen, however, we find that
the opposition to the Stoics, whose materialism was an enemy to
Christianity, has grown stronger. Origen seems unwilling to use the
Stoic term ἀπάθεια freely,[15] even with the revised meaning given it
by Clement. In fact, we find direct denials that God is ἀπαθής. "Quae
est ista, quam pro nobis passus est, passio? Caritatis est passio. Pater
quoque ipse . . . multum misericors et miserator, nonne quodammodo
patitur? Ipse Pater non est impassibilis. . . ."[16] Here the Stoicizing
terminology is abandoned and the God of Love is free to be thought of
more directly in terms of Platonism, the only philosophy of the third
century which reckoned with love in any form.

Ἔρως for the Platonist is normally that sublimation of physical
passion that reaches out for the Good, though we have seen traces of
a different meaning both in Plato and in Plotinus. We have seen also
that the Good for Plato and Plotinus has, at the least, certain affinities
with both Being and "What is beyond Being." It is not surprising,
therefore, that these same difficulties are to be found in Origen.

[10]De Faye, *Clement d'Alexandrie* 276 n.2. Cf. Merki, ΟΜΟΙΩΣΙΣ 49, and Rüther,
Sittliche Forderung 65ff. For the benefits to man of being ἀπαθής, cf. Osborn, *Clement
of Alexandria* 105–106.
[11]Clem. *Paed.* 1.2.4.1–2.   [12]Casey, "Clement of Alexandria," 76.
[13]Clem. *Strom.* 4.151.1. Cf. Irenaeus, *Adv. Haereses* 2.28.4.
[14]Casey, "Clement of Alexandria," 63.
[15]Cf. Crouzel, *Théologie* 244. When Origen does use ἀπάθεια, he defines it as
καθαρειότης ψυχῆς ἐκ χάριτος θεοῦ. (*in Psalm.* 17.12,63).
[16]*Homilies on Ezekiel* 6.6. On the superiority of Love to "Apathy" in Origen, cf.
Völker, *Vollkommenheitsideal* 153–156.

Origen, as a Christian, believes that God is personal, that He is personal Love; we have already noticed the passage from the homily on Ezekiel on this theme. Such texts support the view that God is in the realm of Being, for love, if we know anything of it, is in the realm of Being. Doubtless Origen would have accepted this, had it not been for the Platonic tradition and the desire to place Him ἐπέκεινα τῆς οὐσίας. This desire, however, leads him back to the Platonizing phrases about "beyond Being" that we find in Clement. The following passage from the *Contra Celsum* is representative of his thought:[17]

Moreover, God does not even participate in being. For He is participated in, rather than participates; and He is participated in by those who possess the Spirit of God. Our Saviour also does not participate in righteousness; but being righteous, he is participated in by the righteous. However, there is much to say which is hard to perceive about being, and especially if we take "being" in the strict sense to be unmoved and incorporeal. We would have to discover whether God "transcends being in rank and power," and grants a share in being to those whose participation is according to His Logos, and to the Logos himself . . . . (Trans. Chadwick.)

In this passage, Origen leaves it an open question whether he regards God as "beyond Being" or as Being, but he toys with the Platonic phrase, and quite probably is unwilling to appear too lenient towards Platonism when dealing with his Platonist adversary Celsus. Elsewhere, however, he accepts the notion of God's being ἐπέκεινα τῆς οὐσίας with little hesitation.[18]

It is likely enough that Origen's use of the phrase ἐπέκεινα τῆς οὐσίας to indicate the nature of God is a product of the syncretistic philosophy of the day and that he would only use it in philosophical contexts. Normally he would be content with the Johannine formula that God is Love ('Αγάπη). But the two did not seem to be contradictory. Origen probably regarded love in its aspect of *diffusivum sui* as identical with what is ἐπέκεινα τῆς οὐσίας since all *Being* involves *acquisitive* love. We are again facing problems like that of the Demiourgos' motive for creation and the nature of the "Ερως and "Ερως αὐτοῦ that is the Plotinian Absolute. The One, we remember, though formally "beyond Being," still retains certain of those aspects of the Platonic Form that makes each of those Forms a perfect example of οὐσία. It is something "beyond Being" with which Being is essentially involved. It is "Ερως and "Ερως in the sense of *diffusivum sui*. To Plotinus, "Ερως is the bridge between Being and hyper-Being.

If Plotinus took the step of enlarging the current doctrines of "Ερως with reluctance and perhaps did not realize the full implications of

[17]*Contra Celsum* 6.64.
[18]*Comm. in Johan.* 19.6. *Contra Celsum* 7.38. Cf. *De principiis* 1.1.

taking it, we need attribute no such hesitation to Origen. His Christianity already taught him that God is Love, and if some kind of love has been shown to bridge the gap between Being and what is "beyond Being" for a pagan Platonist, it is highly probable that this kind of *rapprochement* would be welcome to the Christian. If Origen had been able to read Plotinus he would have been delighted to find the pagans being forced by their philosophy to turn to doctrines that Christians could learn by Faith.

But if the emphasis in φιλο-σοφία is to be transferred from σοφία to φιλία, then the narrowness of the Platonic circle can be abandoned. Platonism is perhaps only available to a few, but love is available to all. The Platonic preliminary studies are therefore unnecessary; they can be replaced by Faith. Such is Origen's normal belief, and it is one which, according to the Platonists, excluded Christians from the society of philosophers. Celsus is full of scorn for this ἀνεξέταστος βίος: "They [the Christians] use such expressions as 'Do not ask questions, only believe and your faith will save you,'" he complains.[19] Similarly, Galen writes: "If I had in mind people who taught their pupils in the same way as the followers of Moses and Christ teach theirs—for they order them to accept everything on faith—I should not have given you a definition."[20]

Origen wavers in his opinions about the Platonic special sciences and about philosophy itself, as is clear both from his works and his actions, for at one time he is supposed to have destroyed the manuscripts and the materials for scholarship that he possessed. De Lubac is right in declaring that it was Origen's opinion that "Quant à la sagesse de ce monde, qui consiste dans les sciences, et les arts profanes, poésie, grammaire, géométrie, rhétorique, musique, et peut-être médecine, elle est dangereuse."[21] Dangerous it certainly was, if it fell into the wrong hands—as Plato believed dialectic was dangerous when handled by the young and inexperienced—but it might, if used with proper moderation, have some value as a handmaid of Christianity. The Holy Scriptures teach, urges Origen, that we ought to study dialectic.[22]

His view of philosophy as a supplement, valuable but inessential, is perhaps shown most clearly by a passage recorded in the *Philokalia*, where we read as follows:[23] "What the children of the philosophers say about geometry and music, grammar and rhetoric and astronomy, that

[19]*Contra Celsum* 1.9.   [20]Cf. Walzer, *Galen* 48–56.
[21]De Lubac, *Histoire* 80.   [22]*Contra Celsum* 6.8.
[23]*Philokalia* 13.1 (Cf. *Rep.* 533D). In this passage Origen appears to grant even geometry and astronomy some very small value.

they are the handmaids of philosophy, let us say is true about philosophy itself in relation to Christianity." This passage affords us the clearest possible evidence both of the relative unimportance of philosophy vis-à-vis faith, and of the relative importance that Origen assigns to the Platonic system within the general framework of thought, for it is clearly to Plato that he refers.

Simple faith is enough, though certain more fortunate individuals will be able to support their faith by the sciences and by philosophical disciplines. Most of Origen's Christian contemporaries denied that this supplement could be of any benefit to its possessor. Origen, however, placed great value on it, for without it one could not delve into the allegorical interpretations of Scripture, with the help of which, he claimed, a man can proceed further in the spiritual life than his unlearned fellows. And here the learned or philosophic élite which he had condemned in the Platonic tradition comes back in a new guise. Not every Christian²⁴ could follow in the steps of Philo, who interpreted the *Song of Songs* in terms drawn from Plato's *Symposium*. Origen disregards this contradiction. He explains that, in general, Scripture has three interpretations, one literal (σωματικόν) for the "simple" believers, the second moral (ψυχικόν), and the third spiritual (πνευματικόν). Only the spiritual sense will illuminate Faith with complete understanding and lead to a true Γνῶσις or Σοφία.²⁵

It is not our concern here to go into Origen's allegorical interpretations of Scripture in general, for they are in the realm of the theologian rather than of the student of Neoplatonism. Historically they endeared Origen to many ascetics of a later age, since they acted as a support for that inner life of the spirit which flourished in a climate of thought where the creation of Man κατ᾽ εἰκόνα τοῦ θεοῦ²⁶ was particularly emphasized. Doubtless much Platonism, especially that of Philo,²⁷ is involved in them, but we shall not linger over the details of a spirituality which is not our immediate concern. For the student of Platonism, what is important is that Origen resembles Plotinus in his use of the *via negativa* as a guide to the spiritual life, and that he is in accordance

²⁴Hanson, *Allegory* 214, maintains that there is no evidence that the "simple believers" will ever for Origen attain to higher knowledge. For a contrary view, cf. De Lubac, *Histoire* 86.

²⁵De Lubac (*Histoire*, chapter 4, sec. 3), Cadiou (*Jeunesse* 46), and Bigg (*Platonists* 170) all maintain that Origen *always* preserves the literal sense as well as the spiritual. This is denied by Hanson (*Allegory* 240), whose evidence seems incontrovertible.

²⁶See especially Crouzel, *Théologie, passim*.

²⁷Daniélou, *Origen* 164, attributes the three senses of Scripture to Philo.

with the general Platonic tradition of mysticism in saying nothing of a Dark Night of the Soul. This latter omission is lamented by many historians of Christian mysticism as a defect, and Daniélou[28] believes that it proves that Origen's "Theology of Spiritual Life" is only speculation on "the way the mind is illumined by the gnosis." "It is not," he thinks, "a description of mystical experience" which is "an account of the way the presence of the hidden God is felt in the darkness by the soul as it reaches out and touches Him." Daniélou and others lament that there is no explanation of Mount Sinai as an allegory of the Dark Night of the Soul, but do not attempt to explain the omission. The darkness, as Daniélou points out, had already occurred in Philo and in Clement, and it is therefore more surprising than we might otherwise suppose for Origen, writing in a Judaeo-Christian tradition, to have omitted it. As scholars do not hesitate to adduce the influence of Greek philosophy in other matters, however, there seems to be no reason for refusing to do so here.

We know that Plato often thought of the Good metaphorically in terms of Light. The passage on the Sun in the *Republic* is the most obvious instance. We know too that both those philosophers who derived their Platonism from the Master himself and those who took it through the mediation of Posidonius[29] would have found metaphors of Light, but never metaphors of Darkness, used to describe the passage to the Good. Then may it not be justly assumed that the Dark Night of the Soul is missing from Origen because it is in general missing from Plato and the Platonic tradition? It is true that Carlyle's remark "Plato is very much at his ease in Zion" and Russell's addition[30] "while Plotinus is always on his best behaviour" remind us of the fact that by the third century of our era, even the Platonists were beginning to lose their philosophic optimism in the presence of the Divine. Nevertheless no pagan Platonist could have accepted the association of Darkness rather than Light with the approach to God or the Good. That is a tradition apart from Greek philosophy, and it is significant that Origen ignores it. His unconcern with the Dark Night of the Soul is in accord with the Plotinian view that a part of man's soul remains constantly clear of the plane of material existence and proneness to sin. Socrates had asserted that no man does wrong "willingly." Sin is an error[31] for the Platonists, and to raise oneself is, as Henry has

[28]*Ibid.* 297. Cf. Origen's homilies on Genesis, Exodus, and Numbers.
[29]Witt, "Plotinus," 198ff.
[30]Russell, *Western Philosophy* 312.
[31]Cf. *Enn.* 5.1.1.

said, a "denudation rather than a sacrifice."[32] That Origen held such
a view of the basic purity of the soul is unlikely, but his belief that all
souls, even those of demons,[33] will eventually be saved, probably
derives from such a Platonic way of thinking.

Although the means of ascent proposed by Origen are not always
those of Platonism, there is a marked similarity in the τέλος of the
soul's quest. Merki[34] has pointed out that the phrase ὁμοίωσις θεῷ does
not occur very frequently in Origen, who prefers to speak of οἰκειοῦσθαι
θεῷ but several passages show that he was aware of its importance for
the philosophers and accepted it.[35] We even meet the word θεοποιεῖσθαι[36]
in a description of the achievement of the "spiritual" (πνευματικός)
Christian. This, according to Merki, need not mean "Gottwerden" but
"eine Teilnahme an der Gottheit, eine unio mystica." If Origen is
orthodox on this point, a question I am not competent to decide,
θεοποιεῖσθαι means no more than "attain to eternal life," since death-
lessness to the Greeks is the prime feature of a god. If he is heterodox,
however, he is probably teaching in the Platonic manner a nearer
kinship between the soul and God than Merki would admit. For
Origen, man is created as an εἰκών of God, and attains by purification
to ὁμοίωσις.[37]

In treating of the culminating stage of the spiritual life, Origen
continually reverts to the Platonic tradition. I refer in particular to
the mystical and allegorical interpretation he gives to the *Song of
Songs*. Origen is the first to teach that this poem of the love of the
Bride for the Bridegroom is a figure of the Soul's desire for God. The
particular method of allegorical interpretation is largely unplatonic,
and, so far as concerns Origen, is derived rather from the work of
Philo. Socrates' refusal to allegorize the story of Boreas[38] and Orithyia
in the *Phaedrus* shows that Plato regards such a method with dis-

---

[32]Henry, "Plotinus' Place," xxxvi. Cf. Trouillard, "L'impeccabilité," 19–28, and
pp. 176–178 of this study.

[33]*Comm. in Johan.* 13.59. Cf. *De Princ.* 1.8.3.

[34]Merki, ΟΜΟΙΩΣΙΣ 61.

[35]Cf. *In Gen.* 1.26: "Hi qui deum colunt et confidunt in eo, similes ei fiant." Also
Comm. in Johan. 20.17; *De Princ.* 3.6.1.

[36]Merki, ΟΜΟΙΩΣΙΣ 63. *Comm. in Johan.* 32.37. Cf. Epilogue.

[37]*Contra Celsum* 4.30; *De Princ.* 3.6.1; *Comm. in Rom.* 4.5.

[38]*Phaedrus* 229D. See Tate, "Plato," 142–154 and *CQ* 24 (1930) 1–10. Tate makes
it clear that Plato, though admitting the possibility of ὑπόνοιαι in ancient texts,
since the poets were divinely inspired, assumed that where these ὑπόνοιαι are present
they express δόξα rather than ἐπιστήμη. Hence the philosopher need not trouble
much about them. See my comments in the introduction to this essay.

favour, but when this is admitted, we have not shown that the theory involved in the allegorization is itself unplatonic. The theory might still be Platonic, even though the method of illustrating it by the mystical reading of a text is not.

Certain scholars, however, will not even go as far as that. They dismiss the whole of Origen's love-imagery as unplatonic. Here is Inge once again, in the Bampton Lectures. He writes: "Erotic mysticism is no part of Platonism. The 'sensuous love of the unseen' (Pater) which the Platonist often seems to aim at has more of admiration and less of tenderness than the emotion which we now have to consider. . . . Origen really began the mischief [i.e., that the body as well as the soul of the individual was involved in the love of things eternal] in his homilies and commentary on the Song of Solomon."

Is this, we may ask, strictly true? Even if we accept the body-soul dualism of the *Phaedo* which Inge wishes to make the distinguishing feature of Platonism, we should pause before accepting the above interpretation of Origen's contribution. Have we not seen how even for Plato, who clearly desires to raise "Ερως from its physical forms and manifestations and to make it purely of the soul, "Ερως is grounded in the *Symposium* and the *Phaedrus* on a common search for the Good and the Beautiful? Much though Plato wishes to be rid of the physical element, and indeed although he tried to extend the field of "Ερως beyond the scope of human nature when he urged its direction towards what is lifeless and static, yet he was always too realistic to free himself entirely from the physical basis of his theory.

Even more relevant to Origen than the lovers' common search for the Beautiful under the guidance of "Ερως in the *Symposium* are certain passages of love-imagery from the *Republic*. Let us consider for example the following:[39]

'Αρ' οὖν δὴ οὐ μετρίως ἀπολογησόμεθα ὅτι πρὸς τὸ ὂν πεφυκὼς εἴη ἁμιλλᾶσθαι ὅ γε ὄντως φιλομαθής, καὶ οὐκ ἐπιμένοι ἐπὶ τοῖς δοξαζομένοις εἶναι πόλλοις ἑκάστοις, ἀλλ' ἴοι καὶ οὐκ ἀμβλύνοιτο οὐδ' ὑπολήγοι τοῦ ἔρωτος πρὶν αὐτοῦ ὃ ἔστιν ἑκάστου τῆς φύσεως ἅψασθαι ᾧ πλησιάσας καὶ μιγεὶς τῷ ὄντι ὄντως, γεννήσας νοῦν καὶ ἀλήθειαν, γνοίη τε καὶ ἀληθῶς ζῴη καὶ τρέφοιτο καὶ οὕτω λήγοι ὠδῖνος, πρὶν δ'οὔ.

Here indeed we have a whole series of terms relating to physical love, applied to the ψυχή of the philosopher, in the same way as Origen applies the erotic imagery of the Bride in the *Song of Songs* to the Soul in her quest for God. Similarly, a little later, there occurs the personification of Philosophy herself as the maiden deserted by her true lovers and insulted by the wooing of unworthy suitors.

[39]*Rep.* 490A 7ff. Cf. Louis, *Métaphores* 39, 200.

Οὗτοι μὲν δὴ οὕτως ἐκπίπτοντες, οἷς μάλιστα προσήκει, ἐρῆμον καὶ ἀτελῆ φιλοσο-
φίαν λείποντες ... ἄλλοι ἐπεισελθόντες ἀνάξιοι ἤσχυναν τε καὶ ὀνείδη περιῆψαν....
τί δέ; τοὺς ἀναξίους παιδεύσεως, ὅταν αὐτῇ πλησιάζοντες ὁμιλῶσι μὴ κατ᾽ ἀξίαν, ποῖ
ἄττα φῶμεν γεννᾶν διανοήματά τε καὶ δόξας;

Here again the physical and "tender" nature of the metaphors, which
Inge seems to fear, are to be seen in Plato himself. It is inconceivable
that Plato was unaware of the force of the metaphor in πλησιάζοντες,
or that he would have been repelled by the tenderness involved in the
idea of leaving Philosophy "barren and unfulfilled." This latter passage
is moreover particularly striking because the image used is that of
heterosexual relations rather than those of the Ἔρως of the Symposium.
Critics of the passages in Origen who have denied their relationship
with any but the most "debased" forms of Platonism have tended to
do so precisely because the metaphor is from what we should regard
as normal love rather than from the love of man for man. That Plato
should express himself in terms of the former as well as the latter is
clearly important. It shows that the use of such metaphors by Origen
does not in itself put him outside the Platonic tradition, as is implied
by Inge and many others.

Origen is aware that his words may be misinterpreted and perverted
by the literal-minded.[40] He says: "You must not understand the left
and right hands of the Word of God in a corporeal sense, simply
because he is called the Bridegroom which is an epithet of male
significance. Nor must you take the Bride's embraces in that way
simply because the word "Bride" is of the feminine gender." And
again, in commenting on the line,[41] "His right hand shall embrace
me," we find Rufinus the translator interpreting Origen as "Although
the 'Word' of God is of the masculine gender in Greek and neuter with
ourselves (in Latin), yet all the matters with which this passage deals
must be thought of in a manner that transcends masculine and neuter
and feminine. . . . 'For in Christ there is neither male nor female but
we are all one in Him.'" (Gal. 3.28.)

We can now understand how Origen regards himself as speaking
within the Platonic tradition when he treats of love. It is certainly
regrettable that his Commentary on the Song of Songs is only preserved

[40]He is of course justified in his caution, since certain of the Gnostics, who (at
least in Tertullian's view) had some affinities with Plato, were all too ready to introduce Ἀφροδίτη Πάνδημος into Christianity under the guise of Ἀγάπη. Cf. Clem.,
Strom. 3.3.2; Epiphanius, Panarion haer. 26.4; Eus., H.E. 4.7.9; Hipp., Elench.
6.19.5.
[41]Commentary on the Song of Songs, Book 3. PG 13. 163B.

in the Latin of Rufinus, but provided we remember that the Platonic term Ἔρως is normally rendered by *amor* or *cupido*, and that Ἀγάπη becomes *dilectio* or *caritas*, we shall not go far wrong. As will be seen, it will be because of Origen's scrupulous regard for both the Christian and the Neoplatonic traditions that he will be led to a denial of the Ἔρως-Ἀγάπη antithesis that many of the moderns regard as entirely a Christian innovation. But first let us see how he places himself in the Platonic tradition. He writes as follows:[42]

Among the Greeks, many of the sages, desiring to pursue the search for truth in regard to the nature of love,[43] produced a great variety of writings in this dialogue form, the object of which was to show that the power of love is none other than that which leads the soul from earth to the lofty heights of heaven, and that the highest beatitude can only be attained under the stimulus of love's desire. Moreover, the disputations on this subject are represented as taking place at meals between persons whose banquet, I think, consists of words and not of meats. And others also have left us written accounts of certain acts, by which this love might be generated and augmented in the soul. But carnal men have perverted these arts to foster vicious longings and the secrets of sinful love.

Again, later, we find Origen speaking of the inner man who worships Aphrodite Ourania, and the outer who prefers Aphrodite Pandemos. "There is one love," he says,[44] "known as carnal and also known as Cupid by the poets, according to which the lover sows in the flesh; so also there is another, a spiritual love, by which the inner man who loves sows in the spirit[45]. . . . And the soul is moved by heavenly love and longing when, having clearly beheld the beauty and the fairness of the Word of God, it falls deeply in love with His loveliness and receives from the Word Himself a certain dart and wound of love."

The series of passages quoted above should be sufficient evidence that Origen often thinks of Plato when he treats of love. References to banquets and to the distinctions between earthly and heavenly love cannot but show that his mind was drawn either to Plato himself or to later writers influenced by him. Origen, however, being well aware that the Christian tradition was suspicious of Platonic terms, of which Ἔρως was one of the most prominent, writes, in the translation of Rufinus, as follows:

Videtur autem mihi divina scriptura volens cavere, ne lapsus aliquis legentibus sub amoris nomine nasceretur, pro infirmioribus quibusque cum, qui apud sapientes saeculi cupido, seu amor dicitur honestiori vocabulo caritatem vel dilectionem nominasse.[46]

---

[42]*Ibid*. Prologue, 64BC.   [43]The Latin word is *amor*.   [44]*PG* 13, 67AB.
[45]Cf. *Galatians* 6.8; *Contra Celsum* 4.39; Plato, *Symp*. 203B–E.
[46]*PG* 13, 67D–68A.

He holds that Scripture is careful not to use the word Ἔρως where
there is a danger that it may lead the weaker brethren into trouble;
moreover that the word is avoided not because it is unchristian but
because it is too potent and dangerous except for a select few or in
certain harmless contexts. Where it cannot be read with a "carnal"
interpretation, he finds that Scripture is ready to use it, and he cites
Wisdom 8.2, where, referring to the love of wisdom, the Septuagint
reads ἐραστὴς ἐγενόμην.[47]

Origen, however, cannot see the antinomy between Ἔρως and Ἀγάπη
that is so plain to Nygren. He notes that St. John speaks of *caritas*
(Rufinus' Latin for Ἀγάπη) but adds that he does not think that
anyone could be blamed for calling God *amor* (i.e., Ἔρως) instead, and
he cites a passage from Ignatius to prove that his usage is by no means
an innovation. Ignatius[48] had written "ὁ ἐμὸς ἔρως ἐσταύρωται κ.τ.λ.,"
which, as its context almost certainly proves, means "My earthly
passions have been crucified." Origen believes that ὁ ἐμὸς ἔρως refers
to Christ and interprets the passage accordingly.

How is it that, at the cost of earning the censure of Nygren and
others, Origen is able to pass so freely between the Christian term
Ἀγάπη and that Ἔρως which these critics would like to regard as
nothing but grasping desire? There are two alternatives. One is to
regard the treatment accorded the notion of love by Origen as outside
the "pure" Christian tradition of his day, and a dangerous and
wrong-headed surrender to the forces of Platonism. This solution, in
view of the degree of commitment to things Christian that de Lubac[49]
is able to exhibit as characteristic of Origen, we should be very cautious
of accepting if it is unnecessary to do so. The other possibility is that
Origen was aware that Ἔρως might have a non-appetitive meaning,
a meaning that admittedly does not make it the equivalent of Ἀγάπη
—for the Christian God is personal while the Plotinian One is strictly
beyond Will and Personality—but that at least enables it to imply a
similarly active relationship between the Godhead and the rest of the
Universe. Thus, on our view of the second, non-appetitive meaning
of Ἔρως in the Platonic tradition, Origen would be justified as a
Christian in introducing such an Ἔρως into his account of God, pro-

[47]Origen, however, can only find one other passage where Ἔρως is used. This is
Prov. 4.6. In later times Pseudo-Dionysius, faced with the same problem, was also
limited to these two passages (*DN* 4.12).

[48]Ignatius, *ad Rom.* 7.2. Origen in *PG* 13, 70D.

[49]De Lubac, *Histoire.*

vided that he restored the personal element which the Platonists denied. Furthermore he must have been encouraged to do so by the work of Philo, who frequently discusses the Logos in terms drawn from the *Symposium*.[50] Origen, moreover, speaks in his *Homilies* and *Commentary on the Song of Songs* of the Bridegroom as symbolic of the Logos, though in this matter he could follow the Christian tradition without help from Philo. That he knew of Philo's work and made use of it is certain; also certain is that he could find passages in it that refer to the *Symposium*. Neither certainty, however, proves that his *only* knowledge of the Platonic theories of Ἔρως must have come from Philo. There is no possible reason why he must have been unaware of the duality of the theory from its beginnings in Plato himself.

The above interpretation of Origen's thought, the suggestion that he recognized a downward-flowing Ἔρως as well as the normal Ἔρως which is desire, and that his chief objection to the Platonic *bonum diffusivum sui* was that it is impersonal, is borne out by the terms that he employs to describe God and His Goodness. Besides the usual phrases ἡ ἑνάς and τὸ ἀγαθόν, we find Origen speaking of God as ἡ ἀγαθότης, which, as has been suggested, is probably a conscious contrast to the impersonal Neoplatonic τὸ ἀγαθόν.[51] We should compare Origen's use of ὁ ὤν in preference to the impersonal τὸ ὄν.[52] Furthermore, the downward-flowing love of God is often described by Origen as φιλανθρωπία, almost certainly because, although the few "spiritual" Christians would not have rejected or misunderstood the word Ἔρως if it were used in this context, the simple-minded brethren would have tended to assume from it a God of desire and would thus have been open to the influence of Gnosticism.[53] Certainly Origen's φιλανθρωπία is more than the Plotinian Ἔρως, in that it implies not merely cosmic love of self manifested in creation, but the love of a Saviour. Nevertheless it includes the cosmic Ἔρως.

[50]Cf. Billings, *Philo Judaeus* 40–41 for a list of passages showing Philo's use of the *Symposium*.
[51]The earliest references LSJ can find for ἀγαθότης are from the Bible and Philo. Cf. LXX *Wis.* 1.1; Philo, *Leg. All.* 1.59. It occurs once in Plotinus (*Enn.* 4.8.6) and in Alex. Aphrod., *in Met.* 695.37. Later it came to be used as an expression of respect: ἡ σὴ ἀγαθότης, Your Excellency (Jul. *Ep.* 12.86). This usage suggests that ἡ ἀγαθότης is less impersonal than τὸ ἀγαθόν. The earlier examples suggest its popularity with devotees of a *personal* God.   [52]Cf. *De Princ.* 1.1.6.
[53]*Contra Celsum* 4.17. Cf. φιλανθρωπία and ἀγαθότης in Athanasius (*Or. de inc. verb.* 1. *PG* 25. 97C). For φιλανθρωπία see in general Petré, *Caritas* 209, and for the possible influence of φιλανθρωπία in Plutarch, Koch, *Pronoia* 239.

It is tempting to suppose that this similarity between the views of Origen and Plotinus on one of the aspects of ᾽Ερως can be traced directly to a common source, namely the doctrines of Ammonius Saccas. Others who have found similarities between the Neoplatonist and the Christian have had recourse to this elusive master to explain the connection and thus to strengthen their case.[54] This procedure is, in view of our scanty knowledge of the teachings of Ammonius, of doubtful value; and in any case the work of Daniélou[55] has made it plain that it is impossible to come to conclusions about the common origins of specific teachings that emanated from particular philosophical circles in Alexandria. We shall, therefore, be satisfied to believe that frequently Origen and the Neoplatonists were dealing with the same or similar problems, and thus that each was likely to make use of any advances he considered his contemporaries to have made. Origen, we may be sure, would have been unsatisfied with the ᾽Ερως that is God in the system of Plotinus, but in view of the fact that[56] "He was always reading Plato," and that "The works of Numenius, Cronius, Apollophanes, Longinus, Moderatus, Nicostratus and experts in the Pythagorean philosophy were his mainstay," it is most unlikely that he would have totally neglected any Platonic theory of ᾽Ερως, since such theories were fundamental to the whole Platonic view of the world. Furthermore, although Origen was dead before Plotinus committed his theories to writing, the fact that the two faced similar problems lends credence to the possibility of their seeing similar solutions.

Here it may be noted that the comparison of downward-flowing ᾽Ερως in Origen's and Plotinus' doctrines of God and the One is given added plausibility by another common feature in their theories: the idea of creation by contemplation. That this is a Plotinian doctrine does not need to be proved here, as it is evident from the *Enneads*; that Origen uses it is his Trinitarian theology, however, is additional proof of the importance he attached to Platonist views of the One and Νοῦς. The most important passage is from his *Commentary on St. John's Gospel*, and runs as follows:[57]

᾽Αληθινὸς οὖν θεὸς ὁ θεός [God], οἱ δὲ κατ᾽ ἐκεῖνον μορφούμενοι θεοὶ ὡς εἰκόνες [the angels?] πρωτοτύπου· ἀλλὰ πάλιν τῶν πλειόνων εἰκόνων ἡ ἀρχέτυπος εἰκὼν ὁ πρὸς τὸν θεόν ἐστι λόγος, ὃς ἐν ἀρχῇ ἦν, τῷ εἶναι πρὸς τὸν θεὸν ἀεὶ μένων θεός, οὐκ ἂν

---

[54]Cf. Wolfson, *Church Fathers* 254. Langerbeck, "Ammonius Saccas," 67–74. An accurate estimate of the small amount of knowledge we have of Ammonius is given by Dodds, "Numenius," 24–32.

[55]Daniélou, *Origen* 78.

[56]Eusebius *H.E.* 6.19.8.   [57]*Comm. in Johan.* 2.2 Preuschen. ed. 55.

δ'αὐτὸ ἐσχηκὼς εἰ μὴ πρὸς θεὸν ἦν, καὶ οὐκ ἂν μείνας θεός, εἰ μὴ παρέμενε τῇ ἀδια-
λείπτῳ θέᾳ τοῦ πατρικοῦ βάθους.

As Arnou has said,[58] Origen's interpretation of the text ὁ λόγος ἦν
πρὸς τὸν Θεόν is that "Il [le Logos] ne continuerait pas à être Dieu, s'il
ne persévérait pas dans sa contemplation." For Origen, the Logos is
continually turned towards God in contemplation and thus from all
time receives the illumination of the Divinity that is "Ερως diffusivum
sui. That Origen—perhaps unwittingly—is here teaching a view which
may rightly be termed "subordinationism" by orthodox Christians is
clear; it is also clear, however, that his view is Platonist, so much so
that it proved unacceptable.

We remember from the seventh book of the Republic how careful
Plato tries to be in his choice of those who are fitted to study dialectic,
which is in his view the highest knowledge. We remember too how in
the Symposium, before Socrates' description of that noblest form of
"Ερως which has been revealed to him by Diotima, we hear accounts
of the various inferior versions that commend themselves to lesser
men like Pausanias, Phaedrus, and Eryximachus. If we combine these
two observations, we can conclude that what Plato is looking for is
the best possible love directed to the best possible end, which is exactly
the position of Origen in the Commentary on the Song of Songs.[59]
"When the passion of love is directed to diverse skills, whether manual
crafts or occupations needful only for this present life—the art of
wrestling, for example, or of running—or even when it is expended on
the study of geometry or music or arithmetic or similar branches of
learning, neither in that case does it seem to me to be used laudably.
The only laudable love is that which is directed to God or to the virtues
of the soul."

These words may seem a denial of the Platonic position, and so they
are, if that position be taken to extremes. We have noticed how Origen
regards the Platonic "preliminary studies" as of little value, and from
this passage we can see why. They divert the mind from higher things,
just as, in Plato's opinion, the Pythagoreans[60] tended to be distracted
from the true value of harmony, for example, by an excessive concen-
tration on the technicalities of that science treated as ends in themselves. Origen's complaint here is similar to that of Aristotle[61] that
for "present-day" philosophers philosophy has in fact turned into
mathematics, although still remaining in theory the end to which all

[58]Arnou, "Le thème néoplatonicien," 127.
[59]PG 13, 71BC.
[60]Rep. 7, 531A ff.   [61]Arist. Met. A 992B 1.

the preliminary studies are directed. Again, Origen's position is similar
to that which Plato himself would have taken up towards anyone who
was content that love should remain at the inferior or unreal grades
of reality and waste itself there, in company perhaps with the love of
Pausanias or Phaedrus, and refuse to proceed to the World of Forms
and to the Good. The close of this quotation puts Origen at one with
the Socrates of the *Phaedo*, for whom nothing was so important as
the improvement of the soul by those purifications which were to act
as a μελέτη θανάτου.

We have seen what Origen makes of the term Ἔρως and how he
applies it to his Christianized system. We have seen too how certain
critics have stigmatized his treatment as "erotic" mysticism—meaning
this in a pejorative sense—and how they have regarded it as unplatonic.
Origen, however, does not seem to realize that his work is a specifically
new departure from the philosophical tradition. He shows its kinship
with the *Symposium*, and we have here related it generally to a non-
appetitive view of Ἔρως—a view more akin to the Christian Ἀγάπη.
What the critics of Origen's method should, perhaps, have studied in
more detail, if they wished to prove him unplatonic, is not the emotion
of love, with its physical basis, which he says must fill the soul of the
Bride, but the nature of the object of that love. Here the difference
between Plato and Origen is that, whereas a love of Wisdom or of the
Form of the Good or of the One is a love of what is impersonal, lifeless,
and essentially unresponsive, Origen's Bridegroom is personal. Thus
what the critics of Origen are in fact suggesting is that the love he seeks
to inspire in the soul of the Christian who follows his teachings is
insufficiently sublimated, whereas we have already suggested that one
of the disadvantages of Plato's system was that in demanding love
of the Forms he was making a demand which, if it was not impossible
for all, at least was beyond the capacities of average mortals.

Origen, on the other hand, was generally aware that his creed is
aimed at humanity as a whole, not at a mere élite, and he knew that
whatever Plato's hopes may have been for gaining large-scale support
for his projected reforms of mankind, he had failed to achieve it. He
mentions this point continually during his retort to the charges of
Celsus, in passages of which the following is typical: "If I may venture
to say so, the beautiful and refined style of Plato and those who write
similarly benefits but a few, if indeed it benefits anybody: whereas
that of teachers and writers with a meaner style which was practical
and exactly suited to the multitude has benefitted many. At any rate,
Plato can only be seen in the hands of men who seem to be learned,
while Epictetus is admired even by common folk, who have an inclina-

tion to receive benefit because they perceive the improvement which his words effect in their lives"[62] (Trans. Chadwick).

Plato's style is exclusive, complains Origen. Something more realistic, more in touch with the vast mass of humanity, would have been more appropriate. Origen's correction of the doctrine of Ἔρως is in line with this general criticism. Admittedly, building on the dogmatic foundation of a personal God, he had little alternative to adapting Ἔρως as he did. The fact that he discusses it, however, is a proof both of the strength of the Platonic tradition and of the importance of it to Origen, and at the same time an indication of some weight that all Ἔρως need not be fundamentally antipathetic to Christianity, at least in the view of the Alexandrians.

Thus in brief, though admitting with Inge and the others that Origen introduced certain beliefs into Christianity that in the wrong hands might have become both unplatonic and unchristian, we hope to have shown that the beliefs and theories themselves are at least not entirely unplatonic. Whether they are unchristian is outside the scope of this essay, but that they are both Platonic in spirit and indeed in a sense an exposition and elaboration of Plato himself, is a proposition worthy of reconsideration.[63] To condemn Origen because his doctrine of Ἔρως might be misused by others is equivalent to condemning Plato's *Symposium* because the unworthy teacher Diophanes[64] attempted to derive from it a specious defence of the immorality of Alcibiades. The disgust felt at this performance by Plotinus was directed wholly towards Diophanes; no notion of blame is attached to Plato. Nor is there reason to attach any to Origen.

Besides the *Homilies* and *Commentary on the Song of Songs*, there are other passages in Origen which speak of the culmination of the spiritual life. From our present point of view, perhaps the most important is in one of his *Homilies on Numbers*, where we find the notion of ἔκστασις occurring. The text, unfortunately only given in the Latin of Rufinus, is:[65]

Inde venitur Thara, quod apud nos intellegitur contemplatio stuporis. Non possumus in Latina lingua uno sermone exprimere verbum Graecum, quod illi ἔκστασιν vocant, id est, cum pro alicuius magnae rei admiratione obstupescit animus. Hoc est ergo, quod dicit, contemplatio stuporis, cum in agnitione magnarum et admirabilium rerum mens attonita stupet.

---

[62]*Contra Celsum* 6.2. Cf. Plutarch, *De Alexandri Magni Fortuna vel Virtute* 1, 328E.
[63]The Platonism of Origen, perhaps overemphasized by Bigg and De Faye, has been seriously overlooked in recent works, especially by De Lubac.
[64]Porphyry, *Vita Plotini* 15.
[65]*Homilies on Numbers* 27.12.

The meaning and implications of this passage are much disputed. Völker[66] believes that it implies that Origen himself experienced this ἔκστασις and that its meaning is similar to the notion of transcendence of Self that we find in Plotinus. These claims are disputed by Puech[67] and others. Puech holds that ἔκστασις in Philo can mean either an excessive amazement of the mind, or a complete submergence of that mind such as would be entailed by the transcendence of the νοῦς ἴδιος.[68] The latter meaning is more like, though very far from identical with, the ἔκστασις of Plotinus, but according to Puech, with whom most commentators are in agreement, it is the former that applies to Origen.

Daniélou writes:[69] "Origen stays in the sphere of the gnosis. . . . Or at any rate, Origen's description of the mystical life stops short at the gnosis"—and that is perhaps as far as we can go with certainty. Völker, indeed, points out a passage from the *Commentary on St. John*[70] where Origen speaks of "divine drunkenness," another phrase that has Plotinian echoes. Plotinus, we know, achieved transcendence of the Self on at least four occasions, so that when he speaks of this feeling or experience of being "divinely drunk," we can be more certain about the nature of the ἔκστασις to which he refers, but in the case of Origen the problem is more difficult to resolve. Origen does not speak of "drunkenness" as a transcendence of the self but as a withdrawal from human to divine things. We must, to avoid going beyond the evidence, conclude that the *contemplatio stuporis* is not ecstasy in the normal sense of the word, but is probably a precursor of it. Yet Origen's refusal to give a description of ecstasy itself may well be the consequence of a view that such blessedness can only be experienced, never described. Origen was always a "didaskalos," as Daniélou says. It was not his business to attempt to describe the ineffable heights to which the well-instructed could attain. That was a private matter between the Bridegroom and the Bride, between the Logos and the Soul of the believer.

[66]Völker, *Vollkommenheitsideal* esp. 68 ff.
[67]Puech, "Un livre récent," 508 ff.
[68]Daniélou, *Origen* 302. See above, pp. 188–189.
[69]*Ibid*. 303. See also Crouzel, *Connaissance* 527–535.
[70]*Comm. in Johan.* 1.30 Preuschen ed. 37.

EPILOGUE

Starting with hints and problems in the Platonic text, Plotinus and Origen, as we have seen, widened the scope of Ἔρως to denote a downward as well as an upward force. This process, so well adapted to Christianity, was continued in the following centuries as both Christian and pagan Neoplatonists further shaped the doctrine to suit their own interpretations. So far as we have followed its history, God's Ἔρως has been connected with creation rather than with salvation. In later times, while the creation-motif was maintained and expanded in cosmological discussion, salvationist ideas, fundamental to Christianity, made their way into pagan Neoplatonism too, Plotinus' cautions on the subject notwithstanding.

The notion of creative Ἔρως, deriving from Plato's *Symposium* and even earlier, became confounded with that of Christian Ἀγάπη, as Nygren[1] shows, among the Gnostics. These, however, interpreted Ἀγάπη as the lowest form of Ἔρως and not the most ennobling, and were therefore disowned by orthodox Christians as well as by pagans. None the less, by their treatment of Ἀγάπη as a cosmic force of creation, coupled with the doctrine of downward-flowing Ἔρως or Ἀγάπη in Origen, the Christian Gnostics certainly kept creative Ἔρως before the minds of men. Their doctrine, with its similarity to pagan Neoplatonism, involved one great danger, into which Origen and many others fell. It invited too close an equation of the Second Person of the Christian Trinity with the Second Hypostasis of Neoplatonism, and the corollary of subordinationism. For Origen, where the Father is αὐτόθεος or ὁ θεός, the Son is θεός; where the Father is ἄναρχος ἀρχή, the Son is ὁ δεύτερος θεός.[2] Like the Plotinian Νοῦς, Origen's Christ-Logos stands between the uncreated One and the created Many.[3] The danger

---

[1]Nygren, *Eros* 303–310.

[2]*Contra Celsum* 5.39. For αὐτόθεος and θεός, cf. *Comm. in Johan.* 2.2 Preuschen ed. 54.

[3]*De Princ.* 2.2. The Logos is an εἰκών, and for the Platonists this word implies an inferiority to the παράδειγμα. For fuller textual evidence on Origen's subordinationism, see De Faye, *Origène* vol. 3, 122. Cf. Daniélou, *Origen* 254–257. Daniélou

to Christianity inherent in the adopting of Neoplatonist views of creative emanation is here evident.[4]

The trouble did not end with Origen. All through the fourth century the disputes between the orthodox and the subordinationists continues. Arius, the arch-heretic, went much further than Origen in his subordination of the Second Person of the Trinity to the First. Where Origen had insisted, ὁ σωτὴρ οὐ κατὰ μετουσίαν, ἀλλα κατ' οὐσίαν ἐστι Θεός, and did not envisage a time when the Logos had not existed, Arius thought that the Son attained to divinity by participation,[5] that there was a time before He came into being,[6] and that He was created from nothing.[7] Although Arius probably had little connection with pagan Neoplatonism, he may have been influenced by Origen. The orthodox formulation of Trinitarian doctrine as μία οὐσία, τρεῖς ὑποστάσεις came out strongly against theories such as the Plotinian doctrine of emanation, with its application of οὐσία to the Second and Third Hypostases and not to the First, which is superior to all Being.

The creative Ἔρως of the emanation theory could not survive in orthodox Christianity, unless and until it was cleared of its subordinationist tendencies. In pagan Neoplatonism, however, the direction taken tentatively perhaps, but still recognizably, by Plotinus was followed by his successors. Ἔρως is plainly seen as descending from the higher to the lower hypostases as well as in its original rôle as the upward tendency. Naturally, Nygren wishes to find reasons outside the Neoplatonist tradition for this teaching.[8] He declares rightly that Proclus has been influenced both by Christian Ἀγάπη and by the ancient belief in Providence, and though admitting Plotinus' dictum that "the higher cares for the lower and adorns it," he states dogmatically that since this idea "is never related by Plotinus to the idea of Eros," it "therefore could not influence it."

It seems to have been one of the achievements of Iamblichus to have emphasized the triad μόνη, πρόοδος, and ἐπιστροφή in Neopla-

---

suggests a comparison with Albinus. See also Crouzel, *Théologie* 111–120, where the relationship between Origen's subordinationism and his struggle against the Sabellians is stressed.

[4]For Νοῦς as εἰκών in Plotinus, cf. *Enn.* 5.1.6.7; for the One as ἀρχέτυπος, see *Enn.* 6.8.18.

[5]Athanasius, *Or. contra Arianos* 1.9. (*PG.* 26.28C-32A.).

[6]Socrates, *Hist. Eccl.* 1.5. Arius' view is a direct denial of Origen's as expressed in *De Princ.* 4.4.1.

[7]For this view as a revival of the teaching of Philo, see Wolfson, *Church Fathers* 293, 585.

[8]Nygren, *Eros* 569.

tonism.[9] These terms denote the "remaining, procession, and return" involved in Plotinian theory. The One, for example, while itself "remaining," is the continuous cause of Νοῦς, which thus exists by "procession" and at the same time seeks to "return" to its origin in contemplation. The expression of this theory in formal terms by Iamblichus led to its use in other ways than as an account of emanation and contemplation. It became a general law, with which the whole of reality was involved. In particular it came to be applied to Ἔρως.

We have discussed in detail the Plotinian Ἔρως as both an ascending and a creative force. If this doctrine be treated in terms of the Iamblichean triad described above, the version of Proclus results. Upward and downward loves are linked in a great chain of Ἔρως (ἡ ἐρωτικὴ σειρά).[10] The upward Ἔρως is the normal Platonic love, but Nygren at least professes himself almost stupefied at the descending.[11] "Proclus," he remarks, "says something almost incredible in a Platonist," when he writes ἄνωθεν οὖν ὁ ἔρως ἀπὸ τῶν νοητῶν μέχρι τῶν ἐγκοσμίων φοιτᾷ, πάντα ἐπιστρέφων ἐπὶ τὸ θεῖον κάλλος.[12] If our general interpretation of Ἔρως in Platonism is correct, the shock to Nygren is unnecessary, for Proclus is only systematizing the hints of his predecessors. The phrase Proclus uses for downward-flowing love is Ἔρως προνοητικός, as contrasted with the Ἔρως ἐπιστρεπτικός which leads back to the One. In Proclus' system every god or henad, for example, perfects its products by making them into unities. Such unification shows the gods as gentle and reveals their providential love.[13] Nygren has leaped at the word "Providence" to attempt to explain his amazement at this, to him, new departure, and it is true that the specific equating of downflowing Ἔρως with Providence is unplotinian. He also makes much of the function of this Ἔρως as a "binding" factor in the cosmos, but "to bind" for any Platonist involves "to give unity and form and coherence," in a word "to give Being and Reality." This is precisely what the One gives to the Divine Mind in the Plotinian system.

Nygren's view of Ἔρως is that it always ascends. When he finds a descending Ἔρως in Proclus, he wishes to explain it away or regard it as a new departure, outside the Platonic tradition. Proclus, however, is well read in the works of his predecessors including Plotinus, whom

---

[9]Cf. Proclus in Tim. 2.215.5.

[10]Procl., Comm. in Alcib. 31 Westerink ed. 14. For σειρά, cf. Gregory of Nyssa, De anima et resurr. PG 46, 89A, and for Ἔρωτες, Plot., Enn. 3.5.

[11]Nygren, Eros 570.

[12]Procl., Comm. in Alcib. 52 Westerink ed. 23.

[13]Ibid. 55, 24–25. Cf. Rosán, Proclus 134, 206.

he knows thoroughly. At times he disputes the Plotinian position, for example as to whether the whole soul descends from Νοῦς. Such opposition, however, is only further evidence of his knowledge of tradition and acute awareness of the points at which he diverges from his venerable predecessors. If his view of Ἔρως was a completely new departure and a flagrant contradiction of the tradition, it is unusual, to say the least, that we hear no mention of this. His silence on this point is not positive proof, certainly, but, coupled with the tradition of descending Ἔρως which has been elaborated in this study, it points very strongly to the conclusion that, though Nygren believes descending Ἔρως to be unplatonic, Proclus knew better and was further expounding his predecessors.

"Descending love," says Proclus, "turns all things towards the Divine Beauty." Here then is a reference to the process of the amelioration of the self that Platonism taught from its inception. The turning back to the Divine Beauty may be described as ὁμοίωσις θεῷ. We have already discussed this doctrine in Plato and suggested that man can become a god by being wholly characterized by the Forms that are the source of the Gods' divinity. We have further seen how Plotinus urges us to attain to the Intelligible World, to ταυτότης τίνι θεῷ[14] and to the elimination of all dissimilarities between our souls and the One.[15] Man's soul, for the Platonists, has always existed and is immortal by nature. We must return to our true divinity. We have found the word θεοποιεῖσθαι used by Origen, which leads on to our next point.

As Merki points out,[16] the use of the words θεοποίησις and θεοποιῶ with reference to the culmination of the process of ὁμοίωσις θεῷ occurs frequently as early as Irenaeus. After Plotinus and Origen, there was fought out the struggle between the ὁμοίωσις-motif as understood by the Platonists, involving as it did the belief in the natural immortality of the soul, and the doctrine of a post-creational immortality imparted by Grace which the Christians taught in association with the description in Genesis of man as the image and likeness of God. The interpretation of the upward Ἔρως of the Platonists was thus affected, and we must see briefly how the doctrine was transformed. In doing so, however, we must remember a very great difficulty faced by the theologians of the ancient world. This was that to the Greek mind, as Burnaby[17] reminds us, immortality meant divinization, and things

<hr>

[14]*Enn.* 1.2.5. Cf. *Enn.* 1.2.6.   [15]*Enn.* 6.9.8.
[16]Merki, ΟΜΟΙΩΣΙΣ 131. Cf. Nygren, *Eros* 410–411.
[17]Cf. Burnaby, *Amor Dei* 178. Cf. Wilamowitz (*Platon* 1, 348), "Denn Gott selbst ist ja zuerst ein Prädikatsbegriff." The use of θεός to mean merely "immortal

immortal were called θεός. θεός should often be translated as "immortal being" in both Christian and pagan contexts. Thus the Christians found themselves using the same word θεός both for God and for the souls of men after death—an endless source of confusion. This double usage of the word θεός can be seen clearly in Athanasius. While objecting to the view of divinization taught by the Arians on the ground that it presumes to place man on the same level as God, Athanasius does not deny the "ascent" altogether. While Christ is for him "God" φύσει καὶ ἀληθείᾳ, man only attains to "divinity" κατὰ χάριν. τὰ γὰρ κατὰ χάριν διδόμενα τοῖς ἀνθρώποις, ταῦτα θέλουσιν [the Arians] ἴσα τῆς τοῦ διδόντος εἶναι θεότητος.[18]

The position of Augustine is similar. For him, man has not been immortal from all time, nor is he by nature of the essence of God. His spirit is not πνεῦμα, which is the Holy Spirit, but a created spirit, πνοή.[19] Nevertheless it is, for Augustine, God's plan that by grace men shall become "gods." "Deus enim deum te vult facere: non natura sicut est ille quem genuit; sed dono suo et adoptione."[20] And again: "Homo propter nos factus, qui nos homines fecit; et assumens hominem Deus, ut homines faceret deos."[21] It is hardly too much to compare these passages with those discussed earlier about the fellowship of Gods and souls in the Platonic tradition, and in particular with the account in the *Phaedrus* of the souls in the train of Zeus and the other Gods on their visit to the ὑπερουράνιος τόπος.

A further means of entry by which Neoplatonic influences of an undesirable kind might encroach upon the orthodox Christian view of ὁμοίωσις was closed by Gregory of Nyssa. Christianity and Neoplatonism had been brought together on this matter because the Platonic doctrine of ὁμοίωσις θεῷ was associated very easily with the passage of Genesis which describes man as a creation κατ' εἰκόνα καὶ ὁμοίωσιν τοῦ θεοῦ. Theologians before Gregory—for example, Irenaeus, Clement of Alexandria, and Origen—regarded εἰκών and ὁμοίωσις as distinct.[22] Thus ὁμοίωσις θεῷ for them was the perfection of the original relationship of man to God as an εἰκών. This separation of the terms was abandoned

---

being" may be one reason for Plotinus' occasional hesitation to employ the word to describe the One and his preference in one passage for the phrase πλέον ἔστιν ἤ θεός (*Enn.* 6.9.6).

[18]Athanasius, *Or. contra Arianos* 3.17. *PG* 26, 360A. For θεοποίησις, cf. *ibid.* 2.70. 296A; 3.33. 393A; *Or. de inc. verbi* 54. *PG* 25, 192B.

[19]Augustine, *De civ. Dei* 13.24.

[20]Augustine, *Sermo* 166.4.4.   [21]Augustine, *Sermo* 344.1.

[22]Cf. Merki, ΟΜΟΙΩΣΙΣ 45, 83ff., and Crouzel, *Théologie* 217 ff. Cf. *Contra Celsum* 4.30; *De Princ.* 3.6.1; Irenaeus, 5.6.1; Clem. Al., *Strom.* 2.131.6.

by Gregory,[23] who pointed out that the "divinity" of man is entirely
a product of his *creation*, lost by original sin but restored by grace
through Christ's sacrifice. The Neoplatonic view of ὁμοίωσις is that it
is a return of the self to its divine nature by purification; Gregory, on
the other hand, teaches that it is the recovery of the original ὁμοίωσις
which was "fully existent already in the creational εἰκών."[24] This doctrine
strongly opposes, on Platonic grounds, the more extreme Platonic view
that the object of ὁμοίωσις is to raise man to God's level, for every
Platonist would be bound to admit the inferiority of even the best
possible εἰκών to its παράδειγμα. In Plato himself the παράδειγμα-εἰκών
relationship is a relationship between intelligibles and sensibles, not
between Forms and souls or between the Good and the other Forms.[25]
As Merki says: "Im Neuplatonismus ist die Rückkehr die Wiederver-
gottung, die Apokatastasis der Göttlichkeit beim Nyssener die ὁμοίωσις
und die Gottebenbildlichkeit, das übernatürliche Leben."[26]

Gregory, in dealing with ὁμοίωσις, is plainly aware both of the
Platonic tradition in general, and of the views of Plotinus in particular.[27] Students of his work frequently speak of him as a Platonist.
Yet we can understand from his treatment of the theme of ὁμοίωσις
how much Platonism he was prepared to accept and where he found
himself compelled to draw back. While recognizing the value of the
ascent towards Goodness by purification as taught by the Platonists,
he refused their corollary of the *essential* non-creational kinship of man
and God. οὐ γὰρ δὴ ταὐτόν ἐστι τῷ θεῷ ἡ ψυχή.[28]

Turning back from the "Christian Neoplatonists" to the pagan,
here too we find traces of a decline of confidence that the soul can
make its way unaided, relying only on its natural kinship with God.
We have already commented that the mystic union, as described by
Plotinus, is paid lip-service by Proclus, who, however, appears to
make no claim to the experience. He teaches that in order to attain
to it, we must use a "higher kind of theurgy," namely faith (πίστις).[29]

[23]Cf. Merki, ʹΟΜΟΙΩΣΙΣ. The distinction between εἰκών and ὁμοίωσις is not
employed by Athanasius. Cf. Bernard, *L'Image* 27ff.
[24]Ladner, *St. Gregory of Nyssa* 64. *Parm.* 132D.
[25]Cf. Crouzel, *Théologie* 34.
[26]Merki, ʹΟΜΟΙΩΣΙΣ 111. Cf. Daniélou, *Platonisme* 54.
[27]Cf. Merki, ʹΟΜΟΙΩΣΙΣ 127. A comparison of Plato, *Theaet.* 176AB, Plotinus,
Enn. 1.2.1.ff., and Gregory, *De Oratione Dominica* PG 44, 1145A f.
[28]Gregory of Nyssa, *De an. et resurr.* PG 46, 28A.
[29]Proclus, *Platonic Theology* (Hamburg 1618. Reprint. Frankfurt (1960)) 61–63,
193. Since the original version of this essay was written, Professor Armstrong's paper
"Platonic Eros and Christian Agape" has appeared in the *Downside Review* (Spring
1961, 105–121). Professor Armstrong has been kind enough to acknowledge help

This view, strange as it is in Platonism, appears itself to spring from a lack of confidence. We shall see how Proclus rejects Plotinus' claim that a part of the soul always remains in the realm of Noῦs. In view of this, the need for πίστις becomes understandable. If the soul keeps nothing of its divine origin unspotted, it is not hard to understand how fear could arise that even the purifications might fail to raise its cosmological status. It has been suggested, by Rosán,[30] for example, that Proclus' doctrine of πίστις shows the direct influence of Christianity. Although this seems unlikely, there is no doubt that the fallen nature of man, as understood by Christians, and the fallen soul of Proclus' theology are alike in this, that they both feel the need for the teaching: "Only believe and you shall be saved." Proclus, in the introduction to his commentary on the *Alcibiades*, still piously teaches γνῶθι σεαυτόν, but mere knowledge of one's own nature is no longer adequate as the path to ἔνωσις. For the soul "wholly descended" the only hope, if one is to forgo mere magic, is faith in the ἔρως προνοητικός.

Finally we must return to the question of the descent of the soul. Plotinus teaches that man is a composite being, consisting of soul and the various lower products of soul. To do evil,[31] therefore, is to allow the inferior side of our nature to take temporary control. On such occasions, although still possessing the Intelligible World within us (for we are each a κόσμος νοητός),[32] we decline to make use of our possession. That some part of the soul cannot sin, Plotinus believes, is clear from the fact that if the *whole soul* could sin, we could never attain to the pure world of intellect and should be hopelessly bogged down among material things for all time. Therefore, he thinks, it is a law of the universe that some part of the soul must remain in the Intelligible World. τὸ γὰρ πᾶν αὐτῆς οὐκ ἦν θέμις καθελκύσαι.[33] Although this doctrine does not mean—as has sometimes been suggested—that for Plotinus the will cannot sin, it implies that sin is never the result of a deliberate choice of evil in the knowledge that it is evil, but rather the delusion of the mind by evil under the appearance of good. We are worsted by the inferior part of our nature. We sin under the influence either of desire or of anger or of an "evil image" which prompts action before it is properly considered and known for what it is.

---

received from this essay in its earlier form. He and I disagree, however, on certain points of detail, one of which is the rôle of πίστις in Proclus (cf. Armstrong, 116 n. 15). My position depends on what I regard as the fundamental pessimism of Proclus about the state of the "fallen" soul.

[30]Rosán, *Proclus* 215 n. 152.   [31]*Enn.* 1.1.9.   [32]*Enn.* 3.4.3.
[33]*Enn.* 2.9.1. Cf. 5.1.10. For a discussion of this, see pp. 176–177.

Of the later Neoplatonists, Damascius[34] follows Plotinus in this matter, while Iamblichus, Proclus, and Simplicius refuse to do so. Iamblichus' objection is that if the will sins, the whole soul must be involved.[35] He rejects, in fact, the Plotinian view that sin is a delusion and seems to think of it rather as a deliberate choice of evil. Proclus rejects the view that each of us is a κόσμος νοητός. We cannot, he holds, know the Forms in themselves, as Plotinus taught;[36] we can only know them as images (εἰκονικῶς) and as οὐσιώδεις λόγους.[37] Following Iamblichus, he maintains that the soul has entirely descended.[38]

The consequences of this view for man's ascent are very great. Dodds[39] rightly connects the lower estimate of man's cosmic worth directly with the replacement of the Plotinian intellectual and moral ascent by Iamblichan theurgy—and, he should add, by πίστις. By the power of his own divinity man no longer claims to ascend the path of Ἔρως. He can choose between magic and faith in God's descending Ἔρως for his salvation. Fortunately the doctrine of πίστις—comparable with certain views of the Christians—saved the Platonist, now disillusioned about his natural eternal kinship with the κόσμος νοητός and the uncreated divinity of his soul, from seeking his salvation entirely in θεουργία.

The confusion among pagan Neoplatonists as to the possible kinship of the soul with God provided a weakness which the Christians were not slow to observe. Attacking the Neoplatonic Ἔρως as taught by Plotinus with the criticism that it involved the arrogant notion of self-sufficiency, Augustine maintains that the belief that the soul is by nature, rather than by creation, divine, is itself the cause of the pagan philosopher's failure to know God.[40] For divinization, not the *superbia* of Neoplatonism but the *humilitas* that receives the divine Grace is needed. Proclus' less hopeful view of the potentialities of the human soul and his demand for πίστις suit the Christians well, for the πίστις of a thinker who believes that the soul has "wholly descended" is of little use without Grace and a Saviour. Proclus' Ἔρως προνοητικός must now be personalized, just as Origen personalized the cosmic aspects of the Platonic down-flowing Ἔρως.

---

[34]Damascius, *De Princ.* 400 (Ruelle vol.2, 254).
[35]*Ap.* Proclum *in Tim.* 3.334.7. εἰ δὲ προαίρεσις ἁμαρτάνει, πῶς ἀναμάρτητος ἡ ψυχή;
[36]*Enn.* 6.5.7. νοοῦμεν ἐκεῖνα, οὐκ εἴδωλα αὐτῶν οὐδὲ τύπους ἔχοντες.
[37]Procl. *Elem. Theol.* 194–5.   [38]*Ibid.* 211.
[39]Cf. his edition of *The Elements of Theology* (Oxford 1933) xx.
[40]Cf. *Confessions* 7.20.26.

BIBLIOGRAPHY

The bibliography contains the full particulars of books and articles mentioned in the text or notes, and also includes a number of other relevant studies.

ALLEN, R. E. "Participation and Predication in Plato's Middle Dialogues," *PR* 69 (1960) 147-164.
ARCHER-HIND, R. D. *Plato's Phaedo.* London 1883.
—— *A Commentary on Timaeus.* London 1888.
ARMSTRONG, A. H. "Plotinus and India," *CQ* 30 (1936) 22-28.
—— "Emanation in Plotinus," *Mind* 46 (1937) 61-66.
—— "The Gods in Plato, Plotinus, Epicurus," *CQ* 32 (1938) 190-196.
—— *The Architecture of the Intelligible Universe in the Philosophy of Plotinus.* Cambridge 1940.
—— *Plotinus: A Volume of Selections.* London 1953.
—— "Plotinus' Doctrine of the Infinite," *Downside Review* 231 (Winter 1954-55) 47-58.
—— "Was Plotinus a Magician?," *Phronesis* 1 (1955-56) 73-79.
—— "Salvation, Plotinian and Christian," *Downside Review* (1957) 126-139.
—— "The Background of the Doctrine that the Intelligibles are not outside the Intellect," *Entretiens Hardt* 5 (Geneva 1960) 393-425.
—— "Platonic Eros and Christian Agape," *Downside Review* (1961) 105-121.
ARMSTRONG, A. H., and MARKUS, R. A. *Christian Faith and Greek Philosophy.* London 1960.
ARNOU, R. *Le Désir de Dieu dans la philosophie de Plotin.* Paris 1921.
—— "La séparation par simple altérité dans la 'Trinité' plotinienne," *Gregorianum* 11 (1930) 181-193.
—— "Le thème néoplatonicien de la contemplation créatrice chez Origène et chez S. Augustin," *Gregorianum* 13 (1932) 124-136.

——— "Platonisme des Pères," *Dict. de théologie catholique* (Paris 1935) Vol. 12, 2258-2390.

——— "La Contemplation chez Plotin," *Dict. de Spiritualité* (Paris 1950) Vol. 13, col. 1727ff.

AUBIN, P.   "L'Image dans l'œuvre de Plotin," *Recherch. Scienc. Relig.* 41 (1953) 348-379.

BARDY, G.   "Origène," *DTC* vol. 11, col. 1516-1528.

BERNARD, R.   *L'image de Dieu d'après S. Athanase.* Paris 1952.

BICKEL, E.   "Senecas Briefe 58 und 65," *Rh.Mus.* 103 (1960) 1-20.

BIGG, C.   *The Neoplatonists.* London 1895.

——— *The Christian Platonists of Alexandria.* Second edition. Oxford 1913.

BILLINGS, T. H.   *The Platonism of Philo Judaeus.* Chicago diss. 1919.

BLUCK, R. S.   "The *Parmenides* and the Third Man," *CQ* n.s. 6 (1956) 29-37.

BRÉHIER, E.   "L'Idée du néant et le problème de l'origine radicale dans le néoplatonisme grec," *Revue de Metaphysique et de Morale* 26 (1919) 444-475.

——— *Ennéades,* texte établi et traduit. Paris 1924-38.

——— *Les Idées philosophiques et religieuses de Philon.*[2] Paris 1924.

——— *La Philosophie de Plotin.* Paris 1949.

BURNABY, J.   *Amor Dei.* London 1938.

BURNET, J.   *Greek Philosophy, Thales to Plato.* London 1914.

BURY, J. B.   *The Ancient Greek Historians.* New York 1958.

CADIOU, R.   *Introduction au Système d'Origène.* Paris 1932.

——— *La jeunesse d'Origène.* Paris 1935.

CAIRD, E.   *The Evolution of Theology in the Greek Philosophers.* Glasgow 1904.

CASEY, R. P.   "Clement of Alexandria and the Beginning of Christian Platonism," *Harvard Theological Review* 18 (1925) 39-101.

CHADWICK, H.   Translation with notes of the *Contra Celsum.* Cambridge 1953.

CHERNISS, H.   *Aristotle's Criticism of Plato and the Academy.* Berkeley 1944.

——— *The Riddle of the Early Academy.* Berkeley 1945.

——— "The Relation of the *Timaeus* to Plato's Later Dialogues," *AJP* 78 (1957) 225-266.

CHEVASSE, C.   *The Bride of Christ.* London 1940.

CILENTO, V.   "La Contemplazione," *La Parola del Passato* 1 (1946) 197-221.

CLARK, G. H.   "Plotinus' Theory of Empirical Responsibility," *The New Scholasticism* 17 (1943) 16-31.

CORNFORD, F. M.   *Plato's Cosmology*. London 1937.

——— *Plato and Parmenides*. London 1939.

——— *The Unwritten Philosophy and other Essays*. Cambridge 1950.

—— *Principium Sapientiae*. Cambridge 1952.

COUTURAT, L.   *De Platonicis Mythis*. Paris 1896.

CROUZEL, H.   *La Théologie de l'image de Dieu chez Origène*. Paris 1956.

——— *Origène et la Connaissance mystique*. Bruges 1961.

——— *Origène et la Philosophie*. Paris 1962.

DANIÉLOU, J.   *Platonisme et Theologie mystique*. Paris 1944.

—— *Origène*. Translated by W. Mitchell. New York 1955.

D'ARCY, M. C.   *The Mind and heart of love* . . . . London 1954.

DE CORTE, M.   *Aristote et Plotin*. Paris 1935.

DE FAYE, E.   *Clément d'Alexandrie*. Paris 1898.

——— *Origène, sa vie, son œuvre, sa pensée*. Paris 1923, 1927, 1928.

DE KEYSER, E.   *La signification de l'art dans Plotin*. Louvain 1955.

DE LUBAC, H.   *Histoire et Esprit (L'intelligence de l'Ecriture d'après Origène)*. Paris 1950.

DE ROUGEMENT, D.   *Passion and Society*. Translated by M. Belgion. London 1939.

DE VOGEL, C. J.   "Neoplatonic Platonism," *Mind* 62 (1953) 43-64.

DENIS, M. J.   *De la philosophie d'Origène*. Paris 1884.

DODDS, E. R.   "The *Parmenides* of Plato and the Origins of the Neoplatonic One," *CQ* 22 (1928) 129-143.

——— *Proclus, Elements of Theology*. Oxford 1933.

——— *The Greeks and the Irrational*. Berkeley 1951.

——— "Numenius and Ammonius," *Entretiens Hardt* 5 (Geneva 1960) 3-61.

DÖRRIE, H.   "Zum Ursprung der neuplatonischen Hypostasenlehre," *Hermes* 82 (1954) 331-342.

DYROFF, A.   *Die Ethik der Alten Stoa*. Berlin 1897.

EDELSTEIN, L.   "The function of the Myth in Plato's Philosophy," *JHI* 10 (1949) 463-482.

Entretiens Hardt pour l'Antiquité Classique, Les Sources de Plotin. Vandoeuvres-Genève 1960.

FESTUGIÈRE, A. J.   *Contemplation et vie contemplative selon Platon*. Paris 1936.

——— *Epicurus and his Gods*. Translated by C. W. Chilton. Oxford 1955.

FIELD, G. C.   *Plato and his Contemporaries*.² London 1948.

FRUTIGER, P. *Les Mythes de Platon*. Paris 1949.

GAYE, R. K. *The Platonic Conception of Immortality and its Connection with the Theory of Ideas*. London 1904.

GEACH, P. T. "The Third Man Again," *PR* 65 (1956) 72-82.

GOLDSCHMIDT, V. *La religion de Platon*. Paris 1949.

GOULD, J. *The Development of Plato's Ethics*. Cambridge 1955.

GRUBE, G. M. A. "On the authenticity of the *Hippias Major*," *CQ* 20 (1926) 134-148.

——— "The Logic and Language of the *Hippias Major*," *CQ* 24 (1929) 369-375.

——— *Plato's Thought*. London 1935 and Boston 1958.

GUTHRIE, K. S. *The Philosophy of Plotinus*. Philadelphia 1896.

GUTHRIE, W. K. C. "Plato's Views on the Immortality of the Soul," *Entretiens Hardt* 3 (1955) 4-22.

HACKFORTH, R. "Plato's Theism," *CQ* 30 (1936) 4-9.

——— *Plato's Phaedrus*. Cambridge 1952.

——— *Plato's Phaedo*. Cambridge 1955.

HADOT, P. "Etre, Vie, Pensée chez Plotin et avant Plotin," *Entretiens Hardt* 5 (Geneva 1960) 107-157.

HANSON, R. P. C. *Allegory and Event*. London 1959.

HARDER, R. "Zur Biographie Plotins" in *Kleine Schriften* (Munich 1960) 275-295.

HARDIE, W. F. R. *A Study in Plato*. Oxford 1936.

HARNACK, A. VON *A History of Dogma*. Second edition. Third German edition translated by N. Buchanan and J. Millar (London 1897).

HEINEMANN, F. *Plotin*. Leipzig 1921.

HENRY, P. "Le Problème de la liberté chez Plotin," *Rev. Néosc. de Phil.* Second series. 33 (1931) 50-79, 180-215, 318-339.

——— "Dernière Parole de Plotin," *Studi Classici e Orientali* 2 (1953) 113-130.

——— "Plotinus' Place in the History of Thought," Introduction to MacKenna's translation of the *Enneads*[2] (London 1956) xxxiii-li.

HENRY, P. and SCHWYZER, H. R. *Plotini Opera*. Volumes 1 and 2. Paris and Brussels 1951, 1959.

HIMMERICH, W. *Die Lehre des Plotins von der Selbstverwirklichung des Menschen*. Würzburg 1959.

HIRSCHBERGER, J. *Die Phronesis in der Philosophie Platons vor dem Staate*. Leipzig 1932.

HOFFMANN, E. *Platonismus und Mystik im Altertum*. Heidelberg 1935.

INGE, W. R.   *Christian Mysticism*. Bampton Lectures 1899.
——— *The Philosophy of Plotinus*. Third edition. London 1929.
JAEGER, W.   *Aristotle, the History of his Philosophical Development*. Translated by R. Robinson. Oxford 1936.
JENSEN, C.   *Ein neuer Brief Epikurs*. Berlin 1933.
JONES, R. M.   *The Platonism of Plutarch*. Chicago diss. 1916.
——— "Posidonius and the Flight of the Mind through the Universe," *CP* 21 (1926) 97-113.
——— "The Ideas as the Thoughts of God," *CP* 21 (1926) 317-326.
JOSEPH, H. W. B.   *Essays in Ancient and Modern Philosophy*. Oxford 1935.
KATZ, J.   *Plotinus' Search for the Good*. New York 1950.
KOCH, H.   *Pronoia und Paideusis: Studien über Origenes und sein Verhältnis zum Platonismus*. Berlin-Leipzig 1932.
——— "Origenes," *RE* 18² (1939) col. 1036-1059.
KRAKOWSKI, E.   *L'Esthétique de Plotin et son influence*. Paris 1929.
KRAEMER, H. J.   *Arete bei Platon und Aristoteles*. Heidelberg 1959.
KRISTELLER, P. O.   *Der Begriff der Seele in der Ethik des Plotin*. Tübingen 1929.
LACEY, A. R.   "Plato's Sophist and the Forms," *CQ* n.s. 9 (1959) 43-52.
LADNER, G. B.   "The Philosophical Anthropology of St. Gregory of Nyssa," *Dumbarton Oaks Papers*, Harvard (Cambridge, Mass. 1958).
LANGERBECK, H.   "The Philosophy of Ammonius Saccas," *JHS* 77 (1957) 67-74.
LIESKE, A.   *Die Theologie der Logosmystik bei Origenes*. Münster 1938.
LODGE, R.   *Plato's Theory of Art*. London 1953.
LOENEN, J. H.   "Albinus' Metaphysics, An Attempt at Rehabilitation," *Mnemosyne* s.4, 10 (1957) 35-56.
LOUIS, P.   *Les Métaphores de Platon*. Paris 1945.
LUCK, G.   *Der Akademiker Antiochus*. Bern-Stuttgart 1953.
LUEDER, A.   *Die philosophische Persönlichkeit des Antiochos von Askalon*. Diss. Göttingen 1940.
MACKENNA, S.   *Plotinus, the Enneads*. Translated by Stephen MacKenna. Second Edition revised by B. S. Page. London 1956.
MARKUS, R.   "The Dialectic of Eros in Plato's Symposium," *Downside Review* 233 (1955) 219-230.
MEIFORT, J.   *Der Platonismus bei Clemens Alexandrinus*. Tübingen 1928.
MERKI, H.   ʿΟΜΟΙΩΣΙΣ ΘΕΩΙ. *Von der platonischen Angleichung an Gott*

226 EROS AND PSYCHE

zur *Gottähnlichkeit bei Gregor von Nyssa*. Freiburg, Switzerland 1952.

MERLAN, P. "Plotinus and Magic," *Isis* 44 (1953) 341-348.

—— *From Platonism to Neoplatonism*. The Hague 1953.

MORE, P. E. *The Religion of Plato*. Princeton 1921.

MOREAU, J. *La Construction de l'idéalisme platonicien*. Paris 1939.

MUGNIER, R. *Le Sens du mot Θεῖος chez Platon*. Paris 1930.

MURRAY, G. *The Literature of Ancient Greece*. Third edition. Chicago 1956.

NEBEL, G. *Plotins Kategorien der Intelligiblen Welt*. Tübingen 1929.

NERLICH, G. C. "Regress Arguments in Plato," *Mind* 69 (1960) 88-90.

NOCK, A. D. "Posidonius," *JRS* 49 (1959) 1-15.

NORDEN, E. *Agnostos Theos*. Leipzig 1913.

NYGREN, A. *Eros and Agape*. Translated by P. S. Watson. London 1953.

ONIANS, R. B. *Origins of European Thought*. Cambridge 1954.

OSBORN, E. F. *The Philosophy of Clement of Alexandria*. Cambridge 1957.

OWEN, G. E. L. "The Place of the *Timaeus* in Plato's Dialogues," *CQ* n.s. 3 (1953) 79-95.

PECK, A. L. "Plato and the μέγιστα γένη of the *Sophist*," *CQ* n.s. 2 (1952) 32-56.

—— "Plato's *Parmenides*: Some Suggestions for its Interpretation," *CQ* n.s. 3 (1953) 126-150 and n.s. 4 (1954)31-45.

—— "Plato versus Parmenides," *PR* 71 (1962) 159-184.

PELLOUX, L. *L'Assoluto nella Dottrina di Plotino*. Milan 1941.

PETRÉ, H. *Caritas*. Louvain 1948.

PÉTREMENT, S. *Le Dualisme chez Platon et les manichéens*. Paris 1947.

PISTORIUS, P. V. *Plotinus and Neoplatonism*. Pretoria 1937.

POHLENZ, M. *Die Stoa*. Göttingen 1948.

PUECH, H. C. "Un livre récent sur la mystique d'Origène," *Rev. Hist. Phil. Rel.* (1933) 508ff.

RICH, A. N. M. "The Platonic Ideas as the Thoughts of God," *Mnemosyne* s. 4, 7 (1954) 123-133.

—— "Reincarnation in Plotinus," *Mnemosyne* s. 4, 10 (1957) 232-238.

RIST, J. M. "The Order of the Later Dialogues of Plato," *Phoenix* 14 (1960) 207-221.

—— "The *Parmenides* Again," *Phoenix* 16 (1962) 1-14.

—— "Theos and the One in Some Texts of Plotinus," *Mediaeval Studies* 24 (1962) 169-180.

—— "The Neoplatonic One and Plato's *Parmenides*," *TAPA* 93 (1962) 389-401.

—— "Forms of Individuals in Plotinus," *CQ* n.s. 13 (1963) 223-231.

ROBIN, L.   *La Théorie platonicienne des Idées et des Nombres d'après Aristote.* Paris 1908.

—— *La Théorie platonicienne de l'Amour.*² Paris 1922.

—— *Les Rapports de l'être et de la connaissance d'après Platon.* Paris 1957.

ROBINSON, R.   *Plato's Earlier Dialectic.* Ithaca 1941.

ROSÁN, L. J.   *The Philosophy of Proclus.* New York 1949.

ROSS, W. D.   *A Commentary on Aristotle's Metaphysics.* Oxford 1924.

—— *Plato's Theory of Ideas.*² Oxford 1953.

ROUSSEAU, O.   *Homilies sur la Cantique des Cantiques.* Text, translation, introduction. Paris 1953.

RUSSELL, B.   *History of Western Philosophy.* London 1946.

RÜTHER, T.   *Die Sittliche Forderung der Apatheia.* Freiburg 1949.

RYLE, G.   *The Concept of Mind.* London 1949.

SCHAERER, R.   Ἐπιστήμη et Τέχνη: *Etude sur les notions de connaissance et d'art d'Homère à Platon.* Mâçon 1930.

SCHMEKEL, A.   *Die Mittlere Stoa.* Berlin 1892.

SCHMID, W.   "Götter und Menschen in der Theologie Epikurs," *Rh. Mus.* 94 (1951) 97-155.

SCHUHL, P. M.   *Etudes sur la fabulation platonicienne.* Paris 1947.

SCHWYZER, H. R.   "Die Zweifache Sicht in der Philosophie Plotins," *Mus. Helv.* (1944) 87-99.

—— Plotin, *RE* 21 (1951) col. 471-592.

—— "Bewusst und Unbewusst bei Plotin," *Entretiens Hardt* 5 (Geneva 1960) 343-390.

SELLARS, W.   "Vlastos and the Third Man," *PR* 64 (1955) 405-437.

SHOREY, P.   *Platonism Ancient and Modern.* Berkeley 1938.

SKEMP, J. B.   *The Theory of Motion in Plato's Later Dialogues.* Cambridge 1942.

—— *Plato's Statesman.* London 1952.

SNELL, B.   "Die Ausdrücke für den Begriff des Wissens in der vorplatonischen Philosophie," *Phil. Untersuch.* Berlin 1924.

—— *The Discovery of the Mind.* Oxford 1953.

SOLMSEN, F.   *Plato's Theology.* Ithaca, N.Y. 1942.

SOUILHÉ, J.   *La Doctrine platonicienne d'Intermédiaires.* Paris 1919.

STENZEL, J. *Plato's Method of Dialectic*. Translated by D. J. Allan. Oxford 1940.

STEWART, J. A. *The Myths of Plato*. London 1905.

TATE, J. "Plato and Allegorical Interpretations," *CQ* 23 (1929) 142-154 and *CQ* 24 (1930) 1-10.

TAYLOR, A. E. *Plato, the Man and his Work*. London 1927.

—— *Commentary on Plato's Timaeus*. Oxford 1928.

THEILER, W. *Die Vorbereitung des Neuplatonismus*. Berlin 1930.

TROUILLARD, J. "L'impeccabilité de l'esprit selon Plotin," *Rev. de l'Hist. des Relig.* (1953) 19-28.

—— "La présence de Dieu selon Plotin," *Rev. de Mét. et de Mor.* (1954) 38-45.

—— *La Purification plotinienne*. Paris 1955.

—— *La Procession plotinienne*. Paris 1955.

TUCKEY, T. G. *Plato's Charmides*. Cambridge 1951.

VAN CAMP, J., and CANART, P. *Le Sens du mot Θεῖος chez Platon*. Louvain 1956.

VLASTOS, G. "The Third Man Argument in the *Parmenides*," *PR* 63 (1954) 319-349.

—— "A Reply to Prof. Sellars," *PR* 64 (1955) 438-448.

—— "A Reply to Mr. Geach," *PR* 65 (1956) 83-94.

VÖLKER, W. *Das Vollkommenheitsideal des Origenes*. Tübingen 1931.

WALZER, R. *Galen on Jews and Christians*. London 1949.

WASZINK, J. H. *Calcidius*. London and Leiden 1962.

WHITTAKER, T. *The Neoplatonists*. Second edition. Cambridge 1928.

WILAMOWITZ-MOELLENDORFF, U. VON *Platon: sein Leben und seine Werke*. Berlin 1909.

WITT, R. E. "Plotinus and Posidonius," *CQ* 24 (1930) 198-207.

—— *Albinus and the History of Middle Platonism*. Cambridge 1937.

—— "The Plotinian Logos and its Stoic Basis," *CQ* 32 (1938) 190-196.

WOLFSON, H. A. *Philo*. Cambridge, Mass. 1947.

—— "Albinus and Plotinus on Divine Attributes," *HTR* 45 (1952) 115-134.

—— *The Philosophy of the Church Fathers*. Cambridge, Mass. 1956.

ZELLER, E. *Die Philosophie der Griechen*. Sixth and Seventh Editions. Leipzig 1920, 1923.

INDICES

I. GENERAL INDEX

232 EROS AND PSYCHE

Numenius, 56 n. 1, 61 n. 27, 73, 78 n. 94, 86 n. 125, 112, 188, 208
Nygren, A., 38 n. 67, 79, 80, 83, 85, 99 n. 169, 206, 213–216

ODYSSEUS, 130
Olympiodorus, 14
One, the, 19, 43, 69–87, 95; and Being, 43–46, 54, 80, 88; and Plato's Good, 52; personal and supra-personal characteristics of, 71–73, 86, 87, 97, 109, 110, 198, 206; transcendence and immanence of, 80–92; and Eros, 96–97, 102
Onians, R. B., 40 nn. 71, 73, 108 n. 200, 138, 141
Opinion, 20, 141, 143–151, 154, 164, 167
Orientalism, 7, 56, 104
Origen, 3, 4, 24, 38, 80, 102, 195–212, 213, 214, 216, 217, 220; and Bride of Christ, 28, 202–205, 210, 212; attitude to Plato and Platonism of, 3–4, 24, 195, 199, 201, 208, 210, 211; Christianity and Platonism in, 195; deification in, 202. See also Eros, Agape, etc.
Osborn, E. F., 197 n. 10
Owen, G. E. L., 30 n. 49

PANAETIUS, 163
Pantheism, 14, 81, 104
Pausanias, 27, 209, 210
Peck, A. L., 43–46, 47 n. 84, 52
Pericles, 138
Petré, H., 207 n. 53
Phaedra, 143, 175
Phaedrus, 35, 209, 210
Philebus, 50
Philo, 56 n. 1, 63, 66, 73, 112, 188–190, 200–202, 207, 212, 214 n. 7
Philodemus, 165
Pistorius, P. V., 70, 108 n. 199
Plato, passim; and myths, 7–13; and allegory, 8, 9; lack of system of, 8; deification in, 17–20, 155, 156; contradictions in, 38, 54, 55, 57, 58, 92, 97, 213; two views of love in, 26, 97, 213; contemplation in, 28; demands

on man of, 50, 55, 68, 96, 110; knowledge and vritue in, 115–156; nature of soul in, 105–108, 166. See also Good, One, Ἔρως
Platonopolis, 171–173
Plotinus, 3, 4, 13–15, 19, 24, 31, 32, 42, 43, 50, 53, 54, 56–112, 166, 169–191, 197, 200, 207 n. 51, 208, 211–216, 217 n. 18, 218–220; attitude to Plato of, 3, 4, 13, 24, 57, 58, 92, 105; deification in, 169, 180–191; undescended part of soul in, 175–178; no influence of Christianity on, 31; Forms of individuals in, 109; bias against, 14, 15. See also Ἔρως, One, Knowledge, Mysticism, etc.
Plutarch, 56 n. 1, 64 n. 49, 98 n. 167, 101, 102, 161, 164 nn. 16, 17
Pohlenz, M., 161 n. 9, 164, n. 16
Polus, 12, 127, 140
Porphyry, 57 n. 4, 60, 61, 66, 92, 93, 95 n. 160, 100, 101, 172, 185, 190, 195
Posidonius, 56, 64, 65, 66 n. 52, 74, 162, 163
Proclus, 14, 61 n. 26, 94, 95, 178, 190, 214–216, 218–220
Protagoras, 122, 131, 133, 134, 138, 146
Protarchus, 50, 197
Protogenes, 102
Ps-Dionysius, 70, 206 n. 47
Puech, H. C., 212
Purification, 20, 27, 94; in Plotinus, 86, 89, 92
Pythagoreans, 20, 57, 195, 209

RHADAMANTHYS, 11
Rich, A. N. M., 62, 63, 80 n. 99, 83, 108 n. 199
Rist, J. M., 30 n. 49, 70 n. 63, 109 n. 202
Robin, L., 25, 28, 41 n. 75
Robinson, R., 22 n. 24
Rosán, L. J., 215 n. 13, 219
Rosenmeyer, T. G., 116 n. 4
Ross, W. D., 43, 48 n. 90, 52, 60 n. 18, 125, 158 n. 1
Rüther, T., 197 n. 10
Rufinus, 204–206, 211
Russell, B., 201
Ryle, G., 116, 138, 140, 141

II. INDEX OF PASSAGES QUOTED OR REFERRED TO

INDICES 237

61; (29D) 10 n. 8; (29E) 30 n. 48,
50, 75 n. 83, 155; (35A) 41 n. 75;
(37C) 33 n. 56, 73 n. 74; (39E) 61,
65, 67; (43BC) 27 n. 39; (72D) 106;
(86BC) 149; (90A) 17 n. 5, 186 n.
20; (90D) 22 n. 23; (91) 108 n. 199;
(92C) 62
[Plato]
Def. (411Cff.) 166
Plotinus
Enn. I (1.1.7) 177; (1.1.9) 219 n. 31;
(1.1.12) 171; (1.2.1) 89 n. 131, 135,
90 n. 138, 169, 171, 181, 186 n. 21;
218 n. 27; (1.2.3) 169, 186 n. 21;
(1.2.4) 173–174; (1.2.5) 89 n. 134,
92 n. 149, 186, 216 n. 14; (1.2.6) 89 n.
134, 91 n. 144, 174, 186, 216 n. 14;
(1.2.7) 90 n. 139; (1.3) 90 n. 140;
(1.3.3) 90 n. 142; (1.3.6) 173; (1.4.2)
174; (1.4.9) 163; (1.6.6) 186 n. 21;
(1.6.7) 92 n. 147, 97 n. 165, 190;
(1.6.8) 72 n. 69, 90 n. 141; (1.6.9)
82 n. 111; (1.8.2) 69
Enn. II (2.4.9) 59 n. 13; (2.9.1) 69, 89
n. 136, 219 n. 33; (2.9.2) 177; (2.9.3)
77 n. 86; (2.9.6) 57 n. 5, 61 n. 27,
65 n. 48; (2.9.9) 186
Enn. III (3.2.3) 77 n. 87; (3.2.5) 108 n.
199; (3.2.9) 85 n. 119; (3.4) 108 n.
199; (3.4.3) 219 n. 32; (3.5) 215 n.
10; (3.5.2) 79; (3.5.3) 83; (3.5.4) 79;
(3.5.7) 84 n. 117; (3.62) 174, 177;
(3.6.6) 66 n. 56; (3.7.1) 59 n. 10;
(3.8.1) 86 n. 124; (3.8.4) 170; (3.8.6)
170; (3.8.10) 74 n. 78; (3.9.1) 61 n.
27, 65 n. 48; (3.9.9) 70, 79 n. 88
Enn. IV (4.3.8) 108 n. 199; (4.8.1) 58 n.
9, 111 n. 204, 190; (4.8.6) 207;
(4.8.8) 81 n. 109, 176
Enn. V (5.1.1) 69, 201 n. 31; (5.1.6)
69, 75 n. 80, 87 n. 123, 89 n. 137,
214 n. 4; (5.1.7) 77 n. 88, 87 n. 123;
(5.1.8) 58 n. 7, n. 11; (5.1.10) 176,
177, 219 n. 33; (5.2.1.) 75 n. 80;
(5.3.10) 70 n. 63, 103 n. 182; (5.3.13)
70, 77 n. 88; (5.3.17) 69, 94 n. 159,
95 n. 161; (5.4.1) 69; (5.4.2) 77 n.
88; (5.5) 60 n. 20; (5.5.2) 59 n. 16;
(5.5.6) 70 n. 63, n. 64, 71, 72, 80 n.

105; (5.5.8) 95 n. 162, 189 n. 29;
(5.5.9) 80 n. 104; (5.5.12) 75 n. 83,
80 n. 100, 103 n. 180; (5.6.5) 77 n.
88; (5.7) 109 n. 202; (5.9.1) 169;
(5.9.7) 174; (5.9.12) 109 n. 202
Enn. VI (6.2) 43; (6.2.22) 65 n. 48;
(6.3.16) 174; (6.4.2) 81; (6.4.3) 81;
(6.4.11) 81 n. 107; (6.5.7) 220 n. 36;
(6.6.6) 68 n. 56; (6.7.15) 75 n. 80;
(6.7.22) 50, 74, 86 n. 121, 97 n. 164;
(6.7.31) 89 n. 133, 181; (6.7.34) 94 n.
158, 99 n. 170; (6.7.35) 94 n. 159,
96 n. 163; (6.7.36) 83 n. 113, 88 n.
129, 94 n. 157; (6.7.37) 80 n. 101;
(6.7.38) 70 n. 63; (6.7.39) 42 n. 79,
66 n. 56, 80 n. 102, 84 n. 116, 103 n.
182; (6.7.41) 77 n. 88; (6.8.6) 182;
(6.8.14) 81 n. 108; (6.8.15) 78 n. 94,
82, 104 n. 184; (6.8.16) 69, 98 n. 168;
(6.8.18) 69, 214 n. 4; (6.8.19) 80 n.
101; (6.8.21) 78 n. 93; (6.9.3) 70 n.
66; (6.9.4) 81; (6.9.5) 70 n. 64;
(6.9.6) 69, 71 n. 68, 217 n. 17; (6.9.7)
81; (6.9.8) 86 n. 122, 104 n. 183, 184,
216 n. 15; (6.9.9) 72 n. 70, 102 n.
179, 189 n. 30, 190; (6.9.11) 103 n.
181, 110 n. 203, 183, 189

Plutarch
Adv. Col. (1117A) 165 n. 18
Amatorius (751Eff.) 101 n. 176; (758C)
99 n. 167; (759D) 99 n. 167; (766EF)
102 n. 178; (767DE) 102 n. 177
De Alex. Magni Fort. (328E) 211 n. 62
De An. Proc. (1031B) 65 n. 49
De Prof. in Virt. (83Aff.) 164 n. 17
De Stoic. Repug. (1034C) 161 n. 5
De Virt. Mor. (441Bff.) 164 n. 16
Quaest. Plat. (1007C) 62 n. 28
[Plutarch]
Epit. (Dox. Gr.) (1.7) 62 n. 28; (1.10)
62 n. 35
Porphyry
De Abst. (2.34ff.) 93 n. 155
Vita Plot. (2) 92 n. 150; (9) 101 n. 173;
(10) 93 n. 152; (12) 172; (14) 57 n.
4; (15) 100 n. 172, 188 n. 24, 211 n.
64; (18) 60 n. 22; (23) 93 n. 151,
190 n. 32

PROCLUS
Comm. on Alc. (ed. Westerink) (31 p.
14) 215 n. 10; (52 p. 23) 215 n. 12
Comm. on Tim. (1.13.15) 39 n. 70, 58 n.
8; (1.303.27) 73 n. 77, 86 n. 125;
(1.391.7) 61 n. 26; (2.215.5) 215 n.
9; (4.103.28–32) 86 n. 125; (3.334.7)
220 n. 35
Elements (194–5) 220 n. 37; (211) 220
n. 38
Platonic Theology (ed. Portus) (61–63)
218 n. 29; (193) 218 n. 29
PS-DIONYSIUS
Div. Nom. (2.3–4) 70 n. 62; (4.12) 206
n. 47

SENECA
Ad Marc. (25) 163 n. 15
De Const. Sap. (8.2) 162
Ep. (65) 63 n. 37, 64 n. 44; (65.16)
163 n. 15; (71.6) 160 n. 3; (89.8)
162 n. 11; (102.22) 163 n. 15
Frag. (5) 162
SIMPLICIUS
Comm. on Cat. (237.26) 160 n. 4
SEXTUS EMPIRICUS
Ad. Math. (7.93) 65 n. 49

SOCRATES
Hist. Eccl. (1.5) 214 n. 6
STOBAEUS
Ecl. (1.12.6) 62 n. 35; (2.50ff.) 166 n.
25; (2.59.4) 161 n. 7, 167 n. 30;
(2.75.2) 161 n. 9
STRABO
(2.3.8) 66 n. 52
SYRIANUS
Scholia in Met. 1078B12 (Berlin
Aristotle, vol. 4, ed. Usener) 66 n. 55

TATIAN
Orat. ad Graecos (1.13) 178
TERTULLIAN
Apol. (46) 179
De An. (11) 180; (23) 112 n. 205;
(23–24) 179; (27) 179
THUCYDIDES
(2.87) 118 n. 9; (8.68) 128 n. 22

XENOPHANES
fr. (15 *DK*) 16 n. 1
XENOPHON
Mem. (3.9.4) 130; (3.9.5) 128, 130, 132;
(3.9.8–9) 128; (4.6.1) 129; (4.6.2–3)
129; (4.6.6) 129